KYOTO CSEAS SERIES ON ASIAN STUDIES 17

Center for Southeast Asian Studies, Kyoto University

CENTRAL BANKING AS STATE BUILDING

KYOTO CSEAS SERIES ON ASIAN STUDIES 17
Center for Southeast Asian Studies, Kyoto University

CENTRAL BANKING AS STATE BUILDING

Policymakers and Their Nationalism in the Philippines, 1933–1964

Yusuke Takagi

NUS PRESS
Singapore

in association with

KYOTO UNIVERSITY PRESS
Japan

The publication of this book is funded by the International Program of Collaborative Research at the Centre for Southeast Asian Studies (CSEAS), Kyoto University and the GRIPS Book-Publication Grant Program.

NUS Press
National University of Singapore
AS3-01-02, 3 Arts Link
Singapore 117569
http://nuspress.nus.edu.sg

ISBN 978-981-4722-11-7 (Paper)

Kyoto University Press
Yoshida-South Campus, Kyoto University
69 Yoshida-Konoe-Cho, Sakyo-ku
Kyoto 606-8315
Japan
www.kyoto-up.or.jp

ISBN 978-4-87698-969-0 (Paper)

National Library Board Singapore Cataloguing in Publication Data

Names: Yusuke Takagi. | NUS Press, publisher.
Title: Central banking as state building: policymakers and their nationalism in the Philippines, 1933–1964/Yusuke Takagi.
Other titles: Kyoto CSEAS series on Asian studies; 17.
Description: Singapore: NUS Press in association with Kyoto University Press, Japan, [2016] | Includes bibliographical references and index.
Identifiers: OCN 933267409 | ISBN 978-981-4722-11-7 (paperback)
Subjects: LCSH: Banks and banking, Central—Philippines—History. | Banks and banking, Central—Government policy—Philippines—History. | Nationalism—Philippines—History | Philippines—Colonial influence—History. | Decolonization—Philippines—History.
Classification: LCC HG3316 | DDC 332.1109599—dc23

Cover image: Escolta, the shortest but busiest street in Manila, is seen in the right side of the cover running in parallel with Pasig River. This short street was Manila's commercial center until the 1960s. (Photo courtesy of Lopez Museum, Philippines)

Printed by: Markono Print Media Pte Ltd

CONTENTS

LIST OF TABLES

LIST OF ABBREVIATIONS

ACCP	American Chamber of Commerce in the Philippines
AEA	American Economic Association
BPI	Bank of the Philippine Islands
CB	Central Bank
CIA	Central Intelligence Agency
DA	Democratic Alliance
DFA	Department of Foreign Affairs
DP	Democratic Party
EO	Executive Order
FEATI	Far Eastern Air Transport Inc.
HB	House Bill
HHC	Hare-Hawes-Cutting Act
IMF	International Monetary Fund
ISI	Import Substitution Industrialization Policy
JPCPA	Joint Preparatory Committee on Philippine Affairs
JPAFC	Joint Philippine-American Finance Commission
LP	Liberal Party
MRC	Manila Railway Company
NCP	Nationalist-Citizens Party
NEC	National Economic Council
NEDA	National Economic and Development Authority
NEPA	National Economic Protectionism Association
NP	Nacionalista Party
PACC	Philippine-American Chamber of Commerce
PBC	Philippine Bank of Commerce
PCC	Philippine Chamber of Commerce
PEA	Philippine Economic Association
PES	Philippine Economic Society
PIA	Program Implementation Agency
PNB	Philippine National Bank
PPP	Progressive Party of the Philippines

PSA	Philippine Sugar Association
RA	Republic Act
SB	Senate Bill
SONA	State of the Nation Address
TM	Tydings-McDuffie Act
UP	University of the Philippines
USDA	United States Department of Agriculture
UST	University of Santo Tomas

ACKNOWLEDGEMENTS

While working on this project, more than once I imagined the time when I would be able to acknowledge the people who had helped me in various ways. I thought that this last important task for the book would be relaxed and enjoyable. Now, facing deadlines, I realize that life does not slow down once the book is complete; life seems to go on. Having said that, I am very sure that my professional life would not even have started without a great deal of help from numerous people. It is, therefore, a great pleasure to acknowledge them here. First of all, I appreciate my supervisor, Professor Yamamoto Nobuto. Since first joining his undergraduate seminar, I have been guided by him through his intriguing questions and careful reading of my (often careless) writing. At Keio University, I was given an opportunity to take classes and to have numerous helpful consultations with various professors such as Professors Ohishi Yutaka, Inoue Kazuaki, Izuoka Naoya, Kasuya Yuko and Okayama Yutaka. I was also quite fortunate to work with young scholars who had just finished their doctoral dissertations or were finishing them. Those who taught me how to be a scholar were Shimizu Yuichiro, Nishikawa Masaru, Suzuki Hironao, Karasudani Masayuki, Nobori Amiko, Yamakoshi Shuzo, Sugiura Yasuyuki, Satake Tomohiko, Tega Yusuke and Yamaguchi Shinji. In graduate school, I also met friends with whom I felt the pleasant pressure of competition to be a good scholar. They were Yoshida Shingo, Kadosaki Shin'ya, Imai Makoto, Jera B. Lego, Lauren Richardson, Balkisu Saidu, Shiratori Jyun'ichiro and Goroku Tsuyoshi.

Outside of Keio University, I have been fortunate to receive support from several professors who specialize Philippine studies, such as Professors Nagano Yoshiko (Kanagawa University), Katayama Yutaka (then Kobe University), Temario Rivera (then International Christian University), Patricio Abinales (then Kyoto University), Nakano Satoshi (Hitotsubashi University), Nathan Quimpo (Tsukuba University), Suzuki Nobutaka (Tsukuba University) and Sugaya Nariko (Ehime University). Fellow doctoral students in Philippine studies, such as Azuma Kentaro, Kusaka

Wataru, Kiba Saya, Okada Taihei and Serizawa Takamichi have been a source of inspiration, motivation and an excuse to go out to drink.

As a student of Philippine studies, it is a great pleasure to mention here those who have helped me in the Philippines. Professors Ricardo T. Jose (University of the Philippines), Lydia Yu Jose (Ateneo de Manila University), Tesa Encarnacion-Tadem (University of the Philippines), Julio Teehankee (De La Salle University), Eric Batalla (De La Salle University), Ronnie Holmes (De La Salle University) and Mark Thompson (then University of Erlangen-Nuremberg) gave me opportunities to discuss my research project and helped me to sharpen the argument. The Third World Studies Center, at the University of the Philippines, was the ideal host to elaborate on core arguments because of its rich tradition of accommodating scholars from all over the world. I also appreciate the invaluable support I received from libraries in the Philippines, including the various libraries of the University of the Philippines, Rizal Library of Ateneo de Manila University, National Library, Lopez Museum and Library, and Ayala Museum and Library. Soon Chuan Yean, Roy Mendoza, Merce Planta, Karl Chen Chua and Aaron Moralina often shared their bottles and joy of life with me in Quezon City. Leloy Claudio is one of the most recent buddies who shares my enthusiasm for Philippine studies as well as social science. Just before finishing dissertation, I was given an opportunity to teach at De La Salle University. I appreciate Dean Teehankee (again) for giving me the opportunity to teach lively Filipino students. It was a great experience for me to work with diligent colleagues at La Salle: Charmaine Misalucha, Francis Domingo, Benjamin San Jose, Ron Vilog, Elaine Tolentino, Alvin Camba, Aaron Chang, Lorenzo De los Santos, Phillip Binondo, Al James Untalan and Robin Michael Garcia.

After finishing my doctoral dissertation, I have been fortunate enough to work at the National Graduate Institute for Policy Studies (GRIPS) and also to join the Emerging State Project (ESP), which is an ambitious and exciting research project with economists, historians and political scientists (JSPS KAKENHI Grant Number 25101004). I am deeply grateful to President Shiraishi Takashi of GRIPS, who has provided me with such an opportunity. Let me acknowledge the names of those who have continuously inspired me in various ways at GRIPS: Professors Tsunekawa Keiichi, Sugihara Kaoru, Otsuka Keijiro, Sonobe Tetsushi, Matsumoto Tomoya, Khoo Boo Teik, Kawano Motoko and Veerayooth Kanchoochat. ESP has also given me the opportunities to work with the following distinguished scholars: Caroline Sy Hau, Hon'na

Jun, Okamoto Masaaki, Onimaru Takeshi, Aizawa Nobuhiro, Nakanishi Yoshihiro and more.

In preparing this book manuscript, I am grateful for all the help offered by Professors Hayami Yoko and Shimizu Hiromu as well as Shitara Narumi of Center for Southeast Asian Studies, Kyoto University. I also appreciate comments and advice from anonymous reviewers.

While the faces of many others that I would like to acknowledge come to my mind, there is a limitation of pages. Let me apologize to those that I cannot mention here and note that I am, of course, solely responsible for any mistakes in this work.

This is a revised version of my doctoral dissertation, "Nationalism in Philippine State Building: The Politics of the Central Bank, 1933–1964", submitted to the Graduate School of Law and Political Science, Keio University, November 2013. I appreciate those that have granted me permission to use the following materials from previously published articles.

> Chapter 2 is a revised version of Takagi, Y. "Beyond the Colonial State: Central Bank Making as State Building in the 1930s". *Southeast Asian Studies* 3 (2014): 85–117.
>
> Chapter 4 is a revised version of Takagi, Y. "Politics of the Great Debate in the 1950s: Revisiting Economic Decolonization in the Philippines". *Kasarinlan: Philippine Journal of Third World Studies* 23 (2008): 91–114.
>
> Chapter 5 is a revised version of Takagi, Y. "The 'Filipino First' Policy and the Central Bank, 1958–1961: Island of State Strength and Economic Decolonization". *Philippine Studies: Historical and Ethnographic Viewpoints* 62 (2014): 233–61.

I would also like to acknowledge the generous grants provided by the International Program of Collaborative Research at the Centre for Southeast Asian Studies (CSEAS), Kyoto University and the GRIPS Book-Publication Grant Program.

Lastly, let me dedicate this book to my parents, Takagi Kyo and Michiko, who have always understood and helped me in my long journey in academia.

Yusuke Takagi
Tokyo, October 2015

SELECTED TIME TABLE

Year	*Major Events*	*Form of Government, President*
1872	Three priests (Gomez, Burgos and Zamora) are executed by the Spanish authority.	Spanish Colonial Rule
1888	Filipino Ilustrados establish *La Solidaridad*, which leads to the Propaganda Movement in Spain.	
1892	Andres Bonifacio organizes *Katipunan* in the Philippines.	
1898	After the Spanish-American War, the United States signs a peace treaty with Spain and purchases the Philippine Islands.	American Colonial Rule (Malolos Republic, Emilio Aguinaldo, 1899–1901)
1899	Emilio Aguinaldo establishes the Malolos Republic.	
1902	Organic Act. US President Theodore Roosevelt declares the end of the Philippine "insurrection".	
1907	The Nacionalista Party (NP) led by Sergio Osmena and Manuel L. Quezon wins a majority in the Philippine legislature.	
1916	Jones Law passed. Senate is established and Quezon is elected senate president. *Filipinization* of the colonial bureaucracy begins.	
1929	The Great Depression begins.	
	The Finance Committee of the League of Nations establishes a Gold Delegation to study the gold standard.	
1930	Speaker Manuel A. Roxas organizes *Ang Bagong Katipunan*.	
1933	17 Jan: US Congress overrides the veto against the Hare-Hawes-Cutting (HHC) Act.	
	4 Mar: Roosevelt assumes the office of President of the United States.	
	19 Apr: Roosevelt proclaims a complete embargo on the export of gold.	
	21 Apr: The Philippine Economic Association publishes its study of the HHC Act.	

Selected Time Table Continued

Year	*Major Events*	*Form of Government, President*
1934	Jan: the United States enacts the Gold Reserve Act to set a new parity for the dollar and devalues its currency by 40 per cent.	
	22 Mar: Roosevelt approves the Tydings-McDuffie Act.	
	17 May: Vicente Singson-Encarnacion urges the establishment of a central bank for the first time as the finance secretary.	
1935	14 May: The Filipino people ratify the Constitution.	Commonwealth Government, Manuel L. Quezon
	15 Nov: Inauguration of the Commonwealth government and President Manuel L. Quezon.	
1937	14 Apr: Joint Preparatory Committee (JPC) on Philippine affairs is organized.	
1938	20 May: The JPC makes its recommendations in a report.	
	7 July: The Bank of Commerce is inaugurated with Jose Cojuangco as president and Miguel Cuaderno as manager.	
1939	9 July: President Quezon signs Commonwealth Act No. 458, which provides for the establishment of a reserve bank in the Philippines.	
1940	19 Apr: The National Assembly adopts a resolution authorizing the Philippine president to request the withdrawal and return of Bills No. 1947 and 1244 to assembly.	
1941	Dec: The Japanese military invades the Philippine Islands.	WWII Government in exile, Quezon, Osmena (1944–46)/ The Second Republic, Jose P. Laurel.
1942	3 Jan: Japanese military rule begins.	
1943	14 Oct: "The Second Republic" is inaugurated.	
1944	29 Feb: During the last day of its session, the National Assembly passes a bill to create a central bank but later fails to implement it.	
1945	2 Feb: The US Army enters Manila.	
1945	27 Feb: Restoration of the Commonwealth government.	Commonwealth Government, Sergio Osmena
	2 Sept: The Japanese government surrenders on the battleship USS Missouri.	
	4 Dec: President Osmena announces Proclamation No. 27 to join the International Monetary Fund (CA No. 699).	

continued overleaf

Selected Time Table Continued

Year	*Major Events*	*Form of Government, President*
1946	23 April: In a general election, Manuel A. Roxas of the Liberal Party is elected President of the Republic of the Philippines (Third Republic).	
	30 April: The US Congress approves the Rehabilitation Act for the Philippines and the Philippine Trade Act (Bell Trade Act) of 1946.	
	4 July: The Philippines wins its independence from the United States, the Republic of the Philippines is declared.	Republic of the Philippines, Manuel A. Roxas
	23 Nov: Cuaderno is sworn in as the secretary of finance.	
1947	16 Jan: Joint Philippine-American Finance Commission (JPAFC) begins its research and policy proposals.	
	11 Mar: The parity amendment is approved in a national plebiscite to ratify the Bell Trade Act.	
	14 Aug: President Roxas issues Executive Order No. 81 to create the Central Bank Council.	
	31 Dec: Restoration of the NEC.	
1948	15 Apr: President Roxas dies of a heart attack.	
	15 June: President Quirino signs Republic Act No. 265 to establish a central bank.	
	26 June: Cuaderno and his staff including Leonides Virata leave the Philippines for the United States.	
	Aug: Republic Act 330 import control law.	
	12 Sept: Filemon Rodriguez, General Manager of the National Power Corporation, joins the Cuaderno Mission in Washington.	
	16 Nov: Cuaderno reports on the negotiation with the IBRD regarding the loans for power plants and fertilizer project.	Republic of the Philippines, Elpidio Quirino
1949	3 Jan: The Central Bank of the Philippines opens.	
	5 Nov: Cuaderno returns from a six-month trip to the US and Europe.	
	7 Nov: The presidential election.	
	17 Nov: CB Circular 19 selective credit policy requires a cash deposit of 80 per cent on all letters of credit for less essential and luxury imports.	
	29 Nov: EO 295 is passed to strengthen import controls.	
	9 Dec: CB Circular 19 the exchange controls.	
1950	20 June: the Bell mission comes to the Philippines.	
	14 Sept: Salvador Araneta is appointed Secretary of Economic Coordination.	

Selected Time Table Continued

Year	*Major Events*	*Form of Government, President*
1952	18 Jan: Araneta resigns the Quirino administration.	
1953	21 June: The Democratic Party is launched.	
	25 June: Regulation No. 1 is proclaimed to implement the CB circular 44 (put into effect on July 1).	
1954	9 June: RA 997 establishes the Government Survey and Reorganization Commission.	Republic of the Philippines, Ramon Magsaysay
	20 June: RA 1000 authorizes the President to issue up to P1 billion of bonds for economic development.	
1955	10 Sept: RA 1410 The No Dollar Import Law becomes law.	
1956	1 Jan: The Laurel-Langley agreement is in effect.	
	23 Jan: Magsaysay reveals his support of Cuaderno's policy in SONA.	
	22–23 Feb: Montelibano and then Araneta resign the government.	
1957	17 Mar: President Magsaysay is killed in a plane crash.	
1957	22 June: Garcia vetoes SB 167.	Republic of the Philippines, Carlos P. Garcia
	22 June: RA 1937 President Garcia signs the tariff Act.	
	8 Dec: Cuaderno returns from the US and submits a memorandum to Garcia regarding a study on the stabilization program.	
1958	21 Aug: NEC Resolution 204 Filipino First.	
1960	28 Mar: Cuaderno submits to Garcia the final draft of the decontrol program.	
	2 Oct: Recto dies of a heart attack.	
1962	21 Jan: CB Circular 133 abolishes existing exchange controls.	Republic of the Philippines, Diosdado Macapagal
	22 Jan: Macapagal delivers the SONA.	
	24 Aug: EO 17 establishes the PIA.	
1963	28 Jan: President Macapagal makes his will for land reform public in his SONA.	
	8 Aug: Macapagal signs the RA 3844 Land Reform Code.	
1964	1 Mar: Sixto Roxas leaves the Macapagal administration.	

Sources: Abinales and Amoroso 2005; Abueva 1971; Araneta 2000; Bureau of Banking 1940, 1941; Castro 1974; Cuaderno 1948, 1964; Constantino 1969; Gleeck 1993; Golay 1961; Hartendorp 1958; Hayden 1942; Ikehata 1996; Jenkins 1985; MacIsaac 1993; Macapagal 1968; Malaya 2004; Nagano 2010; Quirino ed. 1938; Philippine Economic Association 1933; Roxas 1958, 2000, 2013; Subramanian 1980; Sudo 2008; Takagi 2008; Valdepenas 1969, 2003; as well as the *Manila Chronicle*, *Official Gazzette* and *Tribune*.

Elpidio Quirino took over Singson Encarnacion and continuously advocated making a central bank as well as organized the Philippine Economic Association in the 1930s. He became the President in 1948. (Photo courtesy of Lopez Museum, Philippines)

Vicente Singson Encarnacion, President, Insular Life Assurance Co., Ltd. and Philippine Guaranty Co., Inc., was appointed the secretary of finance and advocated making a central bank in the Philippines. (Photo courtesy of Lopez Museum, Philippines)

Manuel A. Roxas organized Ang Bagong Katipunan to advocate economic nationalism and was appointed finance secretary before he was elected President in 1946. (Photo courtesy of Lopez Museum, Philippines)

Miguel Cuaderno (left) was appointed the secretary of finance by Manuel Roxas (right). (Photo courtesy of Martin C. Galan)

Miguel P. Cuaderno was a member of the PEA in the 1930s and was appointed finance secretary under Roxas and Quirino administrations before he was appointed governor of the Central Bank of the Philippines. (Photo courtesy of Martin C. Galan)

Salvador Araneta worked together with Miguel Cuaderno but clashed with him during the great debate in the 1950s. (Photo courtesy of Lopez Museum, Philippines)

INTRODUCTION

"I lost my temper and I told Clay that he seemed to forget that our country is now independent"—Miguel P. Cuaderno to Elpidio Quirino.[1]

The above epigraph is part of a confidential letter from the governor of the Central Bank, Miguel P. Cuaderno, to the president of the Philippines, Elpidio Quirino. When Cuaderno met Eugene Clay, an officer at the US embassy, at his office in the Bank, he was asked by Clay to provide favorable foreign exchange allocations to several American firms in the Philippines and was threatened that the US president might withdraw his support for the Philippine government's economic policy. This could have prevented the Philippine government from maintaining the policy under the trade agreement then in effect between the two countries. Knowing the risk, Cuaderno declined the secret deal with the above-quoted words.

While resisting various forms of opposition, the Bank under Cuaderno maintained the economic policy, which supported industrialization under a stable democracy in the 1950s. Cuaderno, who was trained in the Philippine National Bank (PNB) in the 1920s, was not a colorful politician but rather a quiet, skinny lawyer serving as the founding governor of the Central Bank from 1949 to 1960. He won the support of four successive presidents and achieved industrialization for the Philippines while in office. For instance, income from manufacturing increased by 235 per cent in the nine years after 1949 (Golay 1961: 106). The bank occupied the commanding heights of economic policy-making and was therefore assumed to be "an island of state strength" (Abinales and Amoroso 2005: 184).

A study of the Bank's achievement provides a crucial case study through which we can shed a new light on Philippine politics. Such an accomplishment presents a least-likely case scenario, considering the

[1] Cuaderno to Quirino 1950, *EQ*, 6.

dominant framework of Philippine studies (Eckstein 1975).[2] The Bank, in fact, only attracted esteem as the island of state strength in the midst of weak institutional capability among the other parts of the country's state apparatus (Abinales and Amoroso 2005: 184). Therefore, this achievement in the 1950s has been understudied, while failures in different time periods have provided ample evidence to shape the dominant understanding of Philippine politics and economy.[3] The weak state, or the patrimonial oligarchic state, is a prevailing concept highlighting the resilience of domestic or international structural constraints preventing the state from developing. If the Philippine state has been regarded as a patrimonial oligarchy, then why could the Central Bank enjoy autonomy in achieving rapid industrialization in the 1950s? Why did its role change in the 1960s?

In order to address these questions, we should study the policy regime sustained by the Central Bank in the 1950s, the one that Filipino policymakers had prepared for since the 1930s. This preparation began in 1933, when a group of Filipino policymakers seriously attempted to create a central bank. Although they failed this first time, they did not give up. When the Bank was finally inaugurated in 1949, it immediately imposed foreign exchange controls to maintain a strong currency policy that encouraged import substitution industrialization (ISI). The economic policy regime underpinned by the Bank sustained industrialization in the 1950s. When the government lifted controls and devalued its currency in 1962, the commanding heights of economic policymaking fell to the newly established Program Implementation Agency, a predecessor of the National Economic and Development Authority. In other words, the whole process of making and dismantling the policy regime is a political one in which policymakers created an island of state strength and then changed it.

Why did the Central Bank play such an important role? What is the Bank for the policymakers? A clue can be found in Karl Polanyi's

---

[2] Harry Eckstein argues that a crucial case study works well as long as researchers can find a puzzling phenomenon that we cannot expect to work well with existing theories (Eckstein 1975; Kume 2013: 204–11).

[3] There are few book-length studies covering the period when the Central Bank emerged, but they highlight graft and corruption by the Filipino politicians, exploitation by multinational companies, or inefficient economic nationalism (for example, protectionism), and neglect the politics within the Philippine government (Doronila 1992; Gleeck 1993; Hawes 1987; Romero 2008).

classic work of political economy, in which he asserts: "Politically, the nation's identity was established by the government; economically it was vested in the central bank" (Polanyi 1957: 205). Polanyi's insight, originally published in 1944, assumes that a central bank is an expression of nationalism; it emerged just as Filipino policymakers began to advocate central bank making.

For Filipino policymakers, creating a central bank constituted a part of state building. Policymakers faced opposition from American colonial officers as well as from established Filipino politicians who had maintained close relations with American and Filipino businesses enjoying colonial trade. Even after independence in 1946, they continuously faced the lingering effects of the colonial legacy, such as the unequal trade agreement with the United States and colonial economic structure that forced Philippine dependence on the production of primary export products. In the context of colonial rule and neo-colonialism, industrialization sustained by the Central Bank was not only economic policy but also a part of larger project of state building in which aspiring politicians actively participated.

This study covers the whole political process from 1933 to 1964, in which a generation of policymakers emerged, created a policy regime, and was taken over by the successive generation that followed. The rest of this Introduction is composed of three sections. First, a critical review of relevant studies will clarify the reasons why a study of the Central Bank's policy regime is necessary. In addition to studies using the framework of the weak state, it will also review studies of social movements and democracy, as well as studies of American influence in Philippine politics. Second, a review of the role of individual policymakers, policy regimes and state building will lead to a clarification of an analytical framework for this crucial case study. Third, the structure will be shown to clarify the aim of the book.

Revisiting the Weak State and its Criticism

Patrimonial Oligarchic State and Patronage Politics

The Philippine state has been understood as a weak state for decades (Anderson 1988; McCoy 1994; Hutchcroft 1998; de Dios and Hutchcroft 2003; Bello et al. 2004; Kuhonta 2008). According to this argument, in a weak state, politicians who dominate local politics exploit national resources through patronage politics, while the central government fails to create and implement policy to achieve national economic development.

Following in this vein of a weak state, Paul Hutchcroft elaborates on the concept of the Philippine state and invents a new concept—a patrimonial oligarchic state (Hutchcroft 1998). In this scheme, the government in a patrimonial state behaves as if it can hardly distinguish between public and private interests. According to the typology of the patrimonial state, Hutchcroft argues, the Philippine state typifies the patrimonial oligarchic form in which the bureaucracy, a core institution of modern states, fails to develop enough to provide rationality to economic activities, while Indonesia under Suharto and Thailand can be categorized as patrimonial administrative states in which the bureaucracy and military played certain roles to exploit state resources (ibid.: ch. 3). Instead, the Philippines has been characterized as an oligarchy, a type of elite domination in which public interest is sacrificed for the special interests of a few who wield political authority based on their wealth (ibid.: 22). Therefore, one of the most detailed studies of the political economy of the Philippine ISI focuses more on the business sector than on policymakers (Rivera 1994).

The framework of the weak or patrimonial oligarchic state is well accepted by other scholars, partly because it was developed by modifying two dominant frameworks used to understand Philippine politics—the politics of personality and patronage politics. Both of these frameworks were elaborated in an influential work on Philippine political parties published by Carl Lande in the 1960s, in which he asserted that Philippine political parties comprise politicians who share nearly the same ideology, socioeconomic backgrounds and interest structure, which maximizes their patron-client relationships when mobilizing political support among their constituents (Lande 1965). According to Lande's study, political parties in the Philippines are distinguished not by policy orientation but rather by personality.

However, the politics of personality, which sustains patronage politics, does not pay attention to differences in individual personality. Rather, it emphasizes differences between personality politics and politics shaped by ideology or policy preference and assumes that individuals are mere agents of structures or institutions that compel them to join the game of patronage. As Herbert Kitschelt correctly mentions, political actors seek the interests of electoral districts through patronage politics based on clientelist linkage, while they pursue interests beyond a particular district in politics comprised of programmatic linkage (Kitschelt 2000). Owing to the influence of the framework of personality politics, most biographies share a similar plot, which emphasizes rampant patronage politics in general yet make the subjects of biographies exceptions to this common practice.[4] The overemphasis on the achievements of singular figures in biographies has paradoxically reinforced the dominant position of patronage politics as the framework for understanding Philippine politics.

Because of the extensive influence of patronage politics in the literature, subsequent scholars, using various institutional analyses in their studies, have often assumed that the Philippine state is patrimonial (Kang 2002; Hamilton-Hart 2002: 12; Kuhonta 2008: 40–1). For instance, Antoinette Raquiza's comparative work (2012) on Thailand and the Philippines aims to show new dimensions of Philippine political economy but is not so successful at differentiating her concept of "proprietary polity", a framework to understand Philippine polity, from that of the weak state. This is because she adopts a cross-country rather than cross-temporal comparison, as researchers tend to emphasize consistency within a country in order to highlight differences between them.[5] Consequently, she underestimates the role of the Central Bank in the 1950s and highlights the stability of domination by the proprietary class since the colonial era. In addition, she studies technocracy with a focus on institutions but pays minimal attention to human networks. Considering the fact that the Thai technocracy, which she assumes to be more stable than that of the Philippines, depended on the personal network of a central bank governor (Suehiro 2005), the development of the personal networks of economic bureaucrats in the Philippines can also be studied.

In addition, existing studies on Philippine state formation are helpful only to understand the emergence of the weak state. Comparing cases of money politics and state formation in the Philippines and South Korea, David Kang argues that the Philippines has not faced any serious external threat and as a result has followed a different path of development from South Korea (Kang 2002).[6] Facing a serious threat from

---

[4] McCoy claims: "Most Filipino biographies, the potential building blocks for elite-family studies, are more hagiography than history" (McCoy 1994a: 4).

[5] A comparative study of Ferdinand Marcos and Park Chung Hee also enhances the conventional view of the weak state in the Philippines versus the strong state in South Korea (Hutchcroft 2011).

[6] We should distinguish internal developments of the Cold War from external developments as a form of confrontation among nation states. The former requires that the government divide and rule its people, while the latter allows the government to mobilize the people as a whole to face external threats. The Philippines experienced internal developments of the Cold War in the late 1940s when it faced the Huk Rebellion (Takagi 2009), but it did not encounter external threats.

North Korea, political and economic elites in South Korea found that they were mutual hostages and were required to develop the national economy in order to maintain and increase their politico-economic interest. Without a serious external threat, Filipino political and economic elites have failed to establish relationships based on a system of checks and balances and consequently have plundered existing state resources rather than attempt to develop national economy in the Philippines (ibid.).[7] Therefore, in the introduction to a historical-comparative analysis of central banks and state building in Indonesia, Malaysia and Singapore, Hamilton-Hart mentions that the Philippine political economy has been overwhelmed by the patrimonial state (Hamilton-Hart 2002: 12).

Institutional analysis, whether it adopts rational choice, historical institutional, or small-number comparative methods, tends to enhance the argument of the weak state, although scholars who adopt it have often attempted to criticize the concept in various ways. Without studying changes in the Philippines, we may end up reproducing the dominant framework for the study on Philippine politics. A revision of the conventional perspective on Philippine politics will create opportunties for further cross-temporal and cross-country comparative study in future.

Social Movements, Democracy and the Philippine State

Those who study various forms of social movements and democracy have slightly different views on Philippine politics but nonetheless maintain the underlying perspective of a weak state. In contrast, Reynaldo Ileto, in his now-classic analysis of independence movements under colonial rule, established himself as a harsh critic of the weak state perspective (cf. Ileto 1979). In his provocative article, he argues that the notion of a weak state has dominated the narrative of Philippine political studies

[7] On finance and state in South Korea, Jung-En Woo scrutinizes South Korean industrialization in a longer historical framework that begins with Japanese colonial rule, and reminds us of the significance of complex interactions in the historical development of modern state institutions as well as human resources and international relations (Woo 1991). While Woo focuses on industrialization in the 1960s, with much attention paid to historical development since the colonial era, I study state building in the 1950s with a serious consideration of historical development. An analysis of the island of state strength in this study would open the way for a revision of the comparative study of industrialization in these two countries as a topic for future research, because it would show a new perspective on the Philippine state.

(Ileto 2001). This dominance proves the resilience of Orientalism in academia, where observers tend to differentiate themselves from others (ibid.). In a subsequent article, Ileto reminds us of the significance of studying a "history of the inarticulate", which is composed of "the complex interplay of structures and lived experiences" (Ileto 2002: 173–4).[8]

Taking Ileto's criticism seriously into account, Nathan Quimpo published one of the first path-breaking works to revise our view of Philippine politics (Quimpo 2008). Quimpo, also referring to a critical review by Benedict Kerkvliet on the conventional monolithic understanding of Philippine politics (Kerkvliet 1995),[9] argues that conventional studies have been full of stories of the political elites who dominate or exploit national resources, and that now is the time to shift our focus to "contested democracy", which comprises not only "traditional" political elites but also left-wing movements; the latter supposedly represent the voice of the masses and have challenged elite domination (Quimpo 2008).

Quimpo succeeds in enriching our understanding of Philippine politics by broadening our vision but does little to change how we view politics within the government. He often assumes that politics inside government consists of patronage by oligarchs and only briefly mentions the differences within the elite, which comprises traditional politicians engaged in patronage politics and reformists who avoid patronage politics and seek government efficiency as informed by international financial institutions. Moreover, he overlooks analysis of the 1950s when the leftist insurgency was in decline.

Eva Lotta Hedman, meanwhile, touches upon a tradition of business activism since the 1950s in which we find business leaders in certain

[8] The history of the inarticulate in Philippine studies was suggested by Renato Constantino and elaborated by William H. Scott, a distinguished cultural historian of the Cordillera people in Mountain Province in Northern Luzon and the pre-Hispanic Philippines. Scott argues that scholars should read the history of the lived experience of the colonized by reading the "cracks in the parchment" or reading between the lines of official documents written by colonial authorities (Scott 1982).

[9] Kerkvliet has studied the politics of peasants and agricultural laborers in a framework called Everyday Politics (see, for example, Kerkvliet 1990, 2002). There are several studies on the politics of non-elites (see, for example, Ileto 1979). More recently, Kusaka has asserted the significance of a dual public sphere and moral nationalism as an alternative framework to understand Philippine politics (Kusaka 2013). These studies succeed in claiming that there is a broader political sphere but do not address the problems of the monolithic view on so-called elite politics.

roles being critical of cronies or oligarchs and working together with the Catholic Church and the US to maintain their domination of politics and the economy (Hedman 2006). While she reveals the existence of different type of Filipino elites, Hedman does not elaborate on their roles in policymaking that resulted in industrialization. For example, she reproduces the view of a weak bureaucracy (ibid.: 37–8) without a careful review of the development of colonial bureaucracy (for example, Doeppers 1984).

Meanwhile, Mikamo studies reforms in the banking sector from 1986 to 1995, focusing on the roles of individual policy elites and institutions (Mikamo 2005). He does not mention Ileto's criticism but aptly criticizes the argument of the patrimonial oligarchic state and asserts that policy elites, rather than social forces or international pressure, played pivotal roles in the reforms. Although he rightly highlights the role of policy elites under the restored democracy, he simplifies political history before 1986 as a failure and neglects the achievements of the 1950s (ibid.: 39–41).[10]

Conventional studies on social movements, democracy and restored democracy fail to answer the puzzle of the island of state strength. Much of this criticism focuses on political forces that are largely marginalized by the government while presuming that politics within the government is the politics of the elite—which, in turn, is often presumed to take the form of patronage politics in the patrimonial oligarchic state. The works of both Hedman and Mikamo are exceptional in the sense that they pay much attention to the dynamics created by diverse political elites, but they stop short of revising the conventional view on the emergence of the weak state before 1986. In other words, existing criticism of the weak state thesis suggests a rich field beyond elite politics or changes in restored democracy after 1986 but does not challenge the conventional view of elite politics generated through a study of historical developments of the Philippine politics.

Revisiting American Influence on Philippine Economic Policymaking

How have scholars explained ISI, if they have not paid much attention to policymaking? Those who study the origins of ISI have highlighted

---

[10] The writer is grateful to Professor Mikamo Shingo who generously shared his dissertation with him.

the US government's intervention in Philippine policymaking. Sylvia Maxfield and James H. Nolt argue that the US economic survey mission (the Bell Mission) that visited the Philippines in 1950 to deal with the fiscal as well as balance-of-payments crises in 1949 proposed that the Philippine government carry out policies for ISI (Maxfield and Nolt 1990).[11] Even scholars who study the politics of ISI, whenever they explain the introduction of the import and exchange controls in 1949, emphasize the American role, referring to the work of Maxfield and Nolt (Doronila 1992: 52–4; Rivera 1994: 27, 42n10). It is conceivable that the Bell Mission represented a change in US economic policy toward the Philippines (MacIsaac 1993), however, that mission did not drastically change Philippine economic policy. Moreover, if they argue that the Philippine government imposed import and exchange controls in order to respond to the balance of payment crisis, then they should explain why the government could take such swift and efficient measures given the "weak" state apparatus.

In order to know the origins of the economic policy regime, we should study the political process within the Philippine government before 1950. The Bell Mission, for instance, proposed various policy recommendations, including land and tax reforms, although the Philippine government would not follow all of them (Wurfel 1960). Governor Cuaderno mentioned that the two important recommendations of the mission were balancing the budget and revising the Bell Trade Act (Cuaderno 1964: 26). Cuaderno did not argue that the Bell Mission had requested the Bank to change the policy but rather emphasized the mission's support of the Bank's position (ibid.: 25–7). It is also important to know that Cuaderno, who was the finance secretary before he was appointed governor of the Central Bank, had already drawn up the first developmental program seeking industrialization in 1948 (Golay 1961: 350–3). Moreover, Cuaderno faced blunt pressure from American businesses in the Philippines rather than receiving powerful support from the US government, as we saw at the beginning of this study.

The impact of American intervention cannot be understood properly without careful study of the country's domestic politics. Another example of complex Philippine relations with the United States can be found in

---

[11] US Congressman Jasper Bell, author of the Philippine Trade Act of 1946, should not be confused with Daniel W. Bell, president of the American Security and Trust Company, who led the US economic survey mission in 1950.

the Ramon Magsaysay administration (1954–57). It is true that Magsaysay, as the defense secretary (1950–53) and president, was strongly supported by the US government (Abueva 1971; Lansdale 1972). It is also true, however, that Magsaysay began to frustrate the US government once he took his oath as president because he was cool toward the issue of an American military base and because he often sought the advice of the "old guard" of the ruling Nacionalista Party (Gleeck 1993; Cullather 1994). It does not mean, however, that Magsaysay ended up trapped by the resilient oligarchy. He did make progress in curbing graft and corruption and in regaining public confidence in the government (Abueva 1971). The achievement of the Magsaysay administration was impressive, compared to the results of US engagement in the administrations of Cuba's Fulgencio Batista or South Vietnam's Ngo Dinh Diem (Perez-Stable 1993; Dacy 1986). The collapse of these two administrations is a clear example of the limits of US government influence in the Third World.

When it comes to American influence on Philippine economic policymaking, some might recall studies on technocracy (Bello et al. 1982; Broad 1988; Dubsky 1993; Encarnacion-Tadem 2005; Raquiza 2012). Technocrats have been assumed to be Filipino experts who worked closely with the US government and international financial organizations such as the World Bank and International Monetary Fund (IMF), especially after the 1960s. These existing studies, however, do not sufficiently understand the politics of the Central Bank. They focus on the historical development of technocracy only after the 1960s; however, the Central Bank was already held in high regard in the 1950s (Abinales and Amoroso 2005: 184). These studies assume that technocrats are the first professionals to have worked in the government and neglect bureaucrats before the 1960s that had special knowledge in economics and worked in various economic agencies. Filipino professionals familiar with economics have appeared ever since the late 1920s, as we will see in the following chapters.

A memoir by Joseph Smith, a Central Intelligence Agency (CIA) officer who was stationed in the Philippines from 1958 to 1959, recalls how an American intelligence officer understood Philippine politics (1976). Smith claimed that he met all of the potential presidential candidates from the opposition running in the 1961 election but was disappointed with Diosdado Macapagal, who did not have any vision or integrity but instead held power within the opposition party (ibid.: 304).

CIA officers continuously encouraged the close aides of the late President Magsaysay to grab power, but failed. Macapagal prevailed, but the officers remained unimpressed with him in comparison with other reform-minded politicians (ibid.: ch. 17).

What is important here is not the fact that the CIA was disappointed by Macapagal's election as president (1961–65) but rather that the US government dealt with Filipino politicians who acted independently of American interests. The politics of economic policymaking should thus be studied with much attention paid to domestic politics.

Nationalism in Philippine State Building

Policy Regime and the Roles of Individual Policymakers

Patronage politics, which has been intensively studied within the framework of the weak state, is simply one type of politics, according to a classic study of policy process. In this work of policy studies, Theodore Lowi argues that the characteristics of power structures, in which political actors engage in politics, depend upon policy types (1964). Distributive policy, for instance, compels these actors to engage in patronage politics and discourages them from conflicting over broad policy orientations. The type of Philippine politics studied within the framework of the weak state exemplifies patronage politics shaped by distributive policy.

Meanwhile, regulatory policy poses a trade-off for political actors, who must select one option, which can prove beneficial to some sectors and disadvantageous to others.[12] The exchange controls, through which the Central Bank of the Philippines carried out industrial policy, can be seen as having two features—a distributive policy that focused on actors seeking foreign exchange allocations, and a regulatory policy that focused on the decision-making process—for example, whether to adopt the exchange controls. This is because exchange controls have impact on almost all economic activities related to trade.

The study of policy process has been developed into a study of the regulatory policy regime, which is composed of several policies and insti-

[12] Lowi mentions three types of policy, namely, distributive, regulatory, and redistributive. In the case of redistributive policy, political actors tend to behave according to the logic of class conflict. It is important, however, to note that actual policy can have more than one character, something not implied by this concise classification.

tutions that sustain these policies.[13] Eisner, who studies the regulatory regime in the United States, defines regulatory regime as a configuration of policies and institutions developed during a certain period of time, which can shape the structure of interests composed of various state as well as social forces (1993: 1).[14] Eisner's definition raises two points for consideration. First, we should study not a single policy or an institution but rather a cluster of policies and institutions; and second, we should examine a regime as a configuration developed over a certain period of time. By focusing on the regulatory regime governing relations between government and business, Eisner discovers a relatively long process of change in the political order of the United States.[15]

Combining the findings of those who study both the policy regime and also industrial policy, we can argue that the Philippines witnessed various industrial policy regimes. The Philippine government worked for ISI with foreign exchange controls in the 1950s. The government subsequently shifted its strategy: in the late 1960s from ISI to a combination of ISI and export-oriented industrialization (EOI), and in the late 1980s to an accelerated pace of liberalization in cooperation with technocrats from the private sectors (Bello et al. 1982, 2004; Encarnacion-Tadem 2005; Raquiza 2012). However, these studies tend to emphasize the role of the US government or trivialize the change in policy regime into a mere political power struggle among politicians.

Against this background, I focus on roles of individuals who are attempting structural change through policymaking. Scholars who are interested in the role of individuals working outside of the influence of socioeconomic structures or existing institutions study the politics of ideas (Beland and Cox 2011). Mark Blyth, in his comparative work on economic policy change in the US and Sweden, argues that ideas can

---

[13] Policy regime is used in an economist's historical analysis of Japanese foreign currency policy (Adachi 2006). Meanwhile, this study refers mainly to the works of scholars who study American politics. This is because we can find certain similarities between American and Philippine state building.

[14] Although Eisner uses the term "regulatory regime", this study uses the term "policy regime"—the reason being that although a regime can be created through economic policies that not only regulate some activities but also deregulate others, "regulatory regime" sounds like it might neglect the latter.

[15] Paul Pierson, who asserts the significance of studying the temporal dimension of politics (Pierson 2004), examines the concept of policy regime or "clusters of policies with strong elective affinities" when he explains "the impact of early policy initiatives in shaping long-term political process" (Pierson 2006: 120–3).

help political actors figure out various interests and how to achieve them, regardless of existing vested-interest structures, through a process of economic policymaking, especially at a time of uncertain circumstances such as economic crises (Blyth 2002: ch. 1).[16] Industrialization can be seen as a political process whereby policymakers strive to change socioeconomic structures with uncertainty. Moreover, like the politics of regulatory policy, the politics of ideas can often produce clashes among actors because of the uncompromising characteristics of ideas (Green 2001).[17]

The development of a politics of ideas suggests we understand the role of individual political actors in certain contexts because "ideas do not float freely" (Risse-Kappen 1994; Hamilton-Hart 2012). Policymakers study ideas and try to adjust them to fit the particular contexts of actual policymaking. These contexts may shape actors' apprehension of their identities and preferences (Pierson 2004: 169), and they differ from structures. Remembering the words of Ileto (Ileto 2002: 174; Ileto 1979), we can claim that contexts can be drawn from the lived experience of the observed subjects through a study of their words and deeds.

If individual policymakers can play certain roles, however, where are they found in the Philippines? The literature on Philippine state building should be reviewed below.

Revisiting State Building and Nationalism in the Philippines

Patricio Abinales elaborates on the origin of the Philippine state and concludes that the American colonial endeavor ended up establishing a foundation for *cacique* democracy, in which American Democrats familiar with patronage politics in the US took over both the presidency and the majority in Congress and then sent a Democrat to the Philippine Islands in 1912 as governor-general (Abinales 2005a: 173; Anderson 1988). Cacique democracy is a democracy captured by the cacique, who paid the least attention to public policies that promoted the national interest (Golay 1961: 24). Subsequent scholars elaborated on the idea of that cacique democracy resonated with the framework of the weak state. They argue that the early development of decentralized administrative and

[16] Ideas are different from ideology, which is assumed to reflect a stable class structure.
[17] Green, for instance, argues: "the politics of ideas is like lightning, where the friction within public and private life generates a sudden and tumultuous disagreement. Such events fuel intense conflict, where opponents regard each other as worse than enemies and animosity feeds willful misunderstanding" (Green 2001: 1).

political institutions provided institutional bases for the resilience of local power holders based on landholdings or kindred while also preventing the Philippine state from strengthening the central government (Hutchcroft and Rocamora 2003; Abinales 2005a).

However, if the foundation of cacique democracy was consolidated in the American colonial era, how would we regard the origin of the island of state strength after independence? Skowronek, whose study Abinales references (Abinales 2005a), asserts the existence of two phases of American state building, namely, state building as patchwork and state building as reconstruction (Skowronek 1982).[18] State building as reconstruction in American politics followed the period of state building as patchwork, in which several professionals attempted to overcome the problems of machine politics and a decentralized state represented by party and court. Key to the gradual expansion of the national administration was the emergence of university-educated professionals such as bureaucrats, economists and military officers. In state building as reconstruction, reformists could occupy the post of the president, as they did in the early 20th century, thus expanding the capability of the state even though they faced Congress, which mostly comprised of politicians dependent upon patronage (ibid.).

In the literature on the island of state strength, we can also find an important historical context of American political development. Theda Skocpol first proposed the notion of the island of state strength in an article that she co-authored with Kenneth Finegold, entitled "State Capacity and Economic Intervention in the Early New Deal" (1982; Abinales and Amoroso 2005: 5, 17). In their study on American political development in the 1930s, the two authors argue that the Agricultural Adjustment Administration embedded in the US Department of Agriculture (USDA) successfully intervened in economic activities in the agricultural industry, while the Industry Recovery Administration, established directly under the president and staffed with officers appointed from private industry, failed to realize its policy goals (Skocpol and Finegold 1982). Skocpol and Finegold assume that the USDA became the island of state strength because, even before the New Deal era, the USDA had enhanced its capability "for policy research and for centrally coordinated policy

[18] This writer appreciates the suggestion by Professor Patricio Abinales (University of Hawaii) that I read the work of Skowronek (1982).

implementation" through active recruitment of professional experts graduating from the land-grant colleges where students could study agriculture (ibid.: 271–3). While Skocpol widened her focus to states in general rather than elaborate on the concept of islands of state strength, Peter Evans—with whom Skocpol edited a seminal work on states and politics, *Bringing the State Back In* (Evans, Rueschemeyer and Skocpol 1985)—narrowed his focus to the role of states in economic development.

Evans recognizes the existence of institutions that are apparently similar to islands of state strength, although he proposes another term—pockets of efficacy—to describe them, as he does in his comparative study of information-technology industries in Brazil and South Korea (Evans 1995). "Pockets of efficacy" is a metaphor for particular situations in which exceptional institutions make use of expertise in the private sector to realize economic development (Evans 1995; Abrami and Donner 2008: 232). A key concept in Evans's argument about embedded autonomy is that of pockets of efficacy, which is the autonomy of states to intervene in economic activities through the knowledge that they have accumulated via their network in private sectors. Evans argues that in order to develop the economy, states must be autonomous from social forces attempting to exploit state resources for their own special interests while simultaneously remaining embedded in the social network so that they can gather information and develop necessary policy. Therefore, autonomy is relative rather than absolute, in the case of embedded autonomy.

The important assumption behind Evans's argument is the existence of a state, or at least islands of state strength, in which the government can remain autonomous from the social pressures of vested interests. When well embedded in a social network, an island of state strength can function as a pocket of efficacy. It is important, however, to clarify what the social network means. As Evans argues, pockets of efficacy are created by the actors who are involved in policymaking. Therefore, we should study the actual composition of a policymaker's network, which is not necessarily limited to the division of labor in bureaucratic institutions.

Evans's argument helps to advance a revision of the conventional view of the Philippine state, although he does not mention the Philippines. Evans invents three types of states—development, intermediate and predatory—based on their performance in economic development (Evans 1995: ch. 3). While the developmental state is a type of state that achieves economic development underpinned by a capable bureaucracy, the predatory state is one that fails to achieve economic development due to persistent pressure from social forces exploiting state resources.

Intermediate states, somewhere between a development and predatory state, can also be found (ibid.). Evans cites Japan as an example of a developmental state and Zaire as a predatory one (ibid.; Johnson 1982; Wedeman 1997). As for the Philippines, Sidel, who studies political violence by local bosses, assumes that it is predatory (Sidel 1999: 145–7). Predatory and patrimonial states are the same, in the sense that they highlight a lack of state capability to achieve the economic development of the nation, although the former emphasizes political violence while the latter emphasizes rent seeking.

In contrast to Sidel, the literature based on Evans's argument does not categorize the Philippine state as predatory. In fact, Doner and others classify four Southeast Asian states, including the Philippines, as intermediate states based on Evans's work (Doner, Ritchie and Slater 2005). Romero also argues that the Philippine state changed from a predatory to intermediate state beween 1946 and 1965, although he mentions the rise of technocracy only as an indicator of the intermediate state (2008). When Abinales studies Philippine politics after democratization in 1986, he sees "isles of efficacy" created by "coalition politics" composed of a broad network surrounding the president (Abinales 2005b).[19]

Reconsidering the history of Philippine politics, we can notice a moment in the efforts of Filipino professionals in state building. The 1920s was a time when the Philippines witnessed the emergence of a middle class, most of which worked in the colonial government (Doeppers 1984). These colonial bureaucrats began to imagine independence from the United States in a concrete way for the first time in the 1930s. They shared similar educational and occupational backgrounds with their American counterparts, who strengthened the capability of the US federal government in the early 20th century. In fact, the newly appointed American governor-general Leonard Wood (1923–27) was one of the remaining reformists in the United States (Golay 1997: 110–1). Moreover, in the Philippine banking industry, the 1920s was exactly the period of reconstruction following the virtual bankruptcy of the Philippine National Bank in the early 1920s (Nagano 1986: ch. 3; 2003: ch. 8;

[19] While Abinales looks at coalition politics to study the role of the president, I focus on the creation of process of a network among key policymakers (which often include ambitious politicians aiming for the presidency) not based on the president-elect's authority but on shared ideas or goals.

2015: ch. 7). If we can study the process of state building in the Philippines as patchwork as Abinales has done, then we can also study the process of state building as reconstruction.

Looking at the time of reconstruction in the Philippines, we can find nationalism developing among professionals who worked in the colonial state, albeit with certain limitations. Most of these professionals were colonial bureaucrats who shared similar educational as well as professional careers within the American colonial state. In his classic study of nationalism, Benedict Anderson uses the metaphor of pilgrimage to explain the educational and professional careers of colonial administrators who climbed the career ladder but faced colonialism's ceiling at the end of their careers, because they could not climb as high as their colonial masters (Anderson 1991: ch. 4, 7).[20] They understood the colonial administration but could not run it themselves due to colonial rule.

Resil Mojares (2006) beautifully explains the emergence of scholar bureaucrats under American colonial rule. They were students of the *ilustrados*, or the enlightened ones, who were beneficiaries of expansion of educational opportunity in the 19th century and had begun to teach as well as establish their own schools all over the Philippines in the early 20th century. In a sense, these colonial intellectuals were beneficiaries of economic progress under colonial rule but faced "the binaries of collaboration and resistance, acceptance and rejection", which ended up shaping "an autonomous, empowered identity" (ibid.: 499). Ultimately, they aimed to utilize the colonial state in order to change the politico-economic structure of the Philippines. In other words, they worked at state building in order to depart from colonial rule.

By highlighting nationalism in the colonial state, a new dimension of nationalism in the Philippines should be revealed. Before, Philippine studies neglected nationalism among bureaucrats due to a neglect of the state's active role in politics (for example, Corpuz 1957, 1989). As a consequence, nationalist historians on the front lines of academic discourse in the Philippines paid sympathetic attention to rebellion or symbolic

---

[20] In the case of Indonesian nationalism, Anderson convincingly argues the significance of a particular generation of youth, who experienced Japanese occupation in the nationalist movement that followed (Anderson 1972). Brazil mentions Filipino First and the Philippine Economic Association, both of which we address in our study, although he focuses on failure of the planning authorities such as the National Economic Council (1961).

leaders of the opposition party rather than politicians and bureaucrats within the government (Agoncillo and Alfonso 1961; Constantino 1969; Constantino and Constantino 1978; Sidel 2012).

Meanwhile some economists have highlighted economic nationalism in policymaking whenever they explain ISI, however, they define it as an expression of ethnic discrimination or anti-foreign sentiments. Frank Golay, for instance, distinguishes economic nationalism from economic development, saying: "Economic development is concerned with the size of the 'pie' without considering its racial dimensions; economic nationalism is concerned with the racial and ethnic distribution of the 'pie' rather than its size" (Golay et al. 1969: viii). They conclude that economic nationalism was the driving force behind policymaking in Southeast Asia and that it was a cause of the region's underdevelopment (Golay et al. 1969).

The argument of these economists is useful only in understanding particular policies, but it is less so once we take actual policymaking and the bigger picture into consideration. Indeed, there were aggressive advocates for protectionism in the 1930s (de Dios 2002; Sicat 2002), but it is hard to find concrete clues to find direct input from private sectors into policymaking as we will see in Chapter 5. Right after independence, the Philippine government accepted the unequal trade agreement with the United States, as we will see more in detail in Chapter 3. Study of the relations between economic policy, industrialization and economic nationalism gradually lost its influence in the literature that followed, which was taken over by scholars who emphasized American intervention (which I have already criticized). Instead of highlighting social pressure groups, we should study actual policymaking.

Beyond the Weak State

Before explaining the organization of the book, let me briefly mention several caveats. First, I do not assert that the island of state strength can eradicate clientelism or corruption. As Richard Doner and Ansil Ramsay (1997) argue, a coexistence of clientelism and efficient state institutions can create economic growth to a certain extent. They call this coexistence bifurcation, and argue, in the case of Thailand, that clientelism compels political patrons to compete for various resources on behalf of their clients while economic growth is guaranteed by macroeconomic stability sustained by bureaucracy as well as an effective Sino-Thai business elite (ibid.). What I do here is acknowledge patronage politics and examine the role of the state in changing economic structure.[21] While the literature in Philippine studies contains plenty of studies of patronage politics in a patrimonial state, it still lacks studies on policymaking in at least the intermediate state in Philippine studies. By filling this gap in the literature, I do not intend to dismiss the responsibility of policymakers; instead, I aim at revealing to them room for maneuver.[22]

Second, I do not deny the institutional power of the president. In her analysis of the Philippine party system and the presidential term limit, Yuko Kasuya explains that the Philippine president can create a presidential bandwagon in which legislators even change their party affiliation in search of a bigger share of the electorate or quicker execution of so-called pork barrels (Kasuya 2008). While institutional analysis highlights the power relations within executive-legislative relationships in existing institutions, I focus on changing political processes in which policymakers are working to make institutions.

The changing historical context in which policymakers elaborated their own ideas becomes clearer when we revise our conventional view of the Philippine state's historical development. A careful reading of Hutchcroft's work gives us clues about how to reconsider the historical development of the patrimonial oligarchic state. Hutchcroft mainly studies the Marcos administration (1965–86), however, his chapters address several incidents that provide readers with the "historical background" of patrimonial oligarchy that existed before the Marcos administration (Hutchcroft 1998: 6). It is telling that Hutchcroft cites the Macapagal administration (1962–65) as having established the conditions for the Marcos administration's patrimonial behavior through its aggressive liberalization of the banking industry (ibid.: 87–8). If it is the case that predatory behavior by politicians began with policy change, we may find clues that would help us understand the dynamics of Philippine politics through a

---

[21] Doner and Ramsay compare the Thai case with the Philippine one in their short conclusion and argues that Thai state is more institutionalized than the Philippine one (Doner and Ramsay 1997: 273–5). They skip explaining Philippine economic development in the 1950s, partly because they mainly depend on the framework of the weak state to describe Philippine political economy (ibid.: 274, n41, n42).

[22] One implication can be induced from this study for those who are interested in graft and corruption is a search for island of state strength in the field of law enforcement as a topic of coming research.

careful study of the policy change under the Macapagal administration. In addition, we should also remember the study on Philippine technocracy with the assumption that the Philippines witnessed the rise of technocracy in the 1960s. While the 1930s was a historical turning point at which a group of Filipino policymakers began to work for policy regime making, the 1960s can be considered another turning point at which a different set of policymakers began to emerge and to shift the emphasis of the economic policy.

Aim of the Book

The following chapters address questions whose answers lead toward an understanding of the emergence of the island of state strength and its changing nature.

The first question to be addressed is who the Filipino policymakers were. Chapter 1 reviews colonial state building in the Philippines in order to find a path that does not necessarily end with the beginning of the weak state. While the year 1872 marks the beginning of the Filipino nation's history, the year 1933 marks the year when Filipinos faced the first concrete independence act written by the US Congress. We will see, focusing on leading figures and the contexts in which they emerged, the process in which Filipinos emerged to actively take part in colonial state building.

Chapter 2 examines the first attempts by Filipino professionals advocating for a central bank in order to trace the origin of the island of state strength. This presents an academic puzzle here: why did this new generation of policymakers striving for economic decolonization emerge, despite the structural constraints shaped by colonial rule. By scrutinizing the timing of the policymakers' advocacy since 1933, we will see how policymakers emerged, nurtured their network, and strove to make an institution suitable for an independent state.

Chapter 3 examines the emergence of the island of state strength by studying the actual process of building the Central Bank and policymaking of import and exchange controls. It also addresses the conventional view of the politics of independence by studying the process whereby Filipino policymakers aimed to reshape the orientation of the Philippine state by building away from a completely neocolonial trajectory toward greater autonomy despite major constraints. This chapter reviews the context in which the Philippine government accepted the unequal trade agreement with the United States in addition to the subsequent process by which the government endeavored to reinterpret the treaty even before its ratification.

A nature of the Central Bank as the island of state strength is revealed in Chapter 4. A clash erupted between the bank and the export industry, which was not the beneficiary of the bank's industrial policy. The clash manifested as a long policy debate between policymakers—those who sought economic decolonization and those who aimed to maintain the vested colonial economic structure. By asking why Filipino policymakers began to engage in the great debate over the general economic orientation of the Philippines, the character of the Philippine political economy is revealed; not only colonial masters but also Filipino capital invested substantially in economic activities during the colonial era.

If the bank established its autonomy vis-à-vis the export industry, how were its relations with manufacturers, or the beneficiary of ISI? Why did the government proclaim the Filipino First in 1958 rather than 1949? It does not seem so straightforward to find a smooth collaboration between the bank and manufacturers. Actual bank relations with the private sector are studied in Chapter 5 through a case study of the politics of Filipino First, an apparent expression of economic nationalism.

Chapter 6 studies the process by which the policy regime as the island of state strength gradually declined. By studying a time period during which the Central Bank withdrew from its role as the island of state strength, I also examine the significance of studying the ideas of policymakers. Politics under the Macapagal administration has been explained using mutually contradicting frameworks. Some argue that the weak state underestimated the achievement reached by the changes made under the Macapagal administration, while others who highlighting neocolonialism emphasize international intervention by the IMF and the United States. Against this background, this chapter traces the whole process of economic policy regime change, in which clashes among policymakers over ideas shaped political dynamics.

CHAPTER 1

Nationalism and the Philippine Colonial State, 1872–1933

Previous studies have argued that cacique democracy emerged at the American colonial period (1898–1946), during which politicians seeking their own special interests, not policymakers working for the national interest, played pivotal roles in politics. How can we understand the emergence of policymakers in the 1930s? Nationalist-inspired policymakers emerged in that decade, as I suggest in the introduction. However, the historical context in which these policymakers emerged is missing. In order to provide this needed background to the Philippine political economy, this chapter reviews the colonial state building in the late 19th century, which would not end up as the only beginning of a weak state.

The execution of three clergymen in 1872 influenced the ideas of José Rizal, a leading light of Philippine nationalism or the one many have cited as the first Filipino (Anderson 1998: ch. 10). Perhaps a study of the politics of independence could begin here. At the same time, the year 1933 marks an important starting point, because the US Congress passed the first Philippine independence law that year. Following Ileto's suggestion to study "the complex interplay of structures and lived experiences" (Ileto 2002: 174), the structural change in Philippine politics and the initiatives taken by various Filipinos for the sake of this historical transformation of society should be discussed. Therefore, the period between 1872 and 1933 is viewed in this chapter as one continuous time sequence, rather than as two colonial periods, that is, the latter part of the Spanish era from 1872 to 1898 and American time era between 1898 and 1946.[1]

[1] Japan invaded and ruled the Philippines from 1941 to 1945, although it granted the second Philippine republic independence in 1943.

This chapter comprises three sections. First, it traces the emergence of nationalism in the 19th century and its clash with Spanish and US imperialism at the end of the century. Second, it reviews the process of colonial state building under American rule with "tutelary" democracy. Third, it briefly studies the changing situation of colonial rule in the early 1930s, in which key policymakers aimed at going beyond the limitations of tutelary democracy.

The Formative Period of Nationalism

Emergence of Philippine Nationalism and the Malolos Republic

Spain occupied Manila in 1571 and ruled the Philippine Islands until 1898. It colonized the islands but failed to recruit its own people to develop the colony, depending instead on several religious orders to deal with local populations. The only significant economic activity was an intermediate trade between Acapulco, Mexico and other Asian ports, which was known as the Galleon Trade, named after the galleon, a sizeable sailing vessel widely used by European states in the 16th to 18th centuries. The Galleon Trade involved the exchange of Mexican silver, Chinese silk, Indian cotton, and spices from south (Legarda 1999: 33). While Manila became prosperous, the other parts of the islands maintained subsistence economy because of the intermediate nature of the trade.

In the 19th century, however, the colony's Spanish authorities faced the rapidly evolving economic dynamism of East Asia, where the British Empire had established its hegemony over trade a century before (Abinales and Amoroso 2005: 75). Admitting failure in previous attempts to develop the colony on its own initiative, the Spanish authorities decided to enhance trade with other ports in Southeast Asia by opening Manila in 1834, and subsequently Iloilo, Cebu and other major ports in the middle of the 19th century as the development of steam navigation and the opening of Suez Canal accelerated trade in East Asia (Legarda 1999: 110–1, 327).

Growing economic opportunity and Spanish colonial policy in the late 19th century resulted in the emergence of a native middle and upper class, who could distinguish themselves from the rest not only through their wealth but also through their education (ibid.: 213–6). The expansion of trade resulted in a growing demand for clerical skills, or white-collar work. In order to meet the demand, several private educational institutions emerged in Manila, though many parish priests opposed the idea of educating the indios (Abinales and Amoroso 2005: 92–4). One of the new institutions was the Escuela Normal de Maestros, a normal school whose graduates taught Spanish in primary schools newly established in the provinces (Schumacher 1991: 20). Some of the graduates of these local schools proceeded to higher education in the Ateneo Municipal, Colegio de San Juan de Letran, or the University of Santo Tomas (UST) in Manila (ibid.: ch. 3).

The growing mestizo and Filipino population and increasing educational opportunities created political tension, because the two populations were dissatisfied with the unequal treatment of the Spanish colonial authorities, especially the friars who had actually controlled the colony and opposed various social reforms. After a mutiny in the Cavite naval arsenal, three Filipino priests—Mariano Gomez, José Burgos and Jacinto Zamora—were publicly executed in 1872. While the colonial authorities attempted to make the execution a show trial under the colonial master, over time people interpreted it as suppression by the colonizers, and presently the three priests, collectively called Gomburza, became martyrs (Abinales and Amoroso 2005: ch. 5).

Creating martyrs for nationalism, a group of intellectuals not only cast doubt on the Spanish decision in the Cavite mutiny but also publicly stated their dissatisfaction with friarocracy in the Philippines (Schumacher 1997). Moreover, some of these intellectuals, who would eventually be called *ilustrados* (enlightened ones), had studied abroad and had thus been exposed to republicanism, the French Revolution, or anarchism, while at the same time they observed Spain's backwardness relative to France or Germany when they were in Europe (Anderson 2005; Abinales and Amoroso 2005: 105). The frustrated ilustrados finally organized the Propaganda Movement and triggered a fire on independence movements in 1890 (Schumacher 1997).

The impact of the Propaganda Movement and the works of Rizal were felt not only among the rich ilustrados but also by those in other social strata. Andres Bonifacio, who was born in Tondo, possibly the most populated area in Manila, in 1863, absorbed Rizal's views and disseminated these among his fellow common folk (Agoncillo 1996). Bonifacio did not attend university but had worked at several firms as a craftsman, messenger, or commercial agent. While working hard, Bonifacio learned Spanish on his own and read books about the French Revolution, the lives of American presidents, and the works of Rizal (ibid.: 67–71).

After Rizal was deported to Mindanao, Bonifacio organized the *Katipunan* (*Kataastaasan Kagalang-galangang Katipunan na mga Anak ng Bayan* [the highest and most honorable society of the sons of the country]) with fellow workers and students with the aim of bringing down Spanish rule in 1892. The Katipunan was a militant secret society that could mobilize support from peasants and workers because of the leader's background and his deep understanding of the world view of the masses (ibid.; Ileto 1979). Under investigation by Spanish authorities, the Katipunan finally raised a rebellion against the former in 1896, which resulted into the Philippine revolution. In the midst of the revolution Emilio Aguinaldo took over the Katipunan leadership by ordering Bonifacio's execution in the midst of a power struggle. Aguinaldo, in cooperation with ilustrados, accelerated the creation of the Philippine republic in Malolos (the Malolos Republic), the first republic in Asia, in January 1899 (Agoncillo 1997: 241).

Despite the short life of the republic, its history provides clear examples of the Filipino people who attempted to change the status quo. It is important to know what kinds of ideas for state building they had in mind. While most of the ilustrados surrendered to American authorities, as we will see below, Apolinario Mabini worked for the republic until his capture and deportation to Guam. Cesar Majul, the most important biographer of Mabini, reveals fully Mabini's appreciation of the French Revolution and belief in the democratic principles of the republic, and also shares an impressive account of "Mabini's lack of a radical economic program" (Majul 1960: 57–62). Majul, who recognizes that the American invasion deprived the republic of the chance to deal with its economic problems, argues that Mabini's lack of ideas on economic reform came from the nature of the revolution as a political movement triggered by the ilustrados, who had accumulated their knowledge through their own studies, with specialized law or medicine open to them at the UST. A bias in favor of legal education would be found in colonial state building, as we will see below.

American Occupation and Early Colonial State Building

In the midst of the Philippine-American War, which killed "roughly twenty-two thousand Philippine soldiers and half a million civilians" between 1898 and 1902 (Abinales and Amoroso 2005: 117), several leading figures in the Malolos Congress surrendered to the United States and established the Federal Party to advocate a peaceful annexation by the

United States in early December 1901. It is important to know, however, that the Federal Party was not an American creation, although its members collaborated with the Americans when President Aguinaldo was still fighting against the American forces. As Cullinane reveals, the Federalistas (members of the Federal Party) decided to establish their party when they realized that they would not win independence soon because of the Democratic Party's loss in the US presidential election of November 1900 (Cullinane 2003: 63). Moreover, the creation of the Federal Party did not mark the end of militant resistance. President Aguinaldo, in fact, continued to fight, although he had to retreat from Malolos in early March 1899 and moved to the north by the time the Americans captured him in March 1901. While the US government transferred colonial authority from the military to the civilian government on 4 July 1901 and claimed the end of the "Philippine insurrection" in July 1902, the colonial government continuously faced militant resistance in several provinces until around 1910 (Ileto 1979).

From the beginning of its rule, the American colonial authority faced strong pleas for independence by the people who had once organized a republic, and who clarified their visions of independence in various ways. In this context, the US government introduced the "democratic" clause into its organic act, or "An Act temporarily to provide for the administration of the affairs of civil government in the Philippine Islands, and for other purpose", which formed the basic law governing the Philippines until 1916 (Corpuz 1997: 222). William H. Taft designed much of the US colonial policy toward the Philippines as head of the Philippine Commission (1900–02), civil governor (1902–03), secretary of war (1904–09) and president (1909–13), leaving behind a legacy in the history of colonial state building known as the Taft era (Golay 1997: ch. 4).[2] Taft thought that the United States should tutor the Filipino on self-government, although he believed that it would take fifty or a hundred more years for the Filipino to understand what liberty meant for the Anglo-Saxon (10 May 1980).

Tutelary colonialism, a mixture of Philippine reality and American colonial ideas, formed a basic principle of colonization during the Taft era (Go 2008: ch. 1). In the Philippines, the American colonial authority sought legitimacy in the colony where the people had already established

[2] The civil governor was renamed governor-general in 1905 (10 May 1980).

their own republic, a situation that was different from the situation in Puerto Rico (ibid.: 34). In addition, among themselves, the Americans held two sets of ideas. First, most of the Americans involved in colonial rule believed in racial difference but thought that this would be overcome through American tutelage (ibid.: 28–9). Second, these colonizers were active supporters of the progressive movement in the United States, a diverse reform-minded movement aimed at eradicating the machine politics that had been rampant in the late 19th century while enhancing the role of professionals in the federal government (ibid.: 32–3). The progressive movement emerged as a bipartisan movement and did not necessarily oppose colonization. Its advocates believed in a mission to reform US politics and to civilize the colony. Wishing not only to achieve its mission to civilize the "savage blood" in the colony but also to minimize the cost of colonization, the American colonial authority tried its best to induce support from the Filipinos (ibid.: 34–45).

As actual tools for tutelary colonialism, the American colonial authority attempted to introduce universal education and local elections. Beginning in 1901, it introduced free basic education to achieve universal English literacy in the pacified areas (May 1980).[3] After a year, "more than two hundred thousand students were enrolled in primary school", and more than half of them attended the class regularly (Abinales and Amoroso 2005: 120–1). Graduates of the secondary school would be the first generation of Filipino teachers to teach their students in English. Besides, in order to provide opportunities for studies in the US, a scholarship program was introduced in August 1903, which offered what was called the *pensionado* program that sent almost 200 Filipinos to study in the United States between 1903 and 1912 (Agoncillo and Alfonso 1961: 356). Recipients of the scholarship, also known as the pensionados, were beneficiaries of US colonial policy, and they organized their own social club, the Philippine Columbian Club, in 1907.[4]

As the following chapter shows, however, their experience in the United States did not necessarily turn them into pro-American scholars. Carlos Quirino, a leading postwar journalist, asserts that pensionados had become even more nationalistic because of their stay abroad and that

[3] Okada (2014) provides a critical view of the American colonial authority's educational policy.

[4] Homepage of the Philippine Columbian Association. Available at http://www.pcaopen.org/PhilippineColumbian/aboutus.php [accessed 20 August 2013].

"this [Philippine Columbian] club became the focal point in the nationalistic campaign for independence for the next three decades" (Quirino 1987: 39). In this way, tutelary colonialism was interpreted and used by the colonized Filipinos.

The Filipino intellectuals who abandoned "the politics of confrontation" shifted their focus to the efforts of "nation building" (Mojares 2006: 489). Mojares illustrates the initiative of these intellectuals' with several examples. Felipe Calderon, born to a wealthy Manila family in 1868, studied at the UST and played a pivotal role in framing the Malolos Constitution. Before joining the Malolos Congress, Calderon was an established lawyer who founded the Colegio de Abogados de Manila, or the Manila Bar Association, and established Escuela de Derecho, the colony's second law school, in 1891 (ibid.: 475). Calderon was a founding member of the Federal Party but focused more on research and education, especially historical education. He organized the Asociacion Historica de Filipinas (Philippine History Association) in 1905 and worked to establish a history of "the Filipino people" (ibid.: 485; Cullinane 2003: 64). One of Calderon's students was Teodoro Kalaw, of middle-class origin and recognized as an example of "scholar-bureaucrats" (Mojares 2006: 493). Mojares concludes that while the ilustrados under Spanish colonial rule fought the colonial authority, the intellectuals under the American colonial rule worked within the realm of colonial rule (ibid.).

Another example of tutelary colonialism is found in the early introduction of elections. The colonial government implemented local elections up to the level of governors in the provinces, where colonial authorities had suppressed resistance since 1902. The franchise for these local elections was limited to males who had lived in the area for at least six months before the elections and who met any of the following criteria: "individuals who speak, read and write English/Spanish, own real property worth at least P500, or have held local government positions prior to the occupation of the country in 1899" (Abinales and Amoroso 2005: 126). The first criterion reflected the emphasis on education, although the latter criteria apparently represented the conservative nature of the local election.

The introduction of local elections and, later, national elections changed a generation of political elites, which resulted in a change of the leading political party (Abinales and Amoroso 2005: 127). While the Federal Party, renamed the Progressive Party just before the national election, could neither maintain close relations with the new governor-general nor present itself as a party advocating independence, the newly established Nacionalista Party (NP) presented itself as seeking immediate and absolute independence in the first election at the national level in 1907 (Liang 1971: 91).

Emerging figures in the NP represented a new generation of politicians who benefitted not only personal relations with American colonial officers but also the educational reform under the Spanish and colonial state building by the Americans. Two principal figures of the new generation were Sergio Osmeña and Manuel L. Quezon, both of whom led colonial politics throughout the American colonial period (Cullinane 2003). Osmeña was born in 1878 into the distinguished Osmeña family in Cebu. After finishing primary education there, he went to Manila to study at the San Juan de Letran and later at the UST. As the revolution broke out, he went back to Cebu and participated in publishing a newspaper. In 1903 he returned to Manila and was admitted to the bar. After practising law in Cebu, he was appointed acting provincial governor, then fiscal (or prosecuting attorney) of Cebu, which later expanded to fiscal of Negros Occidental. In 1906, he was elected governor of Cebu (ibid.: ch. 8). Quezon was born in 1878 to parents who were both teachers in Tayabas (now Quezon) province. Like Osmeña, he studied at the San Juan de Letran in Manila, but during the Philippine revolution he joined the Aguinaldo army. Afterwards he entered the UST and in 1903 won admission to the bar. Like Osmeña, Quezon practised law and then received appointments as fiscal, first of Mindoro in 1903 and then of Tayabas in 1904, before being elected governor of Tayabas in 1906 (ibid.: ch. 7).

The provincial prosecutor, the post Osmeña and Quezon occupied before being elected governor, was the colony's second-highest office for Filipinos in local government. According to the *Report of the Philippine Commission* (*RPC*): "The policy of the commission in its provincial appointments has been, where possible, to appoint Filipinos as governors and Americans as treasurers and supervisors. The provincial secretary and the provincial fiscal [prosecutor] appointed have uniformly been Filipinos" (*RPC* 1904: 137). While some scholars emphasized the connection between Filipino politicians and American colonial officers, one cannot underestimate the fact that Osmeña and Quezon studied law, became lawyers, and worked as prosecutors in local government. In other words, they were the beneficiaries of the Spanish educational reform that allowed Filipinos to study law at the UST and launched careers as legal bureaucrats in the American colonial government.

The Philippine legislature was almost dominated by lawyers from the very beginning. Table 1.1 shows the occupational background of legislators in various time periods.

Table 1.1 Occupation of Legislators (Selected Years)

	1898	*1907*	*1921*		*1932*		*1946*		*1954*		*1962*	
House	LH	LH	UH	LH	UH	LH	UH	LH	UH	LH	UH	LH
Lawyer	50.6	60.0	87.5	68.8	78.2	68.7	79.1	63.9	78.2	71.2	62.5	75.9
Physician	20.0	5.0	n.a.	6.4	4.3	4.1	—	9.2	4.3	10.8	—	6.7
Agriculturalist	0	22.5	20.8	32.2	21.7	30.2	8.3	15.4	4.3	13.8	16.6	6.7
Teacher	3.5	7.5	0.0	1.0	4.3	2.0	4.1	5.1	21.7	5.9	29.1	9.6
Businessperson	8.3	11.3	0.0	8.6	13.0	11.4	8.3	9.2	13.0	6.9	25.0	18.2
Journalist	0	2.5	33.3	9.6	4.3	5.2	16.6	0.0	4.3	0.9	8.3	6.7
Others	17.6	2.5	0.0	2.1	13.0	3.1	8.3	12.3	8.7	11.8	12.5	17.3
Sum	100.0	111.3	141.6	128.7	138.8	124.7	124.7	115.1	134.5	121.3	154.0	141.1

Notes: a. The writer has categorized occupations according to the classification of Stauffer (1966).
b. The sum often exceeds 100 per cent because quite a few politicians had more than one kind of occupational experience.
c. UH and LH stand for Upper House and Lower House respectively. Their formal names depend upon the era.

Sources: Ocampo 2000; Philippine Assembly 1908; Stauffer 1966.

Based on Table 1.1, we can say, in general, that most of the legislators were lawyers, although the data is not complete. The tendency of lawyers to dominate the legislature persisted even after independence in 1946. The data reveal that family wealth did not guarantee a position, although it might help their children attain higher education. They still had to study hard in law schools in Manila before running for elections in their district. It is also worth mentioning that only two law schools existed in the Philippines in the late 19th century; lawyers thus shared not only their professional experiences but also their college life in Manila, where students from various provinces got acquainted.

Making use of connections they nurtured based on their profession and education, Osmeña and Quezon successfully maintained majorities in the colonial legislature until independence. Table 1.2 summarizes the electoral results during the American colonial period.

Table 1.2 clearly shows the stable strength of the NP throughout the colonial period. Regular elections for the legislature were held during the American colonial period, although there were several changes in the elections based on revisions of the organic act for colonial rule.

Table 1.2 Seat Distribution in the Colonial Legislature, 1907–41

		Nacionalista	*Progressive*	*Democratic*	*Independent*	*Others*	*Total*
1907	LH	58	16		6		80
1909	LH	62	17			2	81
1912	LH	62	16			3	81
1916	UH	22	1		1		24
	LH	75	7	2	6		90
1919	UH	21		1	2		24
	LH	83		4	3		90
1922	UH	12 3		5	4		24
	LH	29 35		26	1	2	93
1925	UH	5 6 3		8	2		24
	LH	64		22	6		92
1928	UH	20		4			24
	LH	61		17	6	1	(94)
1931	UH	6		4			10
	LH	69		12			((81))
1934	UH	3 8					11
	LH	19 67				3	89
1935	LH	19 64			5		(98)
1938	LH	98					98
1941	UH	24					
	LH	95					(98)

Notes: a. LH stands for Lower House, while UH stands for Upper House.
b. In cases of a split within the NP, Osmeña and Quezon led each faction; the left side of the Nacionalista column shows the number in Osmeña's group, while the right side of the Nacionalista column shows that of Quezon's group.
c. Some data since 1928 are lacking. In case the total number is confirmed, though the party affiliation is not confirmed, parentheses are placed around the total. In cases where neither the total number nor party affiliation is confirmed, double parentheses are placed around the total.

Sources: Forbes 1928; Hayden 1942; Liang 1971.

The American colonial authorities, for instance, established the Senate in 1916 based on the Jones Law, abolished it in 1935 based on the constitution, but soon afterward reestablished it by amending the latter in 1941. In terms of party politics, the NP led by Osmeña and Quezon maintained the majority, although it split up twice, which we will study later. Meanwhile, the opposition party failed to obtain the majority in any election. Thus, the colonial legislature was governed by a typical dominant-party system.

Changing the Economy

While the Taft Commission imposed tutelary political rule, it tried to strengthen Philippine-American economic ties. The introduction of duty-free trade was achieved on the strength of Taft's conviction that the Filipino people would prefer to remain under American rule as long as the United States provided good government and access to the US market for Philippine products (14 May 1980). Among his famous remarks is the following:

> If we bring them in behind the tariff wall [of the United States], if they see that association with the United States is beneficial to them, as I verily believe it will be, it is quite unlikely they will desire full independence. (Golay 1997: 96)

The Philippine market was steadily connected to the US market, which had been highly protected (Golay 1997: 82). After the Treaty of Paris expired, the US Congress in 1909 passed the Payne-Aldrich Law, which mandated duty-free trade between the United States and the Philippines, and in 1913 abolished quantitative quotas on Philippine products with the Underwood Simmons Tariff Act. These tariff measures had the effect of transforming the Philippine economy into a typical colonial economy. While the Philippines exported raw materials such as Manila hemp, sugar and coconut, it imported American-made finished products (Nagano 1986: ch. 1). The United States thereafter became the Philippine's largest—nearly the only—trade partner by the end of the American colonial rule.

Philippine lawmakers had mixed feelings about free trade with the United States. Some argued that the arrangement encouraged Philippine exports and would help the country to recover from wartime destruction. Others opposed it, concerned about the political consequences of free trade or the possible lobby of American businesses that would invest in the Philippines in an attempt to retain the colony (Constantino and Constantino 1975: 326–8).

The introduction of free trade with the United States drastically changed the economic structure of the Philippines but did not lead to the complete dominance of an American colonial political economy. This happened partly because the changing economic structure occurred alongside the expansion of Filipino participation in politics under the Democratic Party, which had opposed the colonial policy of the Republican Party and encouraged Filipino participation in politics and business as we will see below.

Formation of the Colonial State

Filipinization and Colonial State Building

Once the Democratic Party won the US presidency in 1912, the colonial government accelerated the delegation of power to the Filipinos both in the executive and legislative branches of government. First, newly appointed Governor-General Francis B. Harrison increased the number of Filipino members in the Philippine Commission to a majority (Hayden 1942: 167). In the colonial bureaucracy, he carried out so-called Filipinization, an aggressive recruitment of Filipinos into the colonial bureaucracy. "As of mid-1913, Americans in the insular service numbered 2,623, of whom 147 were" in major positions, but "six years later there were only 58 Americans remaining in the higher categories" (Golay 1997: 175–6). Meanwhile, "[o]ver this period Filipino[s] in the higher levels of the insular service increased from 859 to 1,080 and in the [lower but] classified service from 6,363 to 12,047. As a result, the proportion of Americans in the colonial civil service fell from 29 to 6 per cent, with those holding higher positions dropping from one-seventh to one-twentieth" by 1919 (ibid.: 176).

Under the Democratic Party-ruled government in the US, the Philippine lawmakers won the Jones Law in 1916—the first act that stipulated the conditions for Philippine independence and guaranteed further autonomy to the Philippine colonial government. Under the Jones Law, the US government abolished the Philippine Commission, appointed Cabinet members who were all Filipinos (except the governor-general and vice governor, who concurrently served as the secretary of public instruction), and established the Senate comprising 24 Filipinos who were elected from larger districts than those created for the Lower House.[5] As a result, the offices of governor-general, vice governor and auditor remained in American hands (ibid.: 202).

While the Jones Law stipulated the separation of the executive and legislative branches, the Nacionalista leaders succeeded in sharing executive power through the establishment of the council of state, which functioned as an advisory body to the governor-general in 1917 (ibid.: 205, 207). The council was composed of the governor-general, the Senate President, the Speaker of the House and cabinet secretaries. The council

[5] The two senators who represented the provinces where non-Christians lived, however, were appointed by the governor-general (Boncan 2000: 95).

convened once a week, and gradually assumed the role of the colony's highest policymaking and decision-making body (Nagano 2003: 49–50).

The Harrison administration enjoyed easy relations with the Filipino politicians enjoying economic prosperity because of the increasing demand for goods caused by World War I. The US market absorbed most Philippine exports (Golay 1997: 212). The administration then actively attempted to develop the Philippine economy. It established, for instance, the Philippine National Bank (PNB) in order to provide developmental loans to private capital. Because of opposition by the US Congress, the colonial government failed to invite American banks to the islands and sought other ways to finance local capital. The major banks in the Philippines were those such as the British-owned Hong Kong and Shanghai Banking Corporation, which served foreign trade rather than local development interests (Nagano 1986: 90–1). The only active local bank was the Bank of the Philippine Islands (BPI), which, however, served export products and did not provide enough loans to develop domestic agriculture (Nagano 1986: ch. 3; 2003: ch. 3; 2015: ch. 2).

Moreover, the administration passed the Infant Industry Law to encourage Philippine capital to invest in new enterprises. It also established several government enterprises such as the National Coal Company, National Petroleum Company and National Cement Company (Golay 1997: 214). Among the national companies, the most important was the National Development Company (NDC), which aimed at providing loans to enterprises in order to develop the country or promote public interest (ibid.: 215).

Filipino politicians made the best use of the expanding economy and government policy, especially after the establishment of the board of control (comprising the governor-general, Senate President and House Speaker), and determined the general policy for all government corporations (ibid.: 215). Quezon, for instance, made use of the Manila Railway Company (MRC), which the government acquired in 1917. The MRC, well managed by a professional trained in Europe and the United States, contributed to the expansion and consolidation of Quezon's political power base (Abinales and Amoroso 2005: 141–2).

Meanwhile Osmeña, who appointed one of his close aides as PNB president, attempted to strengthen and expand his political network through the sugar industry (Abinales and Amoroso 2005: 141). Once the PNB began operations with assets of 12 million pesos in May 1916, the bank vigorously expanded its business and reported assets of 249 million pesos by the end of 1918 (Golay 1997: 213). The sugar industry, which enjoyed huge profits because of the special demand created during WWI, aggressively absorbed loans from the PNB and began to build modern sugar centrals, which milled sugarcane gathered from nearby plantations. Unlike other Southeast Asian economies in which capital from the colonial master played pivotal roles, the Philippines already had established and emerging local capitalists who had accumulated wealth during the time of expanding trade opportunities in the 19th century. These local capitalists made the best use of the expanding opportunities for developmental loans created by the PNB (Nagano 1986: ch. 3).

However, the momentum for prosperity came to a sudden halt in 1919 because of monetary crisis triggered by a sharp slump in commodity prices in the United States soon after WWI ended (Golay 1997: 219–20). However, the crisis was less economic than political, because the economy in general recovered from the sudden slump and expanded throughout the 1920s. The Republican Party regained its clout in the United States and exploited the opportunity it provided to attack and reverse the course of Filipinization as shaped by the Democratic administration. The US government, in which Republicans had recovered their majority in Congress, deployed an investigation mission headed by Leonard Wood and Cameron Forbes. The mission harshly criticized mismanagement of the PNB by claiming that the PNB's failure was the worst in world banking history (Golay 1997: 219–20; Nagano 2003, 2015).[6]

Emergence of a New Generation in Colonial Politics

Philippine lawmakers ended their close relations with American colonial officers and faced the reality of the colony's new situation as soon as the Republican Party won the US presidency in 1920. Leonard Wood, head of the investigative mission for the PNB scandal, was appointed governor-general and carried out his reform of the colonial government. Wood, for instance, vetoed sixteen bills in his first year—three times the number of vetoes exercised by Harrison during his entire term as governor-general (Golay 1997: 237). In terms of economic policy, Wood believed in less intervention by the government, so he attempted to privatize the MRC or transform the PNB from a development bank to a

[6] Nagano uncovered the hidden story of the scandal, in which American colonial officers tried to hide their mismanagement and laid the blame for it on the Filipinos (Nagano 2003, 2015).

savings bank, but failed to do so because of objections from Washington (ibid.: 245–7).

Meanwhile, Quezon, gradually amassing political clout, was determined to challenge the leadership of his rivals in colonial politics. He actually exploited the PNB scandal to challenge the authority of Osmeña, who had enjoyed close relations with Governor-General Harrison (Nagano 2003: ch. 6; 2015: ch. 5). Accusing Osmeña of dominating the decision-making process, Quezon split from the Nacionalista and organized his own Collectivista Party in order to assert his quest for collective decision making in February 1922 (Forbes 1928: 115–6). Quezon and Osmeña both ran for the Senate and won, but Quezon was elected Senate President while Osmeña ended up Senate minority leader. As a result of the internal power struggle within the NP, the Democratic Party, a small opposition party that replaced the Progressive Party, made its presence felt for a while in 1922.

A more important newcomer in the national legislature was Manuel A. Roxas, a 30-year-old former governor of Capiz, who emerged as the leader of a new generation in the Democratic Party. Roxas, born in Capiz in 1891, studied briefly in Hong Kong before graduating from the University of the Philippines (UP) College of Law, passed the bar exam, and practised law in Manila and then Capiz (Lichauco 1952: 9–11). Roxas ran for the governorship of Capiz in 1919 and won, and then for the Lower House as a candidate in Quezon's faction of the NP, which he also won. He took over the speakership from Osmeña, who moved to the Senate following the 1922 election. From then on, Roxas was the third-most powerful figure in colonial politics.

Roxas's educational background followed in the typical career path for his generation. He returned to the Philippines soon after his study in Hong Kong, where several Filipino families sent their children to study English in the early colonial period (Wong 1999: 75). Moreover, he studied at the UP law college, which was established for higher education in 1907 (Jamias 1963: 14–5). The UP College of Law was the third law school established in the Philippines and the first to use English as its medium of instruction. UP became the country's premiere college mainly because of its stiff entry requirements (ibid.: 12–3, 37). Besides Roxas, Jose P. Laurel and Elpidio Quirino, future Philippine presidents, were also early graduates of the college. These men were more than ten years younger than Quezon and Osmeña and had been educated in English as a second language.

These young politicians were not necessarily loyal to their American colonial master, however. They retained memories of the Philippine-American War and maintained a good command of Spanish, and thus possibly nurtured an antagonistic spirit against the former enemy or the United States (Nakano 2007: 125–7). Roxas, for instance, once harshly criticized economic exploitation by American capital, asserting that it "is always ready to pop its ugly head, behind the lady-like innocence of 'civilizing missions' to promote its selfish ends" (Roxas 1985: 402; Nakano 2007: 126). Claro M. Recto, a rising star in the opposition Democratic Party, also belonged to Roxas's generation and became a vocal nationalist critic of neocolonialism in the 1950s. Both Laurel and Recto were from southern Luzon provinces where the American military conducted harsh anti-guerrilla campaigns, including the relocation of residents, torture and the killing of civilians (Nakano 2007: 125–7).

Quezon approached this talented younger generation and consolidated his leadership in the colonial legislature. Then, he concentrated on his fight against the governor-general. In 1923, a Filipino accused an American detective working with the Manila police of official misconduct. Leonard Wood came to the defense of the American, but Jose Laurel, then the interior secretary, resigned because of his dissatisfaction with Wood's position on the issue. Quezon exploited the incident and succeeded in convincing all of the secretaries to resign from government while he and Roxas quit the council of state in July 1923 (Golay 1997: 248). During a special election at the time, Quezon uttered his famous remark: "I prefer a government run like hell by Filipinos to a government run like heaven by Americans" (Constantino and Constantino 1975: 335–6). Quezon's clash with the governor-general secured his position as the leader of the Filipino people, which he would maintain until his death in 1943 (Golay 1997: 249). Nevertheless, Wood was strongly supported by the US president, and he maintained his post until his sudden death in August 1927 (Lichauco 1952: ch. 6; Golay 1997: 272).

In the midst of a series of political battles, Quezon moved to strengthen his ties with the sugar industry. In 1922, owners in the sugar industry organized the Philippine Sugar Association (PSA), which comprised Filipinos and a few Americans in the sugar industry, to act as their political voice (Larkin 2001: 160). The association, whose members included major players in the sugar industry, including the president of the PNB, established close connections with colonial officers and politicians in Manila and Washington (ibid.: 160–1). Exploiting their network, the association worked hard to make Philippine sugar competitive on the world market, which starred top sugar producers like Cuba, Puerto Rico and Hawaii, as well as the American beet in the highly protected US market (ibid.: 160).

Policymakers in the Early 1930s

After the sudden death of Leonard Wood in his office, Quezon and Osmeña flew to Washington to lobby for a new governor-general who would be more cooperative with Filipino politicians. Quezon and Osmeña did not have any legal powers to recommend or appoint a governor-general, but they had experience recommending Harrison and enjoyed close relations with him in the 1910s. They found Henry L. Stimson, the former secretary of war, an ideal candidate, as long as the Republican Party maintained its majority in each house of Congress. At first Stimson was not interested in the post, but was finally convinced to accept it. In December 1927, he was appointed governor-general (Golay 1997: 272–3). While Stimson shared his predecessors' determination to retain the Philippines, he faced a different reality. Stimson, as Taft had done before, believed that duty-free trade would dampen the Filipino plea for independence but recognized its impact on American farmers. It was just a matter of time before the inflow of cheap products and labor from the Philippines generated opposition to colonial policy from American politicians supported by farmers and laborers. To deal with domestic concerns and opposition, Stimson decided to encourage investment and enterprise by Americans in the Philippines. He also raised Philippine tariffs on imports from all other countries except the United States, so that the former could fully share the fruit of tariff walls with the United States (ibid.).

In order to carry out these policies, Stimson abandoned Wood's conflicting policy and reestablished both the council of state and board of controls so that he could cultivate support from Filipino political leaders (ibid.: 274–5). When Stimson invited an American banker to revise a banking regulation, which he had passed, he found that Speaker Roxas quickly understood the problem and helped work for its revision (Lichauco 1952: 55–6). One of Stimson's achievements was, therefore, putting the PNB back on the right track in cooperation with Roxas (ibid.: 56). The PNB, by putting several sugar centrals under its direct control, finally succeeded in making the centrals redeem their loans in the mid-1930s (Nagano 1986: 121–36).

Stimson, however, stayed in the Philippines less than a year before he was appointed secretary of state, and his post was taken over by Dwight Davis. Davis did not have his own position on Philippine policy but followed the lead of the Republican Party to retain the colony (Golay 1997: 283). Davis encouraged industrialization and the diversification of agricultural production, while suggesting that the Philippines voluntarily reduce sugar export.

By the time cooperation between Filipino politicians and American colonial officials was reestablished, the ranks of the Philippine middle class, which comprised white-collar workers in the colonial government, were swelling (Doeppers 1984). The rise of the middle class resulted from two changes that occurred in previous decades. First, the Filipinization policy expanded job opportunities for Filipinos who finished their studies in public schools; many of them took over posts in the colonial government previously held by Americans. Second, economic growth that began in the 1910s provided the colonial government with revenue increase that allowed it to hire more people (Doeppers 1984: 2). According to a survey, Filipinos in the civil service numbered fewer than 3,000 in 1903, but their numbers ballooned to almost 22,000 in 1931 (ibid.: 62). It is true that the rise of the middle class happened mainly in Manila, but its members had come from nearly everywhere on the islands with the development of educational opportunities in the provinces. Although the colonial government failed to provide universal education, as several scholars have pointed out (see, for example, May 1980), it institutionalized the path by which the Filipino youth could study and be employed. In other words, some Filipinos began to assume "education as a means of social mobility" (Golay 1997: 122). Without these colonial bureaucrats, Wood might have been unable to manage the colonial government, which faced hostile politicians led by Quezon.

Miguel P. Cuaderno, who became governor of the future central bank, typifies the middle class that rose during this period. He was born in Bataan in 1890, studied at UP but graduated from National University, became a lawyer in 1919, and was hired at the Bureau of Supply. Although he established his career as a lawyer, he was trained by experience as an economist ever since he was a working student in Hong Kong (Ty 1948). While in Hong Kong, he became a friend of Dee C. Chuan, who was born in the Philippines and established the China Banking Corporation, the first local bank for Chinese businesses in the Philippines, in 1920 (Wong 1999: 75).

Although he was hired at the Bureau of Supply, Cuaderno was no stranger to the banking industry. He had helped an American officer finalize the charter of the PNB in the 1910s as a stenographer and finally transferred to the PNB in 1926, where he energetically dealt with the bank's legal cases, specifically its reconstruction from the financial crisis of the early 1920s (*American Chamber of Commerce of the Philippines Journal* September 1938: 8; Cornejo 1939: 1657–8; Galang 1932: 107). Interestingly, he worked at the PNB when Speaker Roxas cooperated with Governor General Stimson to revise the banking regulation.

Aside from Cuaderno, many emerging economic bureaucrats established their careers in the colonial state. They learned economics either through formal education or from the school of hard knocks. In addition to learning economics in their jobs with the colonial government, there were many bureaucrats who studied in the United States under the revived pensionado system. Professor Abdon Llorente of Far Eastern University stated: "From 1919 to 1930, 379 students were sent by the government to the United States. Of this number, 58 took up the study of different branches of economics....These returned pensionados are now employed as follows; 21 as government employees, 7 as teachers, 1 as practicing attorney, 3 as actuaries, 3 as life underwriters, 2 as newspapermen, 7 in business and 2 as farmers" (Llorente 1935: 16).

Then UP President, Rafael Palma, who was a graduate of the UST and belonged to Quezon's generation, recognized a change in generation. He asserted in his address at a commencement ceremony at UP in the 1920s: "This generation seems to have been destined to work out economic achievements, just as the older generation was called upon to obtain political achievements" (Palma 1985: 381). In Palma's mind there must be several examples of pioneers of economics who worked in various fields. For instance, Conrado Benitez, who studied at the University of Chicago as a pensionado, returned from the United States and graduated from the UP College of Law. He worked at UP as the first Filipino dean of the College of Liberal Arts and became the dean of the College of Business Administration, which was established in 1929 (Cornejo 1938: 1620; Mojares 2006: 491). Meanwhile, Cornelio Balmaceda was an example of a successful pensionado who studied business in the United States and worked in the colonial government. Balmaceda was born in Ilocos Norte in 1896, and studied at Harvard University as a pensionado to obtain an MBA. On his return to the Philippines, he resumed his work at the Bureau of Commerce in 1922. One of the earliest PhD holders was Andres V. Castillo, who was born in 1903, and earned his bachelor degree from UP and PhD from Columbia University. When he returned to the Philippines, he taught at several universities and became the dean of the College of Business Administration at the University of Manila in 1934 (Bangko Sentral ng Pilipinas 1998: 37; *Tribune* 19 August 1934: 17).

In addition to knowing the changing focus from political independence to economic readjustment, it is also significant to understand what kinds of economics they studied. In line with this, Professor Llorente encouraged Filipinos to go to the United States, citing Americans who studied economics in Germany or Austria-Hungary in the 19th century (Llorente 1935: 13). The German school of economics was famous for its nationalist orientation that questioned the effectiveness of free trade for newly independent nations. It was also well known that Alexander Hamilton, the treasury secretary of George Washington's administration, and his economic policy influenced German economists who established the German school of economics that asserted the significance of infant industry protection by the government (Lichauco 1988: 32–49).

Those who studied economics in a country whose economy was highly protected and industrialized most probably cast doubt on the duty-free trade between the Philippines and the United States. As we have seen, the United States maintained a high tariff on imports from other countries except those from its colony. At this point, it was not unusual for Filipino students to be aware of protectionism and American industrial policy and to figure out the double standard in US economic policy: While implementing the protectionism in their country, the United States imposed free trade on its colony.

These early economic bureaucrats and university economists began to discuss tariff and other types of industrial policy and to nurture their network. In February 1928, a group of provincial treasurers published the *Philippine Finance Review* (*PFR*) (Doeppers 1984: 27–31; *PFR* February 1928). Aimed at providing professionals with a variety of information related to finance and commerce, the journal featured various contributions from economic specialists of the time. Cornelio Balmaceda, for instance, advocated protection of infant industries in agriculture and simple manufacturing industry through tariff measures (Doeppers 1984: 27). "Professor Andres Castillo" supported protection and warned that it would be "suicidal" if an independent Philippines continued free trade (ibid.: 28). Moreover, Pator Kimpo, working in the office of the Speaker of the Lower House, picked up Balmaceda's suggestion and asserted that further protection was warranted both for infant industries and advanced manufacturing in order to change the current situation in which the Philippines imported manufactured goods from the United States and exported only raw materials (ibid.: 27). While these were mere discussions in a journal, the ideas exerted a degree of influence on the development of the network of policymakers in the middle of the 1930s.

The Filipinos who discussed policy proposals suddenly faced the politics of independence triggered by the Great Depression, which began in October 1929. The US government, working hard to recover from the Depression, considered a revision of the tariff, which already had been high enough. In a special session on tariffs in late 1929, a senator introduced an amendment to grant independence to the Philippines in order to protect the US market from cheap sugar from the Philippines (Golay 1997: 281). Although the amendment was never realized, the US Congress began to seriously consider abandoning the Philippine Islands because of the rise of protectionism at home and the crisis in the Far East after the Japanese invasion of Manchuria in 1931 (Nakano 1997: ch. 2).

Roxas began to play an impressive role in the changing phase of the politics of independence. He was keen enough to know that economics would become an important agenda alongside political independence, and so he gradually advocated preparation for the adjustment of the Philippine economy. Assuming that the voice of the Americans to cut colonial ties with the Philippines had grown beyond the point of no return, Roxas launched a new political initiative, *Ang Bagong Katipunan* (the new Katipunan), in November 1930 (Golay 1997: 292). Ang Bagong Katipunan advocated the necessary economic adjustment to prepare for independence, which meant the end of duty-free trade with the United States. Roxas's movement was well covered by the *PFR* (*PFR* December 1930: 12, 26–8). For instance, in an article entitled "The Need for a National Economic Policy", Roxas argued that the Philippines needed to launch a new nationalist movement in order to face the changing situation. He advocated greater local production and consumption as well as the conservation of natural resources in the Philippines (*PFR* March 1930: 12). He most probably referred to the various proposals in the previous issues of the *PFR*, as one of the contributors, Kimpo, worked in Roxas's office. Castillo later praised Ang Bagong Katipunan as "the first serious attempt to apply economic principle on a national scale" when he explained the development of economics in the Philippines (Castillo 1934: 15). Ang Bagong Katipunan, however, failed to receive support from Quezon, the sugar industry and American businesses in the Philippines and lost its momentum (Golay 1997: 293).

Although Roxas failed to mobilize support for Ang Bagong Katipunan, he led a series of independence missions in place of Quezon, who suffered the onset of tuberculosis in the middle of the 1920s (Golay 1997: 273, 278, 284, 286, 292). A mission, led by Roxas and Senator Osmeña, which was later called Os-Rox Mission, arrived in Washington in January 1932 and remained for almost a year until it finally brought the Hare-Hawes-Cutting (HHC) Act back to the Philippines. The HHC Act was the first independence law that stipulated the process leading toward Philippine independence. According to the law, the Filipino people would draft a constitution in an elected constitutional convention. After approval from the US president, they would form a commonwealth government that would be run by the Filipino people for ten years after independence (ibid.: ch. 10). As we will see in the second chapter, the passage of the HHC Act gave birth to another political clash between Quezon and Osmeña and was subsequently replaced by the Tydings-McDuffie (TM) Act in 1934. The process toward independence as stipulated by the HHC, however, remained the same, because the TM Act appears almost identical to the HHC Act. In other words, the passage of the HHC Act marks the beginning of the end of colonial rule.

The 19th century was a period when the Philippines experienced rapid socioeconomic change from a subsistence economy to an export economy. This did not result in the consolidation of Spanish control but rather in the emergence of a revolutionary clergy and other intellectuals whose ideas played a significant role in ending Spanish colonial rule. Before the American invasion, the Filipino people had gradually emerged and mounted a revolt against Spain.

US colonial authority, therefore, faced a people on the verge of establishing their own government. While the Americans did not admit Philippine independence, they encouraged Filipinos to practise "self-government" under American guidance. Under tutelary colonial rule, the colonial government included Filipino politicians who were used to the structures of governance. Some had even begun to cooperate with colonial bureaucrats and their numbers gradually but steadily increased.

A new generation of educated politicians and bureaucrats who established their careers under American colonial rule recognized the economic problems they would face following political independence. This is because the American colonization of the Philippines changed the country's economic structure from an export-oriented economy, which was a part of the British empire in East Asia, to a typical colonial economy that depended on the market of its colonial master for its raw-material exports.

While the previous generation focused on political independence, the new generation faced an agenda of economic decolonization in preparation for independence, which necessarily changed economic relations with the colonial master.

Unlike Manuel L. Quezon and his generation, who worked for political independence, policymakers led by Manuel A. Roxas discovered that economic decolonization was next on the agenda for Philippine political leaders. They knew that American colonial officers intended to connect the Philippines with the US market, which was highly protected at the time. The US market was large enough to absorb most of the Philippines' raw materials. When Roxas and other policymakers grew involved in the politics of independence in the 1930s, therefore, they did not begin from scratch. They were no longer revolutionaries; in fact, they emerged from a colonial state. Nonetheless, they were critical of existing structure and working to change the structure.

CHAPTER 2

Beyond the Colonial State, 1933–45

The creation of a central bank was a new idea for the US colony, whose economy previously had been managed without intervention by a central bank.[1] Indeed, central banking was a new idea even in the United States at the time. How did Filipino policymakers discuss the idea of creating a central bank? This chapter studies the flow of new ideas that circulated among Filipino policymakers. The Filipino delegates to the Constitutional Convention of 1934 employed various new ideas in their discussions. Several delegates belonged to a new generation of professionals; therefore, the convention could be called a "national congress" whose members differed from traditional elites (Uchiyama 1999: 201). The inflow of international policy ideas such as economic nationalism (Aruego 1937: 658–69; de Dios 2002) and a strong presidency (de Dios 2002) greatly affected the delegates. Notably, however sensational and well it was accepted at the convention, a truly international inflow of ideas remained

[1] A historical study by a prominent economist, Vicente Valdepeñas, on the development of central banking in the Philippines is helpful (Valdepeñas 2003), but does not pay much attention to the political context. Historians cite attempts to create a central bank in the 1930s (Golay 1997: 397; Nagano 2010: 46), but do not study these in detail. Meanwhile, Lumba studies the relations between the emergence of the image of a national economy and the establishment of the Central Bank of the Philippines (Lumba 2008), but does not study the actual process undertaken by policymakers in the 1930s. Lumba also mentions relations between the American devaluation and Filipino proposal for creating a central bank (Lumba 2013: 275–89), but does not study actual policymaking process in the 1930s.

out of the scope of the existing interest structure that had shaped the patronage politics Quezon used to his advantage (McCoy 1988).[2]

This chapter demonstrates that the emerging professionals, international inflow of policy ideas, and resurgence of nationalism motivated a handful of powerful Filipino policymakers to strive to establish a central bank. Although their proposals failed to materialize before independence, the policymakers developed the idea and by 1949 succeeded in establishing the bank. This chapter explores the development of ideas among policymakers that led to the first proposals to create a central bank in the 1930s. First, the origin of the idea is examined through a study of the early phase of the initiative, from 1933 to 1935, when US policy changes prompted Filipino policymakers to recognize the necessity of autonomy. Second, the period from 1935 to 1945 is examined for the subsequent political contexts in which the key advocates continued to work for their goals despite indifference and opposition from government authorities and the subsequent Japanese occupation.

The Independence Act, US Monetary Policy Change and the First Proposal

The First Independence Act and the Creation of the PEA

In the Philippines, the 1933 passage of the HHC Act in the US Congress led to a political power struggle among leaders of the dominant NP: namely, Senate President Quezon, Senator Sergio *Osmeña* and House Speaker Manuel A. Roxas. The power struggle provided the policymakers with an opportunity to consider the economic consequences of independence. In opposing the HHC Act, Quezon characterized it as a tariff act instead of an independence act (Golay 1997: 320). He said: "All I can say for the present is that the National City Bank [of New York] took an active interest in the passage of the Hawes-Cutting bill" (*Tribune* 1 January 1933: 1, 19).[3] He argued that the National City Bank worked for the passing of the HHC Act in order to protect Cuban sugar at

[2] The appeal for economic nationalism was irrelevant to the agenda of the sugar industry. The sugar industry has usually been assumed to be the country's strongest vested interest, a group that pressured politicians, including Quezon, to seek ways to maintain the status quo (Friend 1963; Golay 1997).

[3] The HHC Act comprised the Hare Bill in the American House and Hawes-Cutting Bill in the Senate, and was sometimes called "Hare Bill" or "Hawes-Cutting Bill".

the expense of Philippine sugar (*Tribune* 1 January 1933: 1, 19; Golay 1997: 320). Quezon's attack was so harsh that a split in the party became inevitable in early January 1933 (*Tribune* 3 January 1933: 1).

Quezon expressed his opposition to the HHC Act on various occasions. When he was invited by a group of economists to a luncheon meeting of the Columbian Club on 17 March, he argued that economic features of the act were so unfavorable to the Philippines that social unrest could develop and result in the resurgence of military over commonwealth government (*Tribune* 18 March 1933: 1). He explained that when the United States imposed the full tariff rate on Philippine sugar three years after the enactment, the US market would virtually shut out Philippine sugar, which would deal a death blow to the Philippine export industry on the heels of massive unemployment and social unrest, and finally culminate with another act of military suppression by the United States (ibid.). Quezon attempted to convince his audience that the HHC Act would result in economic catastrophe.

The audience at the Columbian Club consisted of a group of economists who apparently were the founders of the Philippine Economic Association (PEA), although the group had yet to assume its name. The following supports this assertion: First, Cuaderno points out that the PEA was organized after the passage of the HHC Act (Cuaderno 1949: 1); second, the presiding officer of the day was Elpidio Quirino, who would become the president of the PEA (*Tribune* 18 March 1933: 2; PEA 1934);[4] and third, PEA's first two publications indicate its gradual development as an organization beginning in March 1933 (PEA 1933, 1934). Who, then, were the members of the PEA?

Table 2.1 is a compilation of biographical data on the PEA's founding members whose names were recorded in its first publication (PEA 1933: I). From Table 2.1, we can glean three characteristics about the organization's members. First, the only politician was Elpidio Quirino, although some members had held seats in the legislature. Second, the majority comprised bureaucrats, and there were no visible representatives from any particular industry. Third, most of the members either studied economics or worked for administrations involved in economic issues,

[4] Journalist and biographer Sol H. Gwekoh, in a biography of Quirino, wrote that Quirino organized the PEA to study economic issues (Gwekoh 1949), while the authors of the PEA do not specify any single president or founder in the organization's first pamphlet (PEA 1933).

Table 2.1 Membership of the Philippine Economic Association

	Name	*Educational Background*	*Profession*	*Position, Affiliation**
1	Salvador Araneta	UST / Harvard U.	lawyer, businessman	Partner, Araneta Zaragoza and Araneta (Law firm)
2	Cornelio Balmaceda	Harvard U.	bureaucrat	Assistant Director, Bureau of Commerce
3	Conrado Benitez	UP / U. of Chicago	educator	Dean, College of Business Administration, University of the Philippines
4	Marcelino Bernardo	N.A.	N.A.	N.A.
5	Andres Castillo	UP / Columbia U.	educator	Dean, College of Business Administration, University of Manila
6	Anastacio de Castro	UP / U. of Chicago / Columbia U.	lawyer, bureaucrat	Chief of cooperative marketing and rural credit, Bureau of Commerce
7	Jose L. Celeste	N.A.	bureaucrat, educator	Special Agent, Department of Finance
8	Tomas Confesor	UP / U. of California / U. of Chicago	educator, politician, bureaucrat	Representative, Philippine Legislature / Director, Bureau of Commerce
9	Jose Espino	N.A.	bureaucrat	N.A., Bureau of Customs
10	Vicente Fabella	UP/U. of Chicago / Northwestern U.	accountant, educator	Dean, Jose Rizal College
11	Fermin Francisco	N.A.	educator	Professor, University of the Philippines
12	Mariano Gana	N.A.	educator	Professor, University of the Philippines
13	Guillermo Gomez	Harvard U.	bureaucrat	Undersecretary, Department of Finance
14	Leon Ma. Gonzales	Harvard U.	bureaucrat, educator	Chief of the division of statistics, Department of Agriculture and Commerce
15	Jose M. Hilario	UP / Columbia U.	bureaucrat	Deputy collector, Bureau of Internal Revenue
16	Jacinto Kamantigue	N.A.	bureaucrat	Chief agent of the inspection division, Bureau of Internal Revenue
17	Catalino Lavadia	N.A.	bureaucrat	Director, N.A.
18	Abdon Llorente	N.A.	educator	Professor, Far Eastern University

Table 2.1 Continued

	Name	Educational Background	Profession	Position, Affiliation*
19	Bibiano Meer	N.A.	lawyer, bureaucrat	Chief of the law division, Bureau of Internal Revenue
20	Elpidio Quirino	UP	politician, lawyer	Senator
21	Manuel L. Roxas	UP / U. of Wisconsin	bureaucrat, educator	Professor, UP / Director, Bureau of Plant Industry
22	Hirarion Silayan	UP / U. of California	agriculturalist, bureaucrat	N.A., Bureau of Internal Revenue
23	Nicanor Tomas	N.A.	bureaucrat	Credit Manager, National Development Co.
24	Miguel Unson	UST	bureaucrat, businessman	Secretary of Finance / President, National Life Insurance Company

Note: * The writer has edited information about affiliations in order to specify the characteristics of the members. In some cases the writer has to rely on the sources disclosing the members' affiliations only after 1933.

Sources: Membership data from PEA 1933: I; bibliographical information from Galang 1932; Cornejo 1939; Hayden 1942; Flaviano 1950; Bangko Sentral ng Pilipinas 1998; and *Tribune*, various issues.

and nearly half of them went to the United States to study. All these reflect the political as well as social changes developing in the Philippines under American colonial rule, which we have briefly studied in the previous chapter. Let us further discuss each point.

First, Quirino's political career reflected the shifting phase in the politics of independence. Quirino, born in 1890 in Ilocos Norte, graduated from the University of the Philippines and became a public schoolteacher, a law clerk for the Philippine Commission, a legislator and, finally, a senator. Quirino, who was 12 years younger than Quezon, established his political career under Quezon's tutelage after he met him at the Philippine Columbian Club (Gwekoh 1949: 23). When Quirino became a clerk for the commission he also worked as a secretary at the club and got acquainted with its leading figures. Once elected to the Senate in 1925, he was appointed by Quezon as chairman of the Committee of Accounts and subsequently as chairman of the Special Committee on Taxation, because "a majority of lawyers of the old school [in the Senate] depended not only on the vigor of their young colleagues but on the steady flame of their midnight lamps [to study the new problems of economics]" (ibid.: 31–2).[5] Quirino became so familiar with the economic policy that he was cited as the "high priest of protectionism" in a personal sketch published in the 1930s (Cabildo 1953: 13). Being a close aide of Quezon, Quirino did not collaborate with Roxas, who had failed to mobilize support for Ang Bagong Katipunan and challenged the leadership of Quezon. But Quirino surely belonged to the generation for whom the economic consequences of independence were on the agenda.

Second, 15 out of 24 members were former or incumbent bureaucrats working in various departments in charge of economic policy. For instance, Miguel Unson, born in Iloilo in 1877 and a graduate of the University of Santo Tomas, was a prominent bureaucrat who had been provincial treasurer, and undersecretary and secretary of finance (Cornejo 1939: 2193). Incumbent Undersecretary of Finance Guillermo Gomez was also an original member. There were many PEA members who must have had firsthand information on fiscal conditions as officers of the Bureau of Internal Revenue or Customs, both of which were supervised by the Department of Finance. Meanwhile, Tomas Confesor and Cornelio Balmaceda were director and assistant director of the Bureau of Commerce, respectively, which was supervised by the Department of Agriculture and Commerce. The PEA functioned as a network of bureaucrats from various government economic agencies.

While bureaucrats comprised the majority, a few from the business sector joined the PEA as well. Salvador Araneta, born in Manila in 1902, studied at Harvard University and became a partner at a law firm in the Philippines. The variety of businesses he engaged in included the MRC, a sugar firm, and several mining companies (ibid.: 1602). He was not a representative of any particular industry but was a very active member of the Philippine Chamber of Commerce. He eventually joined in the foundation of the National Economic Protectionism Association (NEPA) in 1934.[6] Unson became another prominent representative of

---

[5] Gwekoh also mentioned that Quirino and Jose P. Laurel (later the president under Japanese military rule) were "the first two graduates of the University of the Philippines to be elected to the Senate and…the first English-speaking senators" (Gwekoh 1949: 30–1).

[6] Araneta did not stick to the interests of a particular industry, although he would become closer to the sugar industry in the 1950s (Takagi 2008). Sicat recorded that Araneta disputed with representatives of the sugar industry in the 1960s (2002: 2).

the business sector when he moved to the insurance industry, however, as mentioned earlier, he established his early career as a bureaucrat.

Third, the members shared a specific knowledge of economics. They learned economics either through formal education or from the school of hard knocks. A member of PEA, Professor Abdon Llorente of Far Eastern University, wrote a column in which he described the dawn of economics in the Philippines, as we have seen in the previous chapter (Llorente 1935). The column suggested that the PEA included most of the pioneering economists of the time, although it did not mention the association directly. Llorente, for instance, praised Dean Conrado Benitez of the UP College of Business Administration, together with Tomas Confesor, Vicente Fabella, Fermin Francisco, and others as "men who crossed the sea in the early days of [the] American regime to delve into the intricacies of economics" (ibid.: 16). Meanwhile, Llorente praised Unson, who led a group of practitioners, including Gomez, because they "began the study of economics from the so-called university of hard knocks" (ibid.).

Nearly half of these men attended school in the United States via either private funding or government scholarship. Those who established the PEA adopted the idea of the positive role of government regulation in economic activities, which the American Economic Association (AEA) represented. American economists who advocated government regulation in economic activities founded the association because they were skeptical of the American Social Science Association, which leaned toward the idea of laissez-faire (Skowronek 1982: 132). The PEA's name most likely derived from that of the AEA, which had established a committee to study the economy of US colonies (Mojares 2006: 490). Llorente asserted that Filipino economists should learn from the United States or Germany, whose governments protected their industries through tariffs (Llorente 1935: 1). In fact, a well-known Filipino buisnssman named Benito Razon mentioned names like Fichte and Friedrich List, both German nationalists, in a speech. Razon was the founding president of the NEPA, for which Llorente later worked as manager (*Tribune* 10 February 1935: 17; 29 May 1935: 16).

PEA members, however, had not yet become radical in their first publication, *The Economics of the Hare-Hawes-Cutting Act: An Analysis* (hereafter, *Analysis*), in which they criticized the independence act instead of proposing their own economic policy (PEA 1933). Part 1, "The National Bonded Indebtedness", studied the Philippine government's fiscal stability as well as its ability to redeem bonds; it concluded: "The present sinking fund arrangement is sufficient to guarantee the ultimate redemption of the Philippine government bonds, and any additional guarantee for their redemption, like the export tax, is not superfluous but is also harmful to national interests" (ibid.: 5). The publication focused on the adversarial effect of the export tax, which the HHC Act required the Philippine government to impose. The subsequent two sections (part 2, "The Export Tax", and part 3, "Effects of Limitations Imposed on Foreign Trade"), to which the authors devoted 28 out of a total of 40 pages, reiterated that the Philippine government could pay its obligation and that it would be faced with difficulty once it was compelled to impose export tax.

The authors criticized the HHC Act as if they aimed at maintaining the status quo. While they admitted that free trade between the Philippines and the United States had contributed to the rapid expansion of export industries such as sugar, they argued "that development [of the export industries] has stood on a weak and unstable foundation" and that free trade would result in "a state of almost complete dependence upon the United States market" (ibid.: 8). They did not yet argue that the Philippines should change its economic structure.

Reflecting the conservative tone of other sections, the authors did not advocate any radical proposal in part 4, "Currency". Here, they concluded: "As long as the present free trade...remains the same there is hardly any need for autonomy in currency legislation because goods like anything else follow the line of least resistance" (ibid.: 38). They hypothetically mentioned that the Philippines would need to depreciate its currency in order to seek new export markets in Asia, especially if the Philippines could no longer export its products to the US market. They recognized: "It is necessary to have our currency at our absolute and free control to provide us with one of the instrumentalities for establishing markets in other countries. We cannot 'remain on a gold island in the midst of a sea of depreciated currency'" (ibid.). They knew what they should do once the current arrangement was abandoned, but stopped short of presenting their own proposals for a comprehensive policy.[7]

The critical but conservative tone of the *Analysis* apparently reflected the political position of Quirino, who was close to Quezon. On the same day Quezon delivered his speech, Quirino asserted that the HHC Act was "a challenge to the Filipinos" (*Tribune* 18 March 1933: 2). It is, however, more important to remember the origin of *Analysis*. The PEA

[7] Regarding their comprehensive policy proposal, see section 1.3.

responded to the US policy change and limited its study to the issue involved. Another US policy change would prompt the PEA to work on another issue. But before examining the PEA's next activity, we shall study an official response within the Philippine government to the US policy change.

US Gold Embargo and the Proposal for a Philippine Central Bank

The year 1933 is pivotal not only because of the HHC Act but also because of a drastic change in the American monetary policy. Facing a series of banking crises after the Great Depression, President Franklin D. Roosevelt became gradually convinced of the need for the country's inflationary policy to recover from the Depression (Eichengreen 1992: 331). Roosevelt, pressured by Congress to adopt a more radical proposal for inflation, embargoed gold exports and endorsed the Thomas Amendment, which authorized the president to take various inflationary measures, on 19 April 1933 (Eichengreen 1992: 331–2). The news was sensationally reported in the Philippines (*Tribune* 21 April 1933: 1).

The Filipino people tried to understand the implications of the US measures. For instance, Andres Castillo drafted a remark that was published as an explanation by a "Filipino political economist" (*Tribune* 23 April 1933: 5). Writing in a relatively pedagogical manner, he explained that inflation would stimulate the domestic economy, although it risked causing hyperinflation of the kind experienced in Germany in 1923 (*Tribune* 23 April 1933: 5, 25).

In the context of this study, it was more interesting that he briefly mentioned: "It cannot be overemphasized that a managed Philippine currency would serve the country best at this time....Unfortunately there is no central bank in the Philippines upon which the task of managing the currency could be very well entrusted" (*Tribune* 23 April 1933: 5, 25). Although it took some time before the currency issue was connected to that of central banking, the policy proposal within the government gradually developed.

Acting Secretary of Finance Vicente Singson-Encarnacion (hereafter Singson), whose name Llorente mentioned as a pioneer of economics (1935: 16), took the lead in handling the situation. Singson was born in 1875 in Ilocos Sur, graduated from the University of Santo Tomas, passed the bar examination, and afterwards became the fiscal of provincial governments and a representative of the Philippine Assembly, as well as a senator (Cornejo 1939: 2143). His career path was similar to contemporaries like Quezon and Osmeña, but it differed from them in two ways. First, Singson was in the minority in the legislature as a member of the Federal Party (Quirino 1987: 44), although he maintained close relations with American colonial officers and became a member of the Philippine Commission from 1913 to 1916.

Second, Singson had vast experience in private business. He was an entrepreneur in the insurance and finance industry. He worked for the Insular Life Assurance Company (hereafter Insular Life), first as a director and later as the president (*Tribune* 15 August 1934: 16). He also worked for the PNB as a board member (Willis 1917: 418; Nagano 2003: 226n15; 2015: 209n15). These two institutions are significant in the historical development of the Philippine finance industry: While Insular Life, founded in 1910, was the first Filipino-owned life insurance company (Batalla 1999: 22), the PNB, founded in 1916, was the first multipurpose governmental bank, as we saw in the previous chapter. After achieving much in private business, Singson was appointed secretary of agriculture and commerce on 1 January 1933.

As agriculture and commerce secretary, Singson promoted local production and domestic commercial activities through the Bureau of Commerce that his department oversaw. Under his leadership, for instance, the government established the Manila Trading Center and organized the first "Made in the Philippines Products Week" in August 1933 with a view to promote local production and domestic trade (Stine 1966: 85). Balmaceda, a member of the PEA and assistant director of the Bureau of Commerce, said that Singson took the initiative to organize the Products Week and to establish the center (*Tribune* 30 December 1933: 6).

Singson was concurrently appointed acting secretary of finance on 21 April 1934, after Rafael Alunan, a representative of the sugar industry, resigned from the post (*Tribune* 15 August 1934: 16). At the finance department, Singson took the initiative to reduce Philippine dependence on the US economy. Informed of a possible change in the Philippine monetary system from the gold exchange standard to the dollar exchange standard in June, Singson expressed serious concerns about its "harmful" effect on the Philippines (Singson to Governor-General 1933, *JWJ*, 2).[8]

[8] The Harry S. Truman Library keeps the *J. Weldon Jones Papers*, the record of an influential American colonial officer of the same name. Professor Yoshiko Nagano (Kanagawa University) kindly shared her copies of the papers with this writer. This writer appreciates her generous support. Hereafter, the writer quotes materials from the collection in the following way: (sender's name to recipients name, written year, *JWJ*, page [if any]) in the text and describes detailed information on each quotation in the reference.

In a memorandum dated 6 July 1933, Singson commented on the following: First, he argued that it was undesirable to link the Philippine currency system to the American one "much more intimately" (ibid.). He was worried that a situation would arise in which the Philippine currency became more vulnerable to US currency policy, since the latter was managed regardless of Philippine conditions. Second, he thought that US inflationary measures would adversely affect the Philippine economy. He asserted: "In many cases, the likelihood is that this country would be the loser in the sense that its currency would depreciate in value..." (ibid.). Based on these considerations, he proposed to invite a monetary expert to consider whether the Philippine Islands should establish an independent monetary system.

Singson aimed to gain autonomy for economic policymaking through the independent currency system. In another memorandum to the governor-general on 5 August 1933, he suggested that the colonial government establish a monetary system sustained by the gold-bullion standard rather than the dollar-exchange standard. He also proposed that the government devalue the peso by half of the current ratio (Quirino to Governor-General 1935, *JWJ*, 2–5). The proposal regarding the gold bullion standard required that the colonial government establish a totally new monetary standard, because the government was on a gold-exchange standard, which functioned through gold deposits in New York prior to April 1933.[9] By adopting the gold-bullion standard, Singson attempted to cut the country's dependence on the US monetary policy, which was managed without any consideration for the Philippine economy. Another proposal, devaluation, was headed in the same direction of reducing Philippine dependence on the United States, because it would encourage Philippine exports to other countries.

While Singson continuously appealed to invite a monetary expert, he created another policy proposal—to create a central bank in the Philippines (MacIsaac 2002: 159). After he came back from the United States, where he joined Quezon's last independence mission, he publicly "advocated the separation of the control over the monetary system from the government, and the establishment of a central bank to assume such control under the government supervision" in a speech at a banquet for Singson and Miguel Unson on 17 May 1934, hosted by the Chamber of

[9] Castillo, in his textbook published in 1941, clearly distinguishes the gold-bullion standard from the gold-exchange standard (Castillo 1949a: 352–4).

Commerce of the Philippine Islands, which was then headed by Eugenio Rodriguez, a future NP party president as well as senate president in the 1950s (*Tribune* 18 May 1934: 1, 7). The proposed central bank, according to Singson, should be a bank of the government, a bank of banks, and a bank whose responsibility was to manage the integrity and stability of the national currency.

Singson emphasized benefits such as the bank's contributions to fiscal discipline and the expansion of commercial credit (ibid.). He argued that because the democratic government tended to carry out inflation-oriented policies to gain support from people, the Commonwealth government would not be able to resist the temptation of falling into inflation finance if it directly managed its currency policy. Regarding the credit market, Singson recognized the existence of doubts over the usefulness of the central bank at a time when the credit market had yet to mature well. He argued, however, that "there is no better instrument to develop credit in a nation than the establishment of a central bank" (*Tribune* 18 May 1934). Where did Singson derive such knowledge and conviction?

In the same speech, Singson mentioned the emerging international policy idea of establishing a central bank. He said: "The body of financial experts and economists of the League of Nations, about five years ago, had recommended the establishment of central banks where such banks do not exist" (ibid.). The Financial Committee of the League of Nations founded a Gold Delegation to conduct research on the problems of the gold standard in 1929 and published the study results in several reports from 1930 (Eichengreen 1992: 250; Sudo 2008: 2–3). For more than a decade after World War I, European and American countries attempted to establish systematic cooperation to respond to international monetary problems (Eichengreen 1992: ch. 6–7). They failed to resolve the problems, but held several conferences and published reports with recommendations.

Singson used the recommendation of the League of Nations for his proposal regardless of the general purpose of the League of Nations. Using examples from other countries, Singson also emphasized the need to establish an independent central bank, citing responsibilities that the existing PNB could not fill. He argued that a central bank should be independent of the government and that the PNB should concentrate on long-term finance for the development of agriculture, as in the case of Greece (*Tribune* 18 May 1934). He elaborated on his proposal through a study of the recommendations of international organizations or cases from other countries.[10] Obviously, he was determined that the Philippines prepare the institutions necessary for an independent state.

In addition to these proposals, Singson also expressed interest in economic planning to change the Philippine Islands' economic structure. On another occasion, Singson stated: "excessive attention was given to the development of the sugar industry while practically abandoning the other industries, so that when the crisis came in sugar, the country faced a great economic difficulty.... What is lacking ... is a plan" (*Tribune* 13 June 1934: 1, 11). He clearly recognized the necessity to change the economic structure that overly depended on the sugar industry, and he publicly announced it. In this context, Economic planning was not only a form of economic preparation for independence but also a political challenge to those supported by the sugar industry.

Singson's multiple proposals to change the economic structure, however, failed to receive support from either Quezon or influential Americans. We cannot find a written document that directly explains Quezon's motive, however, we can still use data that mention two influential groups close to Quezon that opposed Singson's proposals. First, the sugar industry, which had enjoyed easy loans from the PNB and established close relations with Quezon, opposed the idea of establishing a central bank (Cullather 1992: 81). Second, most of the American residents in Manila—the so-called Manila Americans—were beneficiaries of the existing free trade regime and thus opposed Philippine independence (Golay 1997: 332–3).

Moreover, an important American colonial officer, J. Weldon Jones, opposed the idea of creating a central bank, as we shall see below. Jones was the insular auditor and close aide of the newly appointed Governor-General Frank Murphy (Golay 1997: 331). Murphy, a New Dealer supporting the Roosevelt administration, maintained cooperative relations with Quezon and Osmeña but surrounded himself with American advisers who had been in the Philippines for decades and opposed Philippine independence (ibid.: 330–2). Jones was appointed the adviser on currency matters to the governor-general at almost the same time as

[10] From the beginning of its attempt to reshape the banking industry, the colonial government paid much attention to the example of other countries. Nagano mentions that the government asked the American financial expert Edwin Kemmerer to study and make a report on the Agricultural Bank of Egypt when it designed the Agricultural Bank of the Philippine Government, which was established in 1908 and absorbed into the PNB in 1916 (Nagano 2003: 165–7).

Singson began advocating the creation of a central bank (*Tribune* 2 June 1934: 3). Singson left the government without implementing any of his proposals. Governor-General Murphy appointed Elpidio Quirino secretary of finance and Eugenio Rodriguez secretary of agriculture and commerce on 14 July 1934 (*Tribune* 15 July 1934: 1, 7).

PEA, Economic Planning and a Central Bank

Learning from the example of American New Dealers, Quirino had prepared for his advisory committee for economic policymaking. In fact, before his appointment as secretary of finance, he reactivated the PEA. He gathered several additional members into the association in November 1933, when he prepared to join Quezon's independence mission, which Singson had also joined (*Tribune* 3 November 1933: 10). After the last independence mission won another independence act, the TM Act, on 24 March 1934, PEA members began to prepare for a national economic program (*Tribune* 17 April 1934: 2). The members who led the discussion reflected the fact that the association was still composed of prominent bureaucrats—Finance Undersecretary Gomez was the presiding officer of the day and Commerce Assistant Director Balmaceda was the association secretary (*Tribune* 17 April 1934: 2).[11] PEA members paid attention to Singson's proposal and invited him for a discussion when he was still finance secretary (*Tribune* 24 June 1934, 3rd ed.: 4).

Quirino publicly stated that he expected the PEA members to be the "new dealers for the new Philippine Republic" (*Tribune* 2 May 1934: 2). The PEA, with 27 new members, published the results of its study and its policy recommendation in the form of a 270-page book entitled *Economic Problems of the Philippines* (hereafter, *Problems*) in 1934 (PEA 1934). In the preface, Quirino asserted:

> Our national economic structure, with the severance of our relations with the United States, must claim our attention. A comprehensive program of economic planning for the nation is imperative ... it is my hope that the work of the Philippine Economic Association in this regard will be helpful in crystallizing the mind of the people on the necessity of economic planning. (PEA 1934: iv)

Quirino provided a time frame for his proposal and stipulated the deliverables for each period.

---

[11] The article mentions the association as a society, but this author uses only the term *association*, in accordance with the name *PEA*.

Table 2.2 Timetable of Economic Planning

	Time period	*Issues to be Addressed*
1	Period of general preparation	Delimitation, survey and subdivision of public lands. Speedy disposition of cadastral and land registration cases. Colonization of public lands. Extensive vocational education.
2	Period of planning under the Commonwealth	Agricultural readjustment. Rural problems. Development of mines and minerals. Promotion of manufacturing industries. Labor and population. Domestic trade. Transportation and communication. Banks and credit facilities-Central Bank. Currency.
3	Period of planning under the Republic	Foreign trade, trade reciprocity, and treaties. Immigration. Neutrality.

Source: PEA 1934.

Table 2.2 reveals the three steps Quirino had in mind, comprising the period before the establishment of the Commonwealth, that of the Commonwealth and that after independence. Before the establishment of the Commonwealth, Quirino suggested that the government focus on land issues and vocational education. During the Commonwealth period, he proposed a more radical change in economic structure, including the establishment of a central bank. After independence, he planned for the government to do such things as enhance foreign trade and deal with immigration issues. The timetable and agenda show Quirino's intention to comprehensively change the Philippines' economic structure.

In the chapter on banks and other financial institutions, the committee headed by Pedro J. Campos, president of the BPI, Rafael Corpus, president of the PNB, and Cuaderno, assistant general manager of the PNB at the time, asserted that a majority of the local banks agreed on the idea to organize a central bank (PEA 1934: 219). As for the functions of a central bank, "the power of a central bank to control the currency and the credit of the country and to stabilize foreign exchange is a fact recognized by monetary and banking experts" (ibid.). The committee argued that a central bank should be organized to increase credit facilities, stabilize foreign exchange, and meet periodic demands for circulation through note issues, which would help the government achieve credit elasticity.

In its chapter on currency, the PEA reiterated the need for a central bank. The committee headed by Unson and Cuaderno argued that the existing system had failed to provide enough money in 1920 and 1921 and that the Philippines should have a financial organization such as a central bank. While they admitted that the "Philippines is not in a position to adopt an independent currency at this time", they argued that "the main objective, therefore, of an independent system is an adequate management of currency" (ibid.: 242). The PEA apparently distinguished the issue of enhancing the banking system through a central bank from that of establishing an autonomous currency system.

However, it is not true that Quirino gave up on the idea to establish an autonomous currency system underpinned by a central bank. He simply kept his move confidential, because a "wide open agitation coming from above in the discussion of such a delicate matter might invite alarm and misapprehensions to so serious a degree as to shake the confidence of capital in the stability of the financial structure of the country and thus disastrously affect investments and business in general" (Quirino to Governor-General 1935; *JWJ*, 13). Quirino might have abandoned Singson's strategy but not his idea.

In a memorandum to the governor-general on 13 January 1935, Quirino argued that the Philippines should establish an autonomous currency system, quoting Singson's proposal (ibid.: 15). Quirino, following Singson's proposal, took it for granted that the Philippines should establish an autonomous currency system based on the gold standard because, first, the Philippines is a gold-producing country, and, second, because it has a simpler economic structure when compared to the United States and other European countries (ibid.: 17). He also agreed with Singson on the need to devalue the peso. Considering the almost 40 per cent devaluation of the US dollar in January 1934, Quirino suggested a one-eighth reduction of the peso against the US dollar, which would be nearly equivalent to the ratio suggested by Singson in 1933.

Quirino also proposed creating a central bank to conform to the international policy idea as well as to emphasize the merits of national economy. Like Singson, he mentioned:

> [t]he Financial Committee of the League of Nations would entrust a new important role to central banks. It has made these specific recommendations: 'The aim of the Central Bank should be to maintain the stability of international prices both over long periods and over short periods, in other words, they should both keep the average steady over a period of years and avoid fluctuations round this average from year to year.' (ibid.: 21)

Besides, Quirino emphasized, central banks "are necessary ingredients for the promotion of economy and finance of a country", because it would lower the interest rate as well as expand credit supply through rediscounting operations (ibid.: 22).

Like Singon, however, Quirino failed. The colonial government introduced Act No. 4199 on 16 March 1935, stipulating that two pesos should equal one US dollar regardless of the gold content. This marks the official introduction of the dollar-exchange standard, which had come to be the de facto standard of the Islands in the 1920s (Castillo 1949b: 429; Nagano 2010: 45). The currency system of the Philippine Islands "could be considered as representative of the evolving export economy of the Philippines under American rule" (Nagano 2010: 47). Quirino's proposal was overwhelmed by the influence of vested interests in the 1930s.

Moreover, Quezon publicly rejected the idea of establishing an autonomous currency system when he accepted the nomination for the presidency in the election for the Commonwealth government. On 20 July 1935, he declared: "I shall keep our present currency system in all its integrity and will allow no changes that will affect its value.... For the present I can see no reasons for any radical modifications in our monetary system" (*Tribune* 21 July 1935, 3rd ed.: 1, 14). Quezon did not share the idea of seeking currency autonomy with Singson or Quirino, but he did not exactly persuade the policymakers to abandon the idea, either, as we shall see below.

In Search of Autonomy in Economic Policymaking

Early Work of the National Economic Council

After the Filipinos approved the constitution drafted by their delegates at the Constitutional Convention, the Commonwealth government was inaugurated on 15 November 1935. The government, headed by the Filipino president and vice president who were directly elected by the people, prepared a ten-year post-independence plan. Most of the prerogatives of the governor-general were abolished or transferred to the Commonwealth president, while the American high commissioner played the role of supervisor. The government took charge of domestic politics, although decisions related to currency policy needed the approval of the US president. Quezon maintained his dominance in colonial politics and worked hard for the revision of the TM Act. He accepted the TM Act, which was almost identical to the HHC Act except for the condition that the Philippines and the United States would negotiate revision if necessary. Quezon believed that it was necessary to revise it (MacIsaac 1993; Nakano 1997).

The PEA succeeded in persuading President Quezon to organize a central agency for economic planning, although it failed to convince him of the need to create an autonomous currency system. On 18 December 1935, Quezon sent a message to the national assembly, asking them to endorse a bill to create the National Economic Council (NEC), which would be responsible for giving occasional advice to the president on economic affairs as well as proposing comprehensive economic planning. In the message, Quezon mentions a certain limitation to the idea of laissez-faire and emphasizes the significance of the active role of government in economic affairs (Soberano 1961: 185). The government created the Commonwealth Act No. 2, which stipulates the establishment of the National Economic Council, headed by the secretary of finance (NEC 1937, *MAR*; Soberano 1961: 182, 192).[12] The establishment of the NEC and economic planning had been proposed by Singson, Quirino and the PEA (PEA 1934: 213).

When the NEC began operations on 14 February 1936, the secretary of finance and the chair of the NEC changed hands from Quirino, who was appointed secretary of interior, to Antonio de las Alas. Quezon had initially preferred Roxas but instead chose de las Alas after Roxas declined the offer (Romero 2008: 119). De las Alas, born in Batangas in 1889, graduated from the University of Indiana and Yale University as a pensionado, worked for the Executive Bureau, became a lawyer, and was elected representative from Batangas (Cornejo 1939: 1586). Before his appointment as secretary of finance, he was the secretary of public works and communication. De las Alas was close to Quezon, but was not as ambitious as Quirino or Roxas. He seems to have been a more able administrator than aggressive politician.

In the first report of its activity in 1936, the NEC explained its inactivity in an apologetic tone rather than proclaim its achievements (NEC 1937, *MAR*). After mentioning the lack of data, funding, personnel, and so on, the NEC concluded: "The main reason[s], however, why no complete economic program could be formulated at present are the

[12] *MAR* stands for Manuel A. Roxas and refers to the Manuel A. Roxas Papers. The official and private papers of President Manuel A. Roxas are in the Main Library, University of the Philippines, Quezon City, Metro Manila, Philippines. Sources from the Manuel A. Roxas Papers are hereafter referred in the following way: (author's or sender's name to recipient's name [if any], date, MAR, page [if any]).

uncertainty of our economic relations with the United States and the limitations placed upon the powers of the Commonwealth Government by the Tydings-McDuffie Law" (ibid.: 31). The uncertainty came from the ongoing trade conference, while the limitations pointed to the fact that the Commonwealth government could not enjoy any autonomy on tariff and currency issues. Former Governor-General Harrison, who had been appointed as an adviser to Quezon, reported to the United States that the NEC "was 'paralyzed' because all of the energies of the government 'are now bent towards getting a relaxation of the trade sanctions of the Tydings-McDuffie Act'" and that another attempt to promote diversification of the economic structure was opposed by the "influence of the sugar interests and their lobby in Washington" (Golay 1997: 358).

The NEC report is quite intriguing because it reveals that Filipino policymakers never let up on efforts to establish an autonomous currency system and a central bank even under such constraints. The first report on activities in 1936 said that "the peso, under the present system, must follow the dollar for good or for ill, and the Philippines is helpless to influence the American currency policy" (NEC 1937, *MAR*, 33). The NEC advocated:

> The Commonwealth should work for an independent currency system, and if granted, the gold bullion standard should be set up to take the place of the present system....With the establishment of a Central Bank as the necessary accompaniment of an independent currency system, the management of the currency to suit the needs of the Commonwealth and an independent Philippines could be easily accomplished. (ibid.)

It is easy to spot the influence of Singson's proposal in 1934 on this recommendation. Singson was, in fact, a member of the NEC (*Tribune* 2 July 1937: 1).

The idea of an autonomous currency system gradually found sympathizers in the legislature. Assemblymen Benito Soliven and Juan L. Luna, for instance, submitted Bill 2444 "to establish an independent currency system in the Philippines" (Luna and Soliven 1937, *JWJ*). Luna, born in Mindoro in 1894, graduated from the University of Santo Tomas and was a teacher and a lawyer before he became a member of the legislature in the 1920s (Cornejo 1939: 1903). Meanwhile, Soliven, born in Ilocos Sur in 1898, graduated from the University of the Philippines, became a lawyer, and then a member of legislature in the 1920s (ibid.: 2151). These two representatives, however, did not seem to have close relations with Singson or Quirino, although Soliven was from Ilocos Sur where Singson and Quirino were also born. In fact, Soliven would fight and defeat Quirino in the election for the national assembly in 1938 (Espinosa-Robles 1990: 46).

In the explanatory note of Bill 2444, the authors argued that the currency problem was "a grave problem" that was untouched during the trade conference (Luna and Soliven 1937, *JWJ*, 1). They asserted that the devaluation of the US dollar in 1934 caused damage to the Philippines, because the Philippine government would pay more for its debt to other countries. They also asserted that the Philippines needed to establish an independent currency system based on the gold bullion standard. Generally speaking, however, we could find hardly any evidence of the NEC's direct involvement in this bill. The bill's authors didn't mention the NEC's name, although they mentioned the name of Professor Kamantigue, who was a founding member of the PEA when he was still affiliated with the Bureau of Internal Revenue.

The incoherence between legislative and executive actions might have had something to do with President Quezon's convictions about the currency system. A memorandum by Jones records that in April 1937 Quezon told Secretary de las Alas: "Please inform the National Economic Council of my fixed purpose not to recommend or approve during my administration measures establishing a new currency system. The present system will be maintained in its integrity because, after consulting expert advice, I am convinced that it is best for the country" (excerpt from the quarterly report of the High Commissioner 1937, *JWJ*, 1).

Quezon reiterated his position to maintain the status quo of the currency system. In a record from a press conference dated 6 October 1937:

> The Press: How about the currency, Mr. President?
>
> The President: The currency? ~~That is tabooed.~~ [*sic*] That is definitely settled; there is no more talk about that. (Press conference 1937, *MLQ*: 20)

Quezon's brief reply arouses two interpretations: First, the currency issue had already been settled before they recorded the interview, and second, the currency issue was literally considered taboo by someone even though it was struck from the record. It is highly possible that American authorities constrained Quezon from taking a radical position on the matter.

Jones, now the financial adviser to the American high commissioner, criticized Bill 2444 in his memorandum to Washington (Jones to Coy

1937, *JWJ*). Jones stated that the authors of the bill did not understand the existing situation, which prompted the Philippine government to adopt the dollar-exchange standard (ibid.: 1). He reported that there had been no serious problems after the devaluation of the US dollar in 1934, and that it was confusing that the authors condemned the American devaluation but asserted the necessity of a peso devaluation (ibid.: 1–2). The following concluding sentences of the memorandum clearly express Jones's strong conviction about the existing monetary system:

> First, because if any currencies survive in this world of uncertainty we can feel that the dollar and the pound sterling will be included; and second, the economy of the exchange standard and the fact that Philippine foreign trade is so heavily over-balanced by trade with the United States that we can feel that now and for a number of years to come the Commonwealth and the independent Philippines can do more things with a dollar and do them more economically than they can with an actual gold peso. (ibid.: 4)

The outcome was that Bill 2444 failed to gather enough support from both Filipinos and Americans.

Facing strong opposition from the authorities, the NEC shifted the focus of its advocacy from creating an autonomous currency system to creating a central bank. The NEC's second report, a summary of its activities in 1937 when the council held only two meetings (NEC 1938, *MAR*, 6), can be read as a record of its desperate efforts to win support for its ideas. In the report, the authors reiterate that it was an internationally accepted idea to have a central bank. The report states:

> Since the war, under the leadership of the League of Nations, countries that have availed of expert financial advice of the League have established a central bank as one of the principal agencies in effecting the reconstruction of their disorganized economic life. Today, most countries find the central bank an indispensable part of their economic system, and even countries that are not yet independent, like the Dominions, India, and Java, have already established a central bank. (ibid.: 7)

Another point that makes the second report important was the cue it took to figure out key advocates. The NEC mentioned: "Vicente Singson-Encarnacion, a member of the Council, has already framed with the aid of our technical staff the proposed charter for a central bank in the Philippines" (ibid.: 11). Because we know that Singson had been active in advocacy, it is interesting to find out whom the NEC meant by "our technical staff". We can easily assume who the technical staff was, because the NEC report reiterates that the NEC had very few technical staff members. The first report said that Jose L. Celeste served as executive secretary, Castillo as technical adviser and Juan S. Agcaoili as technical assistant (NEC 1937, *MAR*, 14). In the second report they said that after Celeste's resignation in December 1936, Castillo was appointed acting executive secretary of the council (NEC 1938, *MAR*, 1). Two of the three technical staff, Celeste and Castillo, were original PEA members.

The Joint Preparatory Committee

While Singson and others struggled in the NEC, Roxas fought for the expansion of economic autonomy in the trade conference. On 14 April 1937, the Joint Preparatory Committee on Philippine Affairs (JPCPA) was finally formed "to study trade relations between the United States and the Philippines and to recommend a program for the adjustment of the Philippine national economy" (JPCPA 1938: 3). Roxas joined the committee, which was headed by Jose Yulo, Quezon's close aide who would be the Speaker of the House, under instructions from Quezon.

Quezon appointed Roxas as a member of the JPCPA, because of the latter's knowledge and experience and despite their once chilly relations. Another member of the JPCPA and the majority leader of the assembly, Jose Romero, called Roxas "our leading economist" (Romero 2008: 134). Roxas made his thoughts public before he joined the JPCPA in a newspaper contribution published under the title, "Philippine Independence May Succeed without Free Trade" (*Tribune* 1 April 1936 Sec. IV: 1, 2, 4; Roxas 1936). What he wrote was close to the ideas he had advocated when he launched Ang Bagong Katipunan years ago. He argued: "Knowing that we cannot be certain of the continuance of free trade after independence, the logical course for us to take is to reduce as much as possible the relative importance in the national economy of the industries depending for their existence on free trade with America" (Roxas 1936: 14).

However, Roxas failed to gain support for his ideas from a majority in the JPCPA. A comprehensive study of the negotiation within the JPCPA explains that the US economic policy toward the Philippines at the time aimed at expanding American exports while curtailing Philippine imports, concluding: "It was a classic example of economic imperialism" (MacIsaac 1993: 345). Reflecting the American neglect of the Filipino plea, the JPCPA final report said:

> Commercial banking facilities appear to be adequate in Manila and in the larger cities.... In view of the present structure of the Philippine banking and currency systems, there appears to be no necessity at the present time for the establishment of a bank in the Philippines whose functions would be primarily those of a central bank. (JPCPA 1938: 122–3)

This conclusion, however, did not reflect the position of Roxas, who would be appointed the new chairman of the NEC as well as the secretary of finance.

Continuing Attempts to Establish a Central Bank

Roxas did not abandon his idea of changing the Philippine economic structure when he was appointed chairman of the NEC in August 1938 and subsequently finance secretary on 1 December 1938. On 4 January 1939, he held a meeting with local bankers and NEC staff to discuss banking-sector reforms (*Tribune* 5 January 1939: 1, 15). He did not invite bankers from foreign and American banks, because he expected that economic readjustments should be carried out in cooperation with local rather than foreign banks (ibid.: 15). The local bankers Roxas invited included Vicente Carmona, president of the PNB; Bank Commissioner Pedro de Jesus; Pedro J. Campos, president of the BPI; and Miguel Cuaderno, president of the Philippine Bank of Commerce (PBC) (ibid.). The PNB and BPI were the two biggest local banks, while the PBC was a new bank, established only in 1938.

Roxas's plan, revealed on 6 January 1939, proposed to overhaul the role of the PNB (*Tribune* 7 January 1939: 1, 15). He suggested that the government establish a commercial bank, convert the PNB into an investment bank, and "set up a reserve and discount department in the Philippine National Bank which will perform the same functions as those of the federal reserve system [*sic*]" (ibid.). It is impressive that Roxas did not refer to a specific term such as a central bank, and that he did not advocate the establishment of an independent bank but, instead, proposed to set up a new department within the existing structure of the PNB.

His wording, however, did not reflect a retreat from his advocacy to establish a central bank. As a member of the JPCPA, he must have been familiar with the strong opposition from the United States, with whom Filipino policymakers had to negotiate in order to pass any act regarding currency issues under the existing independence act. Roxas seems to have chosen the least controversial way to propose a central bank under this circumstance. What he expected from the department was the enhancement of the banking system and reduction of the interest rate, which were some of the roles that Filipino policymakers had expected the central bank to play.

Shortly thereafter, the bill to establish a Reserve Bank of the Philippines was completed. This time the bill was passed by the Philippine Assembly and signed by President Quezon as Commonwealth Act No. 458, "an act to provide for the establishment of a Reserve Bank in the Philippines", on 9 June 1939 (Bureau of Banking 1940: 21). The Reserve Bank, whose design was taken from the Bank of New Zealand and newly established Bank of Canada (Cuaderno 1949: 4), would function as a central bank in the Philippines. The Commonwealth government could not, however, implement the act immediately because it had to be approved by the US president. Again, Jones opposed the Filipinos' attempts to establish a central bank (Jones to High Commissioner 1939, *JWJ*). He argued in a memorandum that Commonwealth Act No. 458 was against the general policy of the office of the high commissioner, which had been supported by President Quezon and recommended as well by the JPCPA (ibid.: 1).

In the rest of his memorandum, Jones recorded the development of this move and mentioned Cuaderno's name. Jones wrote that A.D. Calhoun, manager of the Manila branch of the National City Bank of New York, had told him that Secretary Roxas pushed the Assembly to pass the bill despite the skepticism of Speaker Jose Yulo. Jones also reported: "Mr. Mike Cuaderno of the Bank of the Commonwealth was the moving spirit behind the agitation. Mike is the more or less discredited former Vice President of the Philippine Bank of Commerce [*sic*]" (ibid.: 6). Jones's hostility toward Cuaderno was obvious. After briefly mentioning the initiative without any comments about Roxas's personality, he emphasized the role of Cuaderno, whom he described as coming from one of "the small banks of the street owned by Filipinos", as well as the uselessness, or even adverse effect, of Commonwealth Act No. 458 on the financial system (ibid.).

In the 1930s, however, Cuaderno was an established lawyer-banker. In addition to his job as the vice manager of the PNB and his participation in the PEA, he was elected in 1934 to the Constitutional Convention as a delegate and became a member of the committee of seven that drafted the constitution (Cuaderno 1937). At the convention, in the committee report of the Committee on Currency and Banking that he chaired, Cuaderno again advocated the creation of a central bank (House of Representatives 1965: 52), although he could not convince other delegates to insert such a clause in the constitution. After resigning from the PNB in 1936, he headed the Finance Mining and Brokerage Company, which was first designed for investment business in the mining industry and was foreseen to become a bank providing financial support to other industries (*Tribune* 6 September 1936: 13). After his experience as a working student in Hong Kong, he nurtured a vision to promote manufacturing rather than commerce in his country.[13]

Cuaderno established the PBC in 1938, the first private bank created with Filipino capital (Reyes-McMurray 1998). The PBC was small in terms of the amount of its business, but it played a significant role, because it provided Filipino practitioners the opportunity to manage a bank at a time when foreigners controlled most of the big banks and did not provide Filipino workers enough opportunities. President Cuaderno of the PBC would actually become the first governor of the Central Bank. The first vice president of the PBC, Alfonso Calalang, became the third governor of the bank (ibid.: 93).[14] Sixto L. Orosa, one of the founding members of the PBC and a prominent banker in the postwar period, later recalled that the PBC was "the Alma Mater of Bankers" (Orosa 1988: 35–6). The above-quoted description by Jones failed to mention any of Cuaderno's credentials and instead worked to discredit him.

In addition to Roxas and Cuaderno, Celeste, a founding member of the PEA, as well as the first executive secretary of the NEC, took action to support the bill. There was a report on the early attempt to make a central bank in the Philippines, which was written by a Japanese officer of the Southern Development Bank (*Nanpou Kaihatsu Kinko*) in 1943 (Awano 1943). According to its postscript, the book was based on *A Reserve Bank of the Philippines* written by "Dr. Celeste" in 1940 (ibid.: 44). It is not misleading to assume that Jose Celeste is the book's author, considering his involvement in the proposal to create a central bank. According to the author, Celeste lists the following four reasons to establish a central bank: the currency system's dependence on the United States, the imperfection of the financial structure, the lack of a credit

---

[13] Interview with Mr Martin C. Galan (a grandchild of Cuaderno) in Makati, Metro Manila, on 6 December 2010.

[14] Calalang was the third governor (Bangko Sentral ng Pilipinas 1998), although Reyes-McMurray wrote that he was the second governor (Reyes-McMurray 1998: 93).

market, and the lack of investment credit (ibid.: 1). Celeste's points reflect the argument made in previous proposals by the PEA. The fact that Celeste wrote this document reflects his continuous commitment.

The act, however, did not receive sincere support from President Quezon and the Assembly. Jones reported the following personal remark of President Quezon regarding Act 458 at a dinner held by the high commissioner. Asked about the act, Quezon told Jones:

> To tell you the truth, Mr. Jones, I did not want to sign the bill. Joe [Speaker Jose Yulo] was not in favor of it particularly. I signed it because I did not wish to indicate any opposition to Roxas. I do not think the Bank will help us any. It is useless unless we have an independent currency. (Jones to High Commissioner 1939, *JWJ*, 8)

What this conversation tells us is that Quezon signed the act only because he didn't like to show his opposition to Roxas. Quezon seemingly avoided any unnecessary confrontation with Roxas, who was still a man of influence especially among politicians who supported the Os-Rox mission in 1933. Considering the resident's lack of support, the national assembly finally adopted a resolution to withdraw Act 458 from US government consideration on 19 April 1940 (Bureau of Banking 1941: 29).

Even after the failure of the Roxas plan, the policymakers continued to advocate the establishment of a central bank whenever they had a chance. In 1941, Castillo published the first comprehensive textbook on economics in the Philippines, which he dedicated to Filipino students (Castillo 1949a; Roxas 2000: 86).[15] In the chapter on central banking, he summarized the historical development of central banking in the world and reiterated its necessity in the Philippines (Castillo 1949a: ch. 19). In this context, he briefly explained: "The Reserve Bank of the Philippines would perform the traditional functions of a central bank and make possible the establishment of a banking system which could adequately and efficiently provide the credit needs of business" (ibid.: 438). Here we find Castillo's deepest convictions expressed.

During World War II, policymakers continuously advocated the bank's establishment. The Japanese, whose military invaded the Philippines in December 1941 and occupied Manila in January 1942, attempted to induce support from Filipino elites who had occupied leading

[15] This author used the edition reprinted in 1949.

positions within the Commonwealth government, while the US government convinced Quezon, Osmeña and other cabinet members to leave the Philippines and establish a government-in-exile headed by Quezon in Washington, DC. The Japanese military nonetheless organized an administration led by Jose P. Laurel and recognized the independence of the Philippine republic with a new constitution in October 1943. The Laurel-led republic was, however, captive to a treaty constraining the republic's sovereignty and the physical existence of 100,000 Japanese military in Manila (Jose 2003: 197). Moreover, there was a secret memorandum that allowed the Japanese to exploit natural resources and public transportation, and stipulated that the Philippines needed to negotiate with Japan over finance and currency issues (Jose 2003: 199).

In this new climate, Filipino leaders in Manila worked to address speculative inflation, resulting in a product shortage after the suspension of trade with the United States and the rampant issue of Japanese military notes. In this context, Castillo proposed that the Philippines establish a central bank that would be "a responsible guardian of our monetary and credit system" (Castillo 1943: 84). The Philippine Assembly finally passed a bill to establish the Central Bank on 29 February 1944 (Cuaderno 1949: 4; National Assembly 1943: 132–8),[16] but the bill was not implemented because the Japanese, who feared losing the prerogative to issue military notes, objected to it (Cuaderno 1949: 4). The diary of Japanese Ambassador to the Philippine Republic Shozo Murata recorded the last efforts of Finance Minister de las Alas and Castillo to appeal for the bill's implementation in an official mission to Japan he joined in April 1944 (Fukushima 1969: 45–8). Meanwhile in the Philippines, Cuaderno, as PBC president, wrote to de las Alas proposing the opening of a central bank in order to curtail inflation in the Philippines (Cuaderno to de las Alas 1944, *MAR*). De las Alas appears to have succeeded in convincing the Japanese minister to establish a central bank, but Philippine cabinet members abandoned Manila in December 1944 before they could implement the act that created it (Jose 2003: 204). President Laurel dissolved the republic on 17 August 1945. The agenda to create a central bank was taken over by the postwar Republic of the

[16] The author would like to extend appreciation to Professor Ricardo T. Jose of the University of the Philippines, who kindly provided him with a copy of the national assembly bill.

Philippines, in which Roxas and Quirino were elected president and vice president, respectively, while Cuaderno was appointed secretary of finance and Castillo the secretary-economist.

As has been discussed in this chapter, two policy changes by the US government prompted Filipino policymakers to perceive the existing constraints on policymaking and made them recognize the need to change the system of crafting policy in 1933. First, the HHC Act prompted Quirino and others to organize the PEA, a network of bureaucrats and professionals who shared common interests in economics, to study the economic consequences of political independence on their own. Second, the US government drastically changed the monetary policy to get out of its serious banking recession. The Filipino policymakers regarded it as a crucial sign of the absence of autonomy, although the American colonial officers assumed that the impact on the Philippine peso was negligible.

Ideas to create a central bank, which were irrelevant to the existing interest structure but had emerged internationally, encouraged the finance secretaries Singson and Quirino to propose the establishment of an autonomous currency system along with a central bank. These beliefs were maintained not only by Singson, who had been outside the center of political power, but also by Quirino, a close aide of Quezon. They aimed to achieve autonomy in policymaking and establish a suitable institution necessary for an independent state.

The Commonwealth period witnessed the continuous endeavors by Filipino policymakers to establish a central bank and the consistent opposition by American colonial officers to it. The persistence of the proposal efforts in the face of objections and failures reveals the fact the bank was the creation of a group of policymakers rather than a single person. Roxas took over the proposal effort from former secretaries Singson, Quirino and de las Alas, and it grew into an agenda that no finance secretary could ignore—one that was worth addressing in order to achieve fame as an emergent political leader. Professionals such as Castillo and Cuaderno, who both scrutinized the idea and developed it into particular policy proposals, found partners in the finance department.

The Japanese occupation was a time to confirm the policymakers' conviction to establish a central bank. Most of the key policymakers remained in the Philippines and sought ways to establish the bank by asserting that the Philippines needed one to curtail raging inflation. They passed the bill to create the bank, but the occupation ended before they could carry out the plan.

The development of the colonial state generated policymakers who went beyond the realm of colonial administration. These policymakers emerged from a changing political context rather than the existing interest structure. They took advantage of internationally accepted policy ideas to which the American colonial officers paid little attention. They were the beneficiaries of the American colonial state, yet at the same time promoters of change in the colonial structure. In sum, central-bank making was an indispensable process of state building by Filipino policymakers.

CHAPTER 3

Departure from the Colonial Economy, 1946–50

On 4 July 1946, the Philippines became independent of the US in accordance with the independence act (TM Act) of 1934. Because of colonial democracy and the independence law passed before the Japanese occupation of 1941–44, few Filipino people believed that the Japanese came to the Philippine Islands to liberate them from American imperialism. Filipino elites collaborated with the Japanese military simply for form's sake, while some of the peasants and agricultural laborers joined one of the best-organized anti-Japanese guerrilla forces in Southeast Asia (Nakano 1997: ch. 6). Japanese occupation and nominal independence under Japanese rule did not change the predominant position of the NP politicians, although the party experienced a split into the NP and Liberal Party (LP), as we will see below.

In terms of independence, therefore, most scholars have emphasized continuity rather than change. Leading historians, for example, have produced works with titles such as *The Philippines: The Continuing Past* (Constantino and Constantino 1978) or "The Philippines: Independence without Decolonization" (McCoy 1981). In addition to the continuity of politicians, neocolonial rule was symbolized by two treaties with the United States—the Philippine Trade Act, or the Bell Trade Act, and the Philippines-US Defense Treaty (Constantino and Constantino 1978; Schirmer and Shalom 1987).[1] The Bell Trade Act, which defined

[1] The Philippines-US Defense Treaty is another important accord used to shape the neocolonial relations according to Constantino and Constantino (1978) and McCoy (1981). This research, however, focuses on the economic aspect of the two-country relations based on differences in contemporary observation. While the Bell Trade Act became a focal point of major political controversy (cf. Takagi 2009), the Defense

Philippine-US economic relations from 1947 to 1974, allowed American businesses in the Philippines to exploit local natural resources in the same way as Filipino businesses and stipulated limited duty-free exports and unlimited duty-free imports to and from the United States.[2]

However, the newly independent Philippines witnessed a generational change in the leadership of the government, and the new generation did not necessarily share the same ideas with their predecessors. Manuel A. Roxas and Elpidio Quirino, whose policy proposal had been neglected or opposed by Manuel L. Quezon and American colonial authorities in the 1930s, were elected president and vice president, respectively, in 1946. President Roxas appointed Quirino finance secretary, but replaced him with Miguel P. Cuaderno in 1947 when Roxas appointed Quirino secretary of the newly established foreign affairs office. As soon as he became finance secretary, Cuaderno appointed Andres Castillo secretary-economist. When Roxas died suddenly in office in 1948, Quirino took over the presidency and retained most of the cabinet. Cuaderno remained as finance secretary until he was appointed governor of the newly established Central Bank, whose charter he mostly designed. The emerging policymakers who had established their network in the 1930s finally occupied leading positions in the late 1940s, and once in power they laid the foundations for the economic policy regime for carrying out industrialization through import and exchange controls managed mainly by the Central Bank (Golay 1961; Valdepeñas 1969; Doronila 1992).

The creation of the policy regime, however, has been understudied because of the influence of the neocolonial perspective highlighting the Bell Trade Act of 1946. Against this backdrop, I focus on the emergence of the economic policy regime through a study of the Joint Philippine-American Finance Commission (JPAFC) of 1947. The JPAFC was created

Treaty was more or less accepted by key policymakers in the late 1940s because they were seriously concerned about another military aggression on account of the memory of WWII (Nakano 1997: ch. 7; 2007: ch. 6). MacIsaac and Nakano shed a new light on the study of Philippine independence by examining the dynamics of American policy toward the Philippines, which, while not categorized under neocolonialism (MacIsaac 1993; Nakano 1997), do not pay much attention to the dynamics of domestic politics in the Philippines.

[2] The Bell Trade Act became effective with an executive agreement between the Philippines and the United States, which was revised and renamed the Laurel-Langley Agreement in 1955 and expired in 1974.

by an agreement between the Philippine and US governments to survey the economic situation in the Philippines and recommend necessary economic measures in a published report.

A shift of focus from the Bell Trade Act to the JPAFC's report prompts us to reconsider the conventional view of the politics of independence. Shirley Jenkins argues that the JPAFC's recommendation differed from the "quasi-colonial character" of the Bell Trade Act, and that it was in "the direction of greater economic sovereignty for the Philippines" (Jenkins 1985: 64, 122).[3] Salvador Araneta, one of the harshest critics of the Bell Trade Act, positively evaluated the JPAFC's achievement, because the commission recommended the creation of the central bank and the imposition of import controls (Araneta 1948: 285). Cuaderno, who led the Philippine section of the JPAFC, left behind an important description in which he argued that the Philippine section prevailed over American opposition regarding the recommendation to create a central bank (Cuaderno 1964: 9–11).

The rest of this chapter comprises two sections and a conclusion. First, it studies the process of creating the JPAFC report and implementing it. Second, it traces the political process of economic decolonization in order to analyze the efforts of the policymakers who gradually crafted the economic policy regime, making use of available tools such as import and exchange controls and the Central Bank.

Reconstruction and Departure from the Colonial Economy

The Roxas Administration and the JPAFC Report

As a consequence of World War II, the Philippine party system changed in 1946. The LP, Roxas's ruling party, split from the NP because of a clash that occurred between those who took a moderate position toward collaborators during WWII and those who attempted to punish them. While Roxas, who had remained in the Philippines during the war, was supported by the former position, the NP led by Osmeña, who took over the presidency of the government-in-exile upon the death of Quezon, and former guerrilla leaders took the latter position. Though the LP won and calmed the collaboration issue by proclaming amnesty in the late

[3] Jenkins does not study the creation process involved in the JPAFC report and implies that the US government imposed the recommendation, including the politically challenging tax reform (Jenkins 1985: 110–22).

1940s, after independence the ruling party would never enjoy the dominant position that belonged to the NP under Osmeña and Quezon, as we shall see in Table 3.1.

Table 3.1 Results of Congressional Elections, 1946–71

		Nacionalista	*Liberal*	*Others*	*Total*
1946	UH	7	8	1	16
	LH	37	49	12	98
1947	UH	1	7	0	8
1949	UH	0	8	0	8
	LH	33	60	7	100
1951	UH	8	0	0	8
1953	UH	5	0	3	8
	LH	58	31	13	102
1955	UH	7	1	0	8
1957	UH	6	2	0	8
	LH	82	19	1	102
1959	UH	5	2	1	8
1961	UH	2	6	0	8
	LH	74	29	1	104
1963	UH	4	4	0	8
1965	UH	5	2	1	8
	LH	41	59	4	104
1967	UH	7	1	0	8
1969	UH	7	1	0	8
	LH	89	18	3	110
1971	UH	2	6	0	8

Note: UH and LH stands for Upper House and Lower House, respectively.

Source: Comelec, n.d.

Table 3.1 shows the results of congressional elections from 1946 to 1971. The constitution stipulated general elections for the president, vice president, a third of Senate (8 out of 24 seats) and all members of the House of Representatives every four years, and midterm elections for politicians of local governments and one-third of the Senate.[4] The Philippines had regular elections based on the constitution following independence in

[4] In order to fill in vacancies caused by WWII, in 1946 the people elected 16 senators.

1946 until the declaration of martial law by President Ferdinand Marcos in 1972. In terms of major parties, while the LP and NP competed for the presidency and a majority in Congress, small minority parties appeared and disappeared, as we shall later see. A Liberal or Nacionalista always took the presidency and maintained a majority in Congress, although there were several cases of divided government in which the president's party differed from the majority party in Congress. An important point here is that the Philippines maintained a stable two-party system, at least in terms of the number of dominant parties.[5]

Just after World War II, Roxas and Quirino, elected president and vice president respectively, took over the reins of the newly independent republic. The Philippines had sustained massive war damage, prompting President Roxas in his inaugural address on 28 May 1946 to note "a dark landscape, a bleak prospect for our future", rather than simply stating his administration's goals (Roxas 2004: 129). After praising the achievements of past presidents Manuel L. Quezon and Sergio Osmeña, Roxas blurted: "Yet look about you, my fellow citizens. The tragic evidence of recent history stares at us from the broken ruins of cities and the wasting acres of soil" (ibid.: 128). As the administration struggled with postwar reconstruction, it faced the controversial US measure to make the passage of the Bell Trade Act a condition of the actual implementation of the Philippine War Damage Act.

The Roxas administration apparently accepted the condition, and vigorously supported the Bell Trade Act in the context of its reconstruction efforts. Roxas's special message to Congress regarding the trade act on 21 June 1946 revealed his efforts to link the act with reconstruction (Roxas 1947: 7–29). In the beginning of his message, he said: "Those two acts [Bell Trade Act and Philippine War Damage Act] provide the pattern of United States aid for our reconstruction and for the rehabilitation of our national economy", as if both of these acts had aimed at reconstruction (ibid.: 7). Roxas assumed that the Philippines could not achieve reconstruction without foreign investment and was determined to clear obstacles that stood in the way of foreign, especially American,

[5] In terms of political cleavage between major parties, the two major parties once differed in their positions toward the collaboration issue and the Bell Trade Act, as we shall see below. However, the major parties gradually bridged the gap in the context of the Cold War, in which the party leaders abandoned the cleavage supposedly representing a class divide (Takagi 2009).

investment (MacIsaac 1993: 385). The administration aggressively supported the Bell Trade Act, and even prohibited several opposition members from taking seats in order to guarantee a two-thirds majority, which was needed to amend the constitution.

Meanwhile, two opposition arguments against the Bell Trade Act arose: One placed priority on attacking the parity clause as undue infringement on sovereignty, while the other cast doubt on the economic benefits of the trade act (Jenkins 1985: 81–96). Opposition parties led by the NP accused the act of betraying the promise of independence. The Democratic Alliance (DA), a small new party, spearheaded the opposition to the Bell Trade Act. DA was mainly supported by the *Hukbalahap* [*Hukbong Bayan Laban sa mga Hapon* (Huk)], which had led anti-Japanese guerrilla warfare in Central Luzon during the Japanese occupation. The Huk liberated some villages, which enjoyed self-government by the peasants who resided there and maintained relations with communists and socialists while it dealt with Filipino collaborators. The US army purged much of the Huk ranks during the liberation, compelling the guerrillas to take both an anti-American and anti-collaborator stance (Takagi 2009).

In the context of this chapter, however, the second group in the opposition is more important. Salvador Araneta, a corporate lawyer, a founding member of the PEA and a leading advocate of economic nationalism in the 1930s, was one of the early critics of the Bell Trade Act. In an article published on 24 June 1947, Araneta reminded Roxas that he had written in 1936 that Philippine independence might succeed without free trade (Araneta 2000: 89–97). Araneta concluded that the Filipinos should not follow the advice of American congressman Bell but instead listen to the economist Roxas, who could have properly evaluated the significance of the local market in 1936. In a different article, Araneta pointed out that the Bell Trade Act would have the effect of preventing US capital from flowing into the Philippines as well as prohibiting the Philippines from protecting its industries. Because of the free-trade stipulation and the high peso-dollar exchange rate, US businesses could export their products to the Philippine market and easily make profit rather than produce in the Philippines. He concluded: "free trade encouraged American entrepreneurs to send consumer goods, not capital, to the Philippines" (Araneta 1948: 281).

The Roxas administration did not overlook the defects of the trade agreement, although it did not reveal these directly and openly. In his inaugural address, as a matter of fact, President Roxas proclaimed:

> But our aim is not alone to rebuild the economy that was broken and destroyed by war. But we know, we have known, that the narrow economy of the past must be broadened. The national structure must be sufficient to house the energies of the whole people. For the Philippines to fit into the pattern of the 20th century, to take its place as an equal among the nations of the earth, we must industrialize, we must make as well as grow. (Roxas 2004: 130)

The administration believed in industrialization as a goal for economic development.

Roxas's commitment to industrialization was expressed by his active cooperation with the Philippine section of the JPAFC headed by Cuaderno. Roxas had requested budgetary and rehabilitation loans from the United States in May 1946, and finally the Philippine and US governments agreed to set up a commission (Hartendorp 1958: 254). While the US government attempted to examine the Philippine government's ability to manage US loans (Jenkins 1985: 115), the Philippine government took an opportunity to change the nature of Philippine-US economic relations from that stipulated in the Bell Trade Act to one shaped by greater autonomy for the Philippine government. Upon returning from a US mission in November 1946, Roxas convinced Cuaderno to accept the post of finance secretary, because he needed Cuaderno on the commission and believed that the finance secretary must head the Philippine delegation (Cuaderno 1964: 4).

Cuaderno accepted the offer, not only because he had confidence in Roxas, but also because he believed that institutional reform for the new country was too exciting to pass up (Cuaderno 1964: 4). In his memoir, Cuaderno revealed that he met with Roxas several times, even before he was appointed finance secretary:

> I emphasized to President Roxas that it would be a mistake to reconstruct the economy along its prewar pattern, and expressed the fear that the country's export-import economy could not be expected to meet the needs of an independent country. I suggested that his administration should begin to plan for a more balanced type of economy. (ibid.: 1)

He criticized the 1938 report of the Joint Preparatory Committee for neglecting the problems caused by an inflexible currency and a decentralized banking system (ibid.: 2). In a meeting with Roxas, he warned the president that the Bell Trade Act "was another great deterrent to the industrialization of the Philippines" (ibid.: 3). Even before leading the

Philippine section of the JPAFC, Cuaderno was determined to depart from its colonial economy by reforming the currency system.

The Philippine section of the JPAFC was composed of Cuaderno; Vicente Carmona, PNB president; and Budget Commissioner Pio Pedrosa. The three had been long familiar with financial and budgetary matters. Cuaderno had worked for the PNB for more than a decade before he founded the PBC in 1938. Carmona, born in Capiz in 1878, established his career mainly as an auditor for various offices in the colonial government, and was appointed undersecretary of finance in 1927 before he was transferred to the PNB as its president (Cornejo 1939: 1642). Pedrosa, born in Leyte in 1900, also had established his career as an auditor for over a decade before being appointed to the budget commissioner's office of the Quezon administration in 1941 (Hidalgo 2000: 16–50). After briefly working for the Philippine Chamber of Commerce (PCC) in the postwar era, Pedrosa was reappointed budget commissioner under the Roxas administration (ibid.: 60). Besides these commission members, both sections of the commission had a technical staff. Table 3.2 lists the technical staff of the Philippine section.

Table 3.2 Membership of the Philippine Section of the JPAFC

		Name	*Position, affiliation*
Member	1	Miguel Cuaderno	Secretary, Department of Finance
	2	Vicente Carmona	President, Philippine National Bank
	3	Pio Pedrosa	Commissioner, Budget Office
Technical staff	1	Andres Castillo	Secretary-economist, Department of Finance
	2	Crispin Llamado	Undersecretary, Department of Finance
	3	Felix de la Costa	Director, Bureau of Banking
	4	Eduardo Romualdez	Assistant Director, Bureau of Banking
	5	Amado R. Briñas	Department of Finance
	6	Gregorio S. Licaros	Executive Office
	7	Delfin E. Silverio	General Auditing Office
	8	Jose Belmonte	Professor, University of the Philippines
	9	Fernando Dizon	Budget Office
	10	Pedro Pacis	Bureau of Customs

Source: Cuaderno 1964: 9.

Table 3.2 reveals the fact that most of the mission members were bureaucrats who were long-term students of Philippine economy during the colonial period. One of the distinguished figures was Andres Castillo, the former executive secretary of the commonwealth's National Economic Council (NEC) and a close aide to Cuaderno as secretary-economist.

Cuaderno noted that the American section was composed of Colonel Edward Crossman, a Wall Street lawyer; John Exter, an economist on the Board of the Governors of the Federal Reserve System; and Arthur W. Stuart of the US Treasury Department (Cuaderno 1964: 9). Although it seems trivial, it is nonetheless interesting to compare the order of the names that Cuaderno wrote and the commission officially recorded in its final report (Cuaderno 1964: 9; JPAFC 1947: iii). While Cuaderno wrote the names of each section's financial specialist (PNB president and Fed economist) next to each chairman, the commission apparently followed conventional protocol order and put the name of a US Treasury representative before that of the Fed representative. Cuaderno apparently was interested more in reforming the banking sector than in dealing with the fiscal problem.

The most impressive initiative that the Philippine section took during a series of meetings of the JPAFC was to prevail on its American counterpart to recommend the creation of a central bank (Cuaderno 1964: 9–11). Cuaderno recorded: "Except for the strong opposition of the chairman [Crossman] of the American group to the establishment of a central bank, the Filipino and American members of this joint commission worked smoothly together" (ibid.: 9). Crossman's objection was a serious matter, because he once succeeded in convincing his American colleagues to not recommend that the Philippine government create a central bank by the time it could balance its budget (ibid.: 9–10).

Crossman, a Wall Street lawyer, reflected the position of American business interests that had invested in colonial Philippines. The Philippine-American Chamber of Commerce (PACC) in New York aggressively supported the Bell Trade Act (Jenkins 1985: 70–80). Cuaderno was later told that the National City Bank of New York attempted to prevent the American section of the JPAFC from recommending the establishment of a central bank (Cuaderno to Quirino 1950, *EQ*, 1; Cuaderno 1964: 11; Espinosa-Robles 1990: 171–2). A.V.H. Hartendorp, a longtime American resident in Manila and editor of the *American Chamber of Commerce Journal* (*ACCJ*) of the American Chamber of Commerce in the Philippines (ACCP),[6] argued that the adoption of the managed-currency

[6] PACC and ACCP were different entities, although they often shared interests and ideas.

system marked "[a] radical change from a relatively free banking system and a virtually automatic gold exchange-currency standard, the safest in the world, to a system of direct government control over both currency and credit" (Hartendorp 1958: 255). He was certain: "It is a very risky system of any kind that must depend almost entirely on the good judgment of a few men" (ibid.: 256). Hartendorp represented those who supported colonial liberalism and attempted to maintain American business prerogatives established during colonial rule (Maxfield and Nolt 1990).

Facing stiff opposition from the head of the American section, Cuaderno finally asked President Roxas to intervene and prevail over the American position. Roxas, disgusted with the attitude of the American section, asked Cuaderno how much time he needed to prepare a separate report. Before Cuaderno could reply to Roxas, two other American members said that they would accept the suggestion to establish a central bank (Cuaderno 1964: 11). Without decisive support from President Roxas and Cuaderno's firm conviction about the creation of a central bank, the commission could very well have acquiesced to the American businesses.

In addition, the Philippine section and its American counterpart clashed over the evaluation of general economic situations. Cuaderno again directly appealed to Roxas to examine the draft report carefully in order not to send an inaccurate message. In a memorandum dated 27 May 1947, Cuaderno asserted: "there are still some passages in the last draft which must either be deleted or rewritten. I consider it important that the Philippine Section does not subscribe to those portions which picture Philippine conditions in too bright a hue, as this might make it difficult for us to approach them if we should find that we simply have to ask them for another loan" (Cuaderno to Roxas 1947, *MAR*, 1).

Cuaderno quoted and criticized several parts of the draft in this memorandum. For example, he contended: "I [Cuaderno] could not agree that 'there is at the present time a general air of prosperity' in the Philippines" (Cuaderno to Roxas 1947, *MAR*, 1). This is the very expression Roxas condemned in his inaugural address almost a year before, when he said:

> The coincidence of easy money and high prices gives to some of our people the false illusion of national prosperity and the mad notion that we have time to dally and debate. The prosperity of money and prices is hallucination, a nightmarish dream resulted from the scarcity of commodities and the influx of half a billion dollars of troop money. Soon, very soon, we must awake from that dream. (Roxas 2004: 129)

Apparently reflecting opposition by Roxas and Cuaderno, the commission deleted the expression from the final report, while retaining phrases such as "this paradox" to juxtapose with the item citing heavy damages caused by the war and the existence of abundant dollar resources (JPAFC 1947: 3).

The commission published its final report on 7 June 1946. Table 3.3 lists the report's contents.

Table 3.3 Contents of the JPAFC Report

1	Introduction
2	The Philippine Economic Problem
3	The Philippine Economy—A Description
4	The Budget
5	Taxation
6	Domestic Borrowing
7	The Monetary System and a Central Bank
8	Banking and Credit Facilities
9	Conservation of Foreign Exchange
10	Economic Development
11	Financing Government Expenditures

Source: JPAFC 1947: v–vi.

Among the issues taken up by the commission, the last two items are important when reconsidering the politics of decolonization. In the section on foreign exchange, the report admits that the Philippines enjoyed abundant foreign reserves but assumed there were "serious potential dangers in this situation" (JPAFC 1947: 65, 67). Its members therefore proposed that the Philippine government impose import controls, although they recognized that "[s]uch controls would be a sharp departure from traditional Philippine practice" (ibid.: 68).

The expression "a sharp departure from traditional Philippine practice" is quite intriguing, although the commission did not delve deeply into this. Considering that the US colonial government managed economic policy based on the idea of free trade (for example, Giesecke 1987), and that the Bell Trade Act followed the same idea, the proposal to impose government import controls indeed signifies a sharp departure from the colonial tradition. The commission apparently avoided a detailed explanation in public, especially just after the Philippine government mobilized all of its forces to win the plebiscite that would amend the constitution in order to put the Bell Trade Act into effect.

In fact, import controls signify a deviance from the policy orientation established by the Bell Trade Act. For instance, Jose Romero, then the commissioner of the Philippine Surplus Commission and future president of the Philippine Sugar Association, opposed the controls because he was concerned about possible retaliation by the United States against Philippine sugar exports to the country. He argued: "the controls were a technical violation of the Bell Trade Act" (MacIsaac 1993: 534).[7] Bello and others mentioned that import and exchange controls were beyond the context of the Bell Trade Act (Bello et al. 1982: 128). A historian more bluntly concluded that the JPAFC's recommendation "violated both the multinationalist principles that the [US] State Department was advocating in international forums and the bilateralist policies of the Philippine Trade Act" (Cullather 1994: 68).

These observations help us read between the lines of the report. The report took the trouble to state that the Bell Trade Act "contains no provision which would prevent the Philippine government from imposing import controls" (JPAFC 1947: 69). The commission members clearly recognized the uneasiness of the import-control proposal and tried to put it in the least controversial way possible in the report. As if vowing not to take bolder actions, the report even stated: "The Commission does not recommend the imposition of controls over foreign exchange transactions" (ibid.: 71).

The section entitled "Economic reconstruction and development" is also worth studying, although it is not straightforward because of its excuse. The report said: "It is not within the Commission's terms of reference to develop detailed plans for the economic development of the Philippines. It has seemed desirable, however, for the Commission to attempt some integration and summation of the economic planning of various public and private agencies and concerns" (ibid.: 72). In the summary, the report asserted that the development program "would make the economy less dependent on its present exports, which are subject to wide fluctuations in price, and facilitate adjustment to the gradual loss of preference in the United States market after 1954 [when the Philippine and US government gradually began to impose the tariff]"

---

[7] This writer highlights the fact that the sugar industry opposed the controls, although MacIsaac emphasizes the gradual change of its position toward the controls by 1954. This is because, obviously, the sugar industry was not a beneficiary of the policy and because it would support the opposition against the Central Bank's monetary policy in the 1950s (Takagi 2008).

(ibid.: 73). The report inserted a different policy orientation that emphasized the departure from the export-oriented economy at the cost of coherence.

The pros and cons of the JPAFC recommendations, therefore, reversed the evaluation of the Bell Trade Act. Araneta, who had pioneered the attack on the trade act, admitted the commission's achievement, especially supported the idea to create a central bank and carry out import controls, for he assumed that such measures would allow the Philippine government to protect local industries (Araneta 1948). He hoped "that it [the Commission's report] rather than the Trade Act expresses the spirit that will shape future American economic relations with the Republic of the Philippines" (ibid.: 285). Meanwhile, beneficiaries of the Bell Trade Act, such as American businesses, had a different opinion of the report. Hartendorp mentioned that the report "was roundly criticized in Manila business circles", although the criticism was not made public (Hartendorp 1958: 256). The ACCP in Manila, unlike the PACC in New York, needed to pay attention to sentiments in Philippine society and avoid public complaints about the report (Jenkins 1985: 80). Hartendorp publicly asserted, but only in the 1950s: "The Joint Finance Commission's Report urged the Philippines well down the road to a government 'planned' and 'managed' economy, as opposed to the system of free enterprise" (Hartendorp 1958: 256). Despite pressure from American vested interests, Filipino policymakers henceforth steadily departed from the colonial tradition.

The Roxas administration was, however, not in a position to proclaim its shift in economic policy, because it was still working hard to win a majority in the plebiscite on the Bell Trade Act scheduled for March 1947. The administration could not convince the public if it loudly declared the proposal of the JPAFC, which revealed the defects of the trade act. Because the administration prioritized receiving war damage compensation and direct American investment, it could not project itself as an administration seeking economic development based on protectionism.

Industrialization and Import Controls

Roxas was actually keen enough to consider the possibility of imposing import controls. Before the JPAFC pointed it out, Roxas had already recognized the seriousness of the balance-of-payments problem. Roxas must have been keen on solving the problem, because he was finance secretary from 1938 to 1941 when the Commonwealth experienced an excess of imports because of the TM Act and other US trade measures (Cuaderno to Quirino 1948, *AMD* Appendix 20; MacIsaac 1993: 343–4; 2002: 162). He mentioned, therefore, the balance-of-payment deficit in his inaugural address: "Every day, that money is being siphoned from our land by more and more imports—not productive imports, but imports of consumption. The well-being of the tradesman alone is not the well-being of our people. Disaster awaits us tomorrow if we do not rouse ourselves and get back to work, to productive work" (Roxas 2004: 130). In other words, Roxas recognized the need for import controls, and in fact he attempted to restrict the inflow of imports from the United States but failed because of American pressure even before the passage of the Bell Trade Act (MacIsaac 1993: 519–20). Aware of the sensitive nature of the controls in connection with the act, Roxas tried to convince the American ambassador in a meeting on 17 December 1947 that the Philippine government would need to impose import controls but it would not endanger the special agreement of the Bell Trade Act (*Foreign Relations of the United States* [hereafter *FRUS*] 1947: 1125).

The NEC, which was revived on 31 December 1947, began to work for import controls in January 1948 (NEC 1948, *MAR*, 1). The NEC was headed by Vice President Elpidio Quirino, chairman; Finance Secretary Cuaderno, vice chairman; and 13 other members with a temporary secretary, Amando M. Dalisay (NEC 1948, *MAR*, 1). Dalisay, who took over the post from Castillo, graduated from Harvard University in 1945, received his PhD in 1946, and was soon appointed chief of the division of economic affairs in the Department of Foreign Affairs (DFA) until 1947 when he was appointed secretary (Jacinto et al. 1957: 155). Like the NEC under the Commonwealth, the NEC under the Republic was led by a young economist trained at a top American university.

After the first meeting on 5 January 1948, the NEC sent a memorandum to President Roxas to report on the projects the council had taken up (NEC 1948, *MAR*, 3). The council reported that it had passed Resolution 1 on a hydropower development, and enumerated other projects such as banking-sector reform including the organization of a central bank, tax reform, measures to conserve foreign-exchange reserves and measures to promote particular agricultural products (NEC 1948, *MAR*, 3). Among these issues, the NEC apparently prioritized working on import controls. Some of the official and private papers of Quirino, who was the chairman of the NEC from January to April 1948, provide clues that help us to understand the process of creating the import-control bills (MacIsaac 1993: 526, 586–7).

The earliest document in the Quirino papers concerns the resolution of the NEC's committee on foreign and domestic commerce dated 30 January 1948. The committee was headed by Placido L. Mapa, who would soon become the secretary of commerce and industry on 12 February 1948 (*Official Gazette* [hereafter *OG*] February 1948: 1005), simply suggested that the president create "an Import Control Board with powers to control the importation of non-essential and luxury articles and to prescribe the manner of such control subject to the approval of the President" (Mapa to Quirino 1948, *EQ*, 1). It reflected the administration's concern about the balance-of-payment problem but not necessarily the will to protect local industry through import controls. This memorandum was, however, not at all final, and by April the NEC continued to study the issue.

Reflecting two different goals of the policy, the NEC prepared two final drafts that were circulated among the relevant government agencies (MacIsaac 1993: 526). A memorandum from Leonides Virata of the DFA to Dalisay dated 2 April 1948 is helpful in understanding the internal discussion within the NEC, because Virata had succinctly summarized characteristics of the two NEC drafts. In the memorandum he mentions two different drafts reflecting two different goals: The first focuses on the balance-of-payment problem, while the second "frankly combines this objective with another aim" (Virata to Dalisay 1948, *EQ*, 1). Why did he put "frankly" before "combines" here? What was the other aim that warranted such frankness from policymakers?

The aim was, frankly, the protection of infant industries. Virata continues: "The original feature of the second draft that is not found in the first is, as stated before, a frank recognition of the necessity of special governmental assistance for the establishment and development of nascent industries" (ibid.). Virata was concerned about negative implication of such frankness and wrote: "this interpretation [protection of local industry] would be viewed as too strained considering the objective and general theme of the whole bill" (ibid.). He suggested: "An open declaration of a protectionist policy at this time should not prejudice the current government policy of attracting American productive capital to the Philippines.... A protectionist policy at this time should not induce repercussions damaging to our exports of primary products" (ibid.: 3). Virata, however, did not oppose the second draft and only suggested moderate revisions in its expression (Virata to Dalisay 2 April 1948, *EQ*, 3).

Dalisay, in his memorandum to Quirino on 3 April 1948, suggested that the government focus only on the balance-of-payment problem rather than expand the policy goals for the protection of the infant industries (Dalisay to Quirino 1948, *EQ*, MacIsaac 1993: 526, 586–7). Although there is no record telling us the reason why Dalisay dropped the second draft, it is not difficult to assume that the NEC, as a part of the executive branch, had decided to go with the draft that was more loyal to the formal policy of the administration, which encouraged foreign investment and which attempted to reduce obstacles to it.

Within the cabinet, however, Finance Secretary Cuaderno supported import controls not only as an urgent measure to curtail imports but also as a policy tool to promote local industries. He was reported as saying: "The measure is considered timely for a country like the Philippines[,] which is just rehabilitating its economy and seeking to establish a trade position which will in effect give impetus to infant industries at home" (*Manila Times* 5 April 1948, LM, *Import Controls*).[8] It is important that Cuaderno, who as finance secretary was in charge of counter measures addressing the balance-of-payment crisis, supported backing the infant industries through import controls.

The policymakers adopted the draft stating the two objectives when Congress began its deliberations on the import control bill (House Bill [HB] 1794) on 26 April 1948. The purposes of the bill were to conserve foreign exchange, develop and reconstruct industries that would sustain balance-of-payments, and "to give special governmental assistance for the establishment, development, or reconstruction of particular industries or particular branches of agriculture" (Sec. 1, HB 1794). Congress had already paid much attention to the promotion of local industries before deliberating on the import control bills. It passed Republic Act (RA) 35, or the tax exemptions law for new and necessary industries, on 30 September 1946 (Golay 1961: 248–50; Valdepeñas 1969: 50–2).

In the background of these congressional initiatives, there was a voice from the PCC led by Gil Puyat (president) and Salvador Araneta (vice president) (Jenkins 1985: 126; MacIsaac 1993: 533). Puyat was a

[8] LM stands for the Lopez Museum in which the news clipping on various issues of the *Manila Times* are restored. This writer thereafter puts *LM*, name of the category of clipping next to the date of the publication of the article when he refers to the article in the collection of the Lopez Museum, because the page is missed in the collection of the Lopez Museum.

son of Gonzalo Puyat, a distinguished figure in business who founded the National Economic Protectionism Association (NEPA) in cooperation with his colleagues in the PCC in order to promote local production and trade in the 1930s. The PCC, in fact, had recommended the idea of import controls to President Roxas in 1946 (Araneta 2000: 161). Araneta delivered a speech on 20 March 1948 in which he recommended that the government impose import controls; it "should frankly [be] provide[d]", he added, "that its purpose is not merely negative, in other words, to limit importation of non-essential commodities, but that it has a positive aim, in other words, to foster the industrialization of the economy" (ibid.: 165–6).

The policymakers clearly characterized import controls as not only a special monetary measure but also another way to promote local industries. In their explanatory note on HB 1794, the sponsors, including Congressman Modest Formilleza, a former colonial bureaucrat with the Bureau of Internal Revenue in the 1930s and then chair of the House Committee on Ways and Means, recognized that there were three measures to protect infant industries: namely, subsidies, tariffs and quantitative controls on import materials. They said that fiscal conditions had never allowed the government to provide subsidies and admitted that the Bell Trade Act prevented the government from imposing tariffs on imports from its largest trading partner, the United States. They therefore stated that, under the circumstances, import controls were the only way to protect infant industries (*Congressional Record: House of Representatives*, hereafter, *CRHR*, 6 May 1948: 1672).

The policymakers accurately recognized the possible repercussions that could arise from private businesses, especially foreign ones. When Congressman Manuel Cases cast doubt on the bill's effectiveness and said that the Manila Junior Chamber of Commerce opposed the bill, Formilleza argued that the PCC, composed entirely of Filipinos, supported the bill, and asserted: "the Manila Junior Chamber is more or less international in membership, and you cannot expect them to be in favor of this bill" (*CRHR* 6 May 1948: 1677–8). Despite possible opposition from the foreign capital, Congress passed the bill on 24 June 1948, and President Quirino, who had succeeded Roxas who had died suddenly on 15 April, approved it as RA 330, or the import control act, on 25 June 1948.

Filipino policymakers made efforts to depart from the Philippines' colonial economic structure through import controls, which deviated from the policy orientation of the Bell Trade Act. This effort to change the colonial economic structure will become clearer when we study the process of creating the central bank.

Establishing the Central Bank

A month after the publication of the JPAFC report, President Roxas created the Central Bank Council by Executive Order 81 on 14 August 1947, and appointed Cuaderno as the council chair. The other members were Jose Yulo, Vicente Carmona, Delfin Buencamino and Alfonso Calalang (*OG* 1947: 3566). Of the four, Carmona and Calalang were known figures in the banking industry. Calalang was a senior bank examiner at the Bureau of Banking in the colonial government, and Cuaderno had brought him to the Finance and Mining Brokerage Company as its vice president in 1936 (Orosa 1988: 1). Cuaderno and Calalang were very close: When Cuaderno became the founding president of the PBC in 1938, Calalang became its vice president (ibid.: 24).

Cuaderno began to collect material about the new types of central banks in 1946 in order to brush up on his knowledge of central banking, because he discovered that the traditional type of central banks established in Latin America after World War I had failed to cope with particular economic conditions in the region (Cuaderno 1964: 86). After joining the council, Cuaderno also consulted with economists with the Fed, which functioned as a consulting agency for those countries attempting to establish new types of central banks in the 1940s (Golay 1961: 217; Cullather 1992: 80). Cuaderno found an article written by Robert Triffin that proved the most helpful, because Triffin, formerly a leading economist at the Fed and later the International Monetary Fund (IMF), assisted the governments of Guatemala and Paraguay in establishing a new type of central bank (Cuaderno 1964: 86). After surveying the latest knowledge about central banking, Cuaderno succeeded in crafting a draft bill in early 1948, and then asked President Roxas to send a special message to Congress to endorse the bill.

In the special message dated 27 February 1948, Roxas appealed to legislators to support the central bank bill (*CRHR* 27 February 1948: 534–5). After claiming, "I had always favored the creation of a central bank to give flexibility to our currency and to provide adequate administration of credit and exchange", Roxas explained that countries like the Philippines, which depended on an international market with just a few export crops, were vulnerable to fluctuations in the international price of these crops. He asserted: "To offset such disequilibria, countries such as ours must adopt compensatory monetary policies in order to maintain domestic levels of income and activity. Without a central bank, the adoption of such compensatory policies is not at all possible" (ibid.). His message apparently reflected the results of a study by the Cuaderno council.

Cuaderno elaborated on his idea in a statement at the joint hearing on the central bank bill conducted by the banking committees of the House of the Representatives and the Senate on 3 March 1948 (Cuaderno 1955: 165–76). Quoting Triffin, Cuaderno explained that the Philippines needed a new type of central bank that was designed for "a relatively small agricultural economy, which is still in an early stage of development and which is particularly vulnerable to disturbances in international trade" (ibid.: 171). Cuaderno referred to the failure of central banks in Latin American countries and explained that the central banks of underdeveloped countries were expected to engage in "active and powerful intervention" in the money market, because they were expected to operate without broad and active private financial markets in a market dominated by foreign banks that paid more attention to foreign trade and less to domestic economic development (ibid.: 174). He concluded his statement by declaring: "Our country is now free and independent [,] and in the exercise of its right of economic self-determination, it is its earnest desire to lay the foundation of our currency and banking system on a sound basis, and to administer it so that the system will 'promote a rising level of production, employment and real income'" (ibid.: 176).

Regarding the source of his study, Cuaderno enumerated the names of central bankers in Latin American countries, including Raul Prebisch of Argentina, together with leading economists in the US Fed (ibid.: 171). Prebisch, born in Argentina in 1901, was a leading economist and adviser to the ministers of finance and agriculture in Argentina, which introduced exchange controls in 1931 and import controls in 1938 (Love 1980: 47–8). He advocated the creation of a central bank with the power to control credit and monetary policy in the early 1930s, and served as the director-general of the Central Bank of Argentina from 1935 to 1943. In his struggle to help his country recover from the balance-of-payment crisis caused by the Great Depression, Prebisch published an article in 1934 that explained how the price of agricultural products was more vulnerable than that of industrial products, an idea he elaborated further after he resigned from the Central Bank in 1943 (ibid.: 50–5). Since the 1930s, before he gained international notoriety as the advocate of the theory of unequal exchange and of ISI as a way to overcome unequal exchange, he had publicized his formative idea not only in Argentina but also in other Latin American countries. In citing the Latin American experience, Cuaderno could present a living example of a new type of central bank with novel policy tools such as exchange and import controls, as well as the supporting idea that agricultural products were more vulnerable than industrial products in terms of fluctuations in international prices.

The congressional debate revealed the significance of nationalism over the technical nature of the bill. In the plenary session in Congress, Congressman Jose J. Roy, chair of the committee on banks and corporations and a sponsor of HB 1704 (the Central Bank bill), played a pivotal role in passing the bill through the House (Valdepeñas 2003: 62–85). In the bill's deliberations, Roy argued in support of the bill along the lines of Roxas and Cuaderno, saying that the Philippine economy, dependent on a few export crops, needed a type of central bank different from those in developed countries. In the relatively pointless discussion in Congress, Congressman Topacio Nueco made an interesting remark that underscores the bill's political context. Admitting to not being a financial expert, he said: "I am inclined to favor this bill because certain foreign interests are against it" (ibid.: 84). The next speaker, Congressman Agripino P. Escareal, revealed Cuaderno's letter disclosing the fact that Crossman, chair of the American section of the JPAFC, opposed the idea of a Philippine central bank (ibid.). After Congress passed the bill, President Quirino signed RA 265 (Central Bank Act) on 15 June 1948.

In his message at the inauguration of the Central Bank on 3 January 1949, President Quirino affirmed the view of the Central Bank as a symbol of independence and a locomotive for industrialization. He reminded his audience of the failed PEA proposal to create a central bank in the 1930s and explained: "The chief impediment [at that time] was the lack of authority to accomplish it" (Quirino 1955: 105). He meant sovereignty, and therefore he stated that the Central Bank Act was a "charter of our economic sovereignty" (Quirino 1955: 105; Cuaderno 1949: 8). He expected the Central Bank to contribute not only to the improvement of monetary policy management but also to economic development in general. He said: "As we carry out our program of development in an effort at total economic mobilization, the Central Bank becomes both a challenge to our ingenuity as a people and an opportunity to show our creative faith in our economic future". He added: "the Bank should encourage the development of infant industries and the establishment of new ones by giving both the proper and due incentive in financing them" (Quirino 1955: 105).

Following the passage of the Central Bank Act, Castillo and Cuaderno published their studies of the Central Bank of the Philippines. First, Castillo contributed a paper entitled "Central Banking in the Philippines" to the academic journal *Pacific Affairs*, which it published in December 1948 (Castillo 1948). In this article, Castillo wrote that the Filipino people had "acquired an instrument for liquidating financial colonialism in their country" (ibid.: 371). Describing the historical development of the banking industry in the Philippines, he argued: "The foreign banks have exercised a far more decisive influence on the banking business in the Philippines than their share of total banking resources would indicate". He added that the foreign banks dedicated financial resources to foreign trade rather than invested them in the long-term development of the Philippines (ibid.: 364). He even briefly mentioned that the Bell Trade Act failed to encourage American capital to invest in the Philippines, and argued that the "Central Bank will create the requisite financial environment for the rapid development of the domestic securities market" (Castillo 1948: 368–9). Castillo expected the Central Bank to be not only the authority on monetary policy but also the organ to encourage domestic investment for the diversification of agriculture and industrialization.

Cuaderno published his monograph on the Central Bank in June 1949 (Araneta 1958: 386), in which he admits the necessity of active intervention by the Central Bank in development projects (Cuaderno 1949). He explains that policymakers in fact added "a special exception" to Section 137 of the Central Bank Act, under which the government can determine "productive and income-producing projects" and provide advances up to 200 million pesos to the banks or people who would carry out those projects (ibid.: 76–7). The policymakers not only recognized the structural difference between developing and developed economies but also strived for structural change through the active participation of the Central Bank.

Aware of such a high level of responsibility and expectation, Cuaderno maximized his long experience in both the private and public sectors in order to bring specialists into the Central Bank. Sixto Roxas, who himself worked for the Central Bank in the early 1950s, asserted: "Cuaderno recruited the earliest team of economists, finance, statistics, and accounting specialists" (Roxas 2002: 86). Cuaderno, for instance, brought Alfonso Calalang and Nicanor Tomas from the PBC as the deputy governor and the superintendent of banks, respectively, due to their long experience in the banking industry (Cuaderno 1964: 90; Orosa 1988: 25). He appointed Castillo the director of the securities market department because of the latter's wide knowledge of central banking (Cuaderno 1964: 90). Cuaderno also recruited Virata from the DFA to be the director of the department of economic research, which was described as "the premiere center of applied economics and statistical research and attracted the cream of local talent" (Roxas 2002: 86). As the governor—the only member who could devote all of his time to the monetary board, the highest governing body of the bank—Cuaderno succeeded during the 1950s in making the board the dominant institution in economic policymaking (Golay 1961: 20).

Emergence of the Economic Policy Regime

Suspended Negotiations with the World Bank and the Developmental Plan

After the formation of the Central Bank Act, Cuaderno, as the finance secretary, made an extra effort to negotiate with the World Bank for a set of loans for hydroelectric projects and a fertilizer project (Cuaderno 1964: 17–21; MacIsaac 1993: 488–98). Although it spent more than a year negotiating with the bank, the Philippine government ultimately gave up on securing the loans. Cuaderno, who led the Philippine mission to Washington, DC from July to November 1948, "submitted a voluminous report to President Quirino, together with a copy of the Program of Rehabilitation and Development which we [Cuaderno and his mission] had prepared in Washington" (Cuaderno 1964: 20). The "voluminous report" comprised 81 pages and 31 appendices, including the first development program by the Philippine government. By studying the report, we can understand what the Filipino policymakers sought and why they finally suspended negotiations with the World Bank.

Cuaderno was originally instructed by President Quirino to lead the negotiation for loans for four hydroelectric power plants and one fertilizer plant that was to be connected to one of the power plants (Cuaderno to Quirino 1948, *AMD*, 1). Once he started negotiations with the World Bank, however, Cuaderno discovered that he was expected to present a comprehensive development program as a precondition to begin a full-scale entry into loan negotiations. In the first meeting, Cuaderno was asked to brief the World Bank on the Philippine economy. He pointed out the following as economic problems:

(1) The large current deficit in our balance-of-trade due to the heavy damage suffered by our export industries and the considerable reduction in the general level of output—a deficit that is being temporarily offset by large amounts of US government payments.
(2) The gradual loss after 1954 of the favored position of Philippine export crops in the American market and the difficulties of adjustment due to high production and shipping costs. (ibid.: 6–7)

The subsequent record of the discussion between the Philippine mission and World Bank officers reminds us of the disagreement between the Philippine and American sections of the JPAFC. While the Philippine mission assumed the above-mentioned problems as "the two problems of paramount urgency on our economic horizon", the World Bank maintained a rather optimistic view of the Philippine economy (ibid.: 6). Cuaderno informed President Quirino that the preliminary report prepared by the World Bank officers "revealed some of [*sic*] erroneous conclusions", including "misleading impressions culled by these [World Bank] men from some biased reports given out by a few foreign interests and local magazines" that they collected in their preliminary research mission to the Philippines in January 1948 (ibid.: 1, 13–4).

Cuaderno was even required to answer questions regarding anti-foreign sentiments in the Philippines. He "countered by pointing out that this alleged [anti-foreign] sentiment could not stem from an ideological antipathy to foreigners in general" (ibid.: 25). He asserted that the Philippine government asked only for "a share of the country's import and export trade and of the retail trade" or efforts to develop resources; moreover, the government repeatedly said that it would "welcome the flow of American capital" (ibid.). Cuaderno attempted to claim that the government's economic policy was far from anti-foreign and criticism of it was pointless.

A debate over the implementation process of the JPAFC report is helpful in knowing how the Philippine government was conscious of the principle of sovereignty. When the World Bank officers demanded that Cuaderno implement the recommendation of the JPAFC as a condition for the development loan, Cuaderno denounced the "condition to be an undue interference with our sovereignty" (ibid.: 67). It is impressive that Cuaderno supported import controls while opposing the World Bank's idea to make the import controls a condition of the development loan. Because of the uncompromising attitude of the Philippine mission, the two parties only agreed to start negotiations on partial loans for the Philippine request the following year (ibid.; MacIsaac 1993: 491–2). In 1949, President Quirino finally decided to reject the condition and instead utilize financing from the Central Bank (Cuaderno 1964: 21).

An important byproduct of the negotiation was the first developmental program crafted by Cuaderno. At first, he tried to avoid losing the focus of the discussion and claimed that the current activities of the government "are in fact in accordance with a short-term program embracing a number of projects that are urgent and critical to the solution of the two major problems which face the nation in the immediate future" (Cuaderno to Quirino 1948, *AMD*, 32). Faced with the unrelenting attitude of the World Bank, however, he finally presented "the Program of Rehabilitation and Development", or Cuaderno Plan, as the country's five-year development program for 1949 through 1954 (Cuaderno 1964: 19–20). The following summarizes the Cuaderno Plan's goals:

> I [Cuaderno] submitted a program of rehabilitation and development designed principally to adjust the Philippine economy to the decline in [US] Government payments by about 1951, and to [provide] the necessary adjustment to the progressive application of American tariffs after 1954. Consequently, this program aims at improving the production conditions of dollar-producing products, at the establishment and encouragement of new agricultural industries yielding dollar-producing crops, at the encouragement of greater food production and light industries as well as handicrafts that will diminish the volume of foreign exchange disbursements. (Cuaderno to Quirino 1948, *AMD*, 32)

This summary is important on two counts. First, it shows that Cuaderno was conscious of the timetable for economic adjustment: In 1951, the War Damage Commission was expected to terminate its activity, marking the end of reconstruction, while in 1954 the Philippine and US governments were supposed to begin to impose tariffs on their imports, signifying the beginning of the final phase of the Philippines' special trade relationship with the United States. Second, the summary reveals that Cuaderno admitted roles for dollar-producing industries, including export industries, but at the same time he encouraged the promotion of food production and light industries, which would eventually save foreign exchange because the Philippines relied heavily on imported foods and products of light industry. Golay, in fact, noticed that one of the features of the Cuaderno Plan, compared with the Yulo Plan that succeeded it, was its emphasis on industrial development (Golay 1961: 350–5). Filemon Rodriguez, general manager of the National Power Corporation, had assisted Cuaderno in the creation of the development program, and he confirmed that more than two-thirds of the investment was to be allocated for industrial development while the rest would be spent for agricultural development (Rodriguez 1967: 35).

Cuaderno supported the idea to change the colonial economic structure. For instance, he asserted: "It is also designed as the first phase in the process of effecting the structural adjustments that are necessary to change an export economy highly sensitive to change in demand and prices of its few agricultural export crops into one that is better fortified against outside pressures" (Cuaderno to Quirino 1948, *AMD*, 32). Let us turn to the import controls which Cuaderno sought to use toward industrialization.

The Central Bank and the Politics of Decolonization

While succeeding in gathering bright talents to the Central Bank, Cuaderno was dissatisfied with the poor implementation of import controls. This is because the government had failed to implement RA 330 immediately; instead, it took more than half a year to proclaim the executive order to carry out the act because of opposition from the private sector (Cuaderno 1955: 216). The ACCP, in particular, was dominated by American importers and exporters who had vigorously opposed the control measures ever since the first attempts of the Philippine government to implement them in 1948 (MacIsaac 1993: 534). The ACCP handed its view directly to President Quirino through the PACC when Quirino visited the United States in September 1949 (*Manila Chronicle*, hereafter, *MC* 11 September 1949: 1). In the letter, the ACCP argued that the chamber could not support the import controls as long as these were used against foreign business (*MC*, 11 September 1949: 1; Jenkins 1985: 130). According to an observation by the US Embassy, Quirino was seriously concerned about losing support from the ACCP in the presidential election in November of same year (Maxfield and Nolt 1990: 66).

It was not the case, however, that the Philippine government was totally prevailed upon by American pressure (Cuaderno 1964: 24). After receiving consent from President Quirino, Cuaderno directly called on American Ambassador Myron Cowen on 29 November 1949, to request him to ask US President Harry Truman to allow the Philippine government to impose exchange controls. After a brief survey by the IMF mission and confidential advice from the US government, the Philippine government finally announced its decision to implement exchange controls with the authority of Section 74 of the Central Bank Act on 9 December 1949.

After the introduction of exchange controls, the Central Bank directly faced the opponents of them. Some of the toughest opponents came from American businesses that resorted to political leverage in the Philippines' US embassy (MacIsaac 1993: 537–9). Lewis Gleeck has an interesting story that shows how the tension eventually resulted in direct pressure by the US embassy on the Central Bank (1993: 98–9). Gleeck recorded that Andres Soriano, a Filipino business tycoon who acquired an American citizenship during WWII, and Joseph Foly of the National City Bank of New York called on the Philippine desk of the US State Department on 28 December 1949. Soriano and Foly condemned the import controls and decried Cuaderno's personality as "arrogant, difficult to get along with and determined to run the bank as his own show" (Gleeck 1993: 98).

On 29 December 1949, the day after Soriano visited the State Department, Ambassador Myron Cowen and Eugene Clay of the US embassy visited Cuaderno's office to demand that the Philippine government return the money that the US Army had deposited in the Philippines by 31 December 1949. Cuaderno was so upset that he fired off a long memorandum to President Quirino on 30 December 1949 (Cuaderno to Quirino 1949b, *EQ*; Espinosa-Robles 1990: 171). Cuaderno doubted that Washington would refuse a Philippine request to extend the transfer and rather lamented the fact that the US embassy had been so affected by the National City Bank's conviction that the Philippine government would devalue the peso in the near future (Cuaderno to Quirino 1949b, *EQ*, 2). Cuaderno assumed that the US embassy attempted to pressure the Philippine government into paying back the peso deposit as soon as possible, because it was afraid of losses caused by devaluation.

Cuaderno, however, had opposed devaluation since the 1930s. In 1937, for instance, he publicly argued that devaluation would not be beneficial for the Philippine government mainly because of the additional burden it placed on the government to pay back loans from the United States (*Tribune* 10 September 1937: 14). He did not change his view after independence. In fact, Cuaderno appealed to Quirino in a letter written during the electoral campaign in October 1949: "[b]ecause the Philippine economy is still highly dependent on imports, the cost of living and the cost of production of local crops and manufactures would go up. This would generate inflationary pressures which will be very injurious at a time when the country is in a development stage" (Cuaderno to Quirino 1949a, *EQ*, 3–4). In this letter, he plainly reiterated his conviction about the needlessness of devaluation.

When the Central Bank grew gradually but deeply involved in the implementation of the control measures in their entirety, the bank's monetary board discussed the objectives of import controls based on a memorandum prepared by Cuaderno on 9 January 1950. In this memorandum, Cuaderno, quoting the report of the JPAFC, explained: "the agency created to administer import controls should be closely coordinated with the Central Bank" (Cuaderno 1955: 218). He clarified that "what is needed to solve our foreign exchange problem is the rapid increase in the country's productive activities" (ibid.: 221), adding that foreign exchange reserves should be built up "in order to restore confidence in our currency" (ibid.: 220). Cuaderno integrated the problems of the balance-of-payments and productivity and assumed import and exchange controls as the remedy.

After the monetary board's discussion, Cuaderno took various opportunities to explain the significance of both the import and exchange controls and also the necessity of adjusting the Philippine economy before the US war damage payments ceased in 1951. In a speech before the Philippine Importers Association on 21 January 1950, Cuaderno mentioned that the importers, 95 per cent of whom he assumed were foreigners, had time to adjust their management before the implementation of the controls, because implementation took more than six months due to pressure from the business sector. He reportedly said that the controls would lead to the development of the Philippine economy run purely by Filipinos and prevent an outflow of pesos (*MC*, 22 January 1950: 1, 4). Such an appeal inevitably raised concerns among foreign businesses.

The ACCP, in its journal of January 1950, warned the Philippine government that "we have come full-turn [of the vicious circle] because under the present controls, especially the exchange control, all hope of any substantial influx of new capital must be abandoned and together with that, all hope of any rapid development of our export industries" (*ACCJ* January 1950: 6). This is because the exchange controls were an example of the "excessively nationalistic government policies" that would cause "the dangerous consequences" (ibid.). According to the editorial of the *ACCJ*, the government could not expect any inflow of capital that the Philippines robustly needed, because the exchange controls were against the natural law of economics (ibid.).

Meanwhile, Cuaderno criticized the ACCP by name in a meeting of the Rotary Club on 26 January 1950 (Cuaderno 1955: 230–4). First, with regard to any nationalistic tendency, he mentioned that the government had always encouraged foreign private capital to invest in the Philippines (ibid.: 231–2). Second, in terms of government intervention, he related the *Journal*'s article with the ideas of Adam Smith; he argued that "[r]ecurring depressions and the continuing paradox of poverty in the midst of plenty are evidence that economic activity cannot regulate itself" and pointed to the New Deal and economic planning in the United States and United Kingdom as good examples of government intervention in the West (ibid.: 233). Cuaderno, who had studied in the UK and worked as a member of the PEA, which was affected by the idea of the New Deal in the 1930s, was quite aware of shifting ideas in economics as shown in the previous chapter.

After finishing his rebuttal against the *ACCJ* article, Cuaderno confessed his dilemma: While Washington demanded the Philippine government to prepare a comprehensive developmental program, the ACCP accused the Philippine government of perpetuating a vicious circle of political intervention into market economy, citing exchange controls as an example (Cuaderno 1955: 233–4). He lamented: "This [conflicting pressure from the Americans] puts the Government between the Scylla of omission and the Charybdis of commission" (Cuaderno 1955: 233–4).

Cuaderno did not, however, abandon the responsibility, and so he requested the cabinet to organize a special committee to study priorities in the actual allocation of foreign exchange on 2 February 1950 (Balmaceda to Cabinet 1950, *EQ*). The committee was composed of Secretaries Cornelio Balmaceda of Commerce and Industry, Mapa of Agriculture and Natural Resources, Prospero Sanidad of Public Works and Communications, Governor Cuaderno and two more government officials. The committee drew up a priority list with consideration for "the basic requirements such as food, shelter, clothing, health, education, and increased production of exports and other dollar-producing industries, and industrial development along selected lines that will decrease imports and save dollars" (ibid.: 3). Balmaceda, who had worked for the promotion of local industry and trade as an officer of the Bureau of Commerce and as PEA secretary since the 1930s, said that the list was only a guide, and that the Central Bank would decide on the items to "serve the common welfare and help strengthen the national economy" (ibid.).

Cuaderno was continuously faced with American opposition and became so annoyed with the actions of the US embassy and the National City Bank that he sent a confidential letter to President Quirino dated 4 December 1950 (MacIsaac 1993: 539; Espinosa-Robles 1990: 171). In the letter, entitled "anomalous position in which Ambassador Cowen and the high officials of the National City Bank have been trying to place the Central bank", he accused the National City Bank of using its influence to pressure the Philippine government to "soft-pedal or even kick me [Cuaderno] out of the Central Bank" (Cuaderno to Quirino 1950, *EQ*, 1). Cuaderno furthermore reported to Quirino the things that happened following the imposition of exchange controls. Cuaderno had apparently been asked by Clay of the US embassy to provide special treatment to several American firms by, among other things, granting a general license to remit funds. When Cuaderno asked Clay to submit proper documents for study, he was told that the US president's permission for the exchange controls was just temporary, and that "it might be revoked if we [the Central Bank] did not grant what the Embassy here asked us to do for American business firms" (ibid.: 5–6). At that moment, "I [Cuaderno] lost my temper and I told Clay that he seemed to forget that our country is now independent" (ibid.). Tensions between Filipino policymakers and Clay illustrate the disgust of the former group with the uncooperative attitude of the US embassy (Cuaderno 1964: 32; Constantino and Constantino 1978: 228; Gleeck 1993: 113). These did not cause the policymakers to abandon import and exchange controls, however.

Meanwhile, lawmakers in Congress had begun work on revising the existing import controls in January 1950 in order to cope with severe criticisms of graft and corruption in the existing administration of import controls. The Quirino administration was roundly accused of graft and corruption as well as electoral fraud in the 1949 election (Gleeck 1993: ch. 3). There were various stories about a bill padding scandal involving government sales of particular medicines, mishandling imported product quotas, and a kind of "so-what" attitude of Senate President Jose Avelino, who ended up losing his position partly because of this attitude in 1949. The 1949 election was remembered as one of the most violent and fraudulent elections in the history of the republic, in which the anti-government movement led by the Huk swiftly increased its support of the people angry at electoral fraud and violence by the administration (Kerkvliet 2002: 211).

In the midst of legitimacy as well as fiscal crisis, Congressman Domingo Veloso, chair of the committee on commerce and industry in the first Congress and Speaker pro tempore in the second Congress, was appointed chair of a special committee on import and price controls on 13 January. For one month, the committee conducted a hearing with the public and private sectors, including the Central Bank. One of the materials to which the committee referred was the IMF report of 20 January 1950, which recommended that the Philippine government implement control measures for two to three years (*CRHR* 18 April 1950: 1164). Finally, the committee submitted HB 900, "An act to safeguard the international monetary reserve of the Philippines", on 14 April 1950 (*CRHR* 8 February 1950: 157; *CRHR* 14 April 1950: 1094).

Although the title of the bill emphasized that its purpose was to safeguard the international monetary reserve, Veloso, as the bill's sponsor, pointed out that there were three other goals: "Firstly, to arrest the alarming drain [on] dollar reserve, [s]econdly to divert dollar reserve from luxuries and non-essential imports to machinery and equipment for the rehabilitation of agriculture and industries, and [t]hirdly, to protect the local industries from competition of imported goods" (*CRHR* 14 April 1950: 1100–1). Veloso further explained that they aimed at drafting a more comprehensive bill that would cover all import products rather than only selected items (*CRHR* 14 April 1950: 1101; Valdepeñas 1969: 107–8). In addition to these changes, Veloso clarified that at least 40 per cent of the licenses were to be allocated to new Filipino importers (*CRHR* 14 April 1950: 1101). The lawmakers attempted to make the revised import control bill a remedy for the balance-of-payment crisis, a tool for industrialization and a means to encourage the nationalization of business. Finally, Congress passed the bill and President Quirino signed it as RA 426, "An act to regulate imports and for other purposes", on 19 May 1950.

Just before Congress passed the revised import control bill, Cuaderno had made another speech in a convention of the National Conference of Trade Unions on 3 May 1950 (Cuaderno 1955: 208–14). In his speech he reiterated his conviction that the government needed to carry out import controls as a vital part of the developmental program. He followed the argument of the inaugural address of late President Roxas, saying that "the prosperity we have been enjoying being artificial cannot last at the same high plane" (ibid.: 212). Unlike Roxas, who could have only warned the audience in 1946, Cuaderno could take pride in the achievement of import and exchange controls. He asserted that "because of the import and exchange controls, new industries are being established now with local capital" (ibid.: 212–3). Although not a few criticized the graft and corruption that allegedly marred the implementation process of import and exchange controls, most of the Filipino policymakers agreed to implement ISI through the controls before they accepted the Bell Mission of the US in June 1950.

To sum up, the acceptance of the Bell Trade Act of 1946 was not the end of the politics of independence. Its acceptance should be understood in the context of the government having exhausted efforts to rebuild the country even in the face of the US government making the act the condition for the rehabilitation act. The inaugural address of President Roxas was informative, in which it reveals that the administration aimed not only at reconstruction but also at industrialization. As we have seen in the previous chapters, Roxas and Quirino had been keen on economic issues and quite prepared for economic decolonization. For them, industrialization represented the departure from the colonial economy. The Roxas administration therefore made the most of the JPAFC, which recommended that the government impose import controls to stabilize the balance-of-payment and establish a central bank to realize a flexible currency system—or the departure from neocolonial relations with the United States stipulated by the Bell Trade Act. In the subsequent policymaking process, the Central Bank, which was expected to be not only the monetary authority but also a locomotive for industrialization, directed the process of industrialization to achieve economic decolonization.

The Filipino policymakers were not necessarily anti-American but were clearly anticolonial. While the Filipino policymakers supported the idea of active intervention by the government, the American businesses stuck to the idea of colonial liberalism. Relentless pressure from American businesses would have ensured that the Philippine government lost the opportunity to depart from the colonial economic policy were it not for the determination of the policymakers. The Filipino policymakers were conscious about sovereignty, although they sought various kinds of assistance from the World Bank, IMF, or Fed. They in fact withdrew their request for the loan when they faced conditions from the World Bank, because they considered the conditionality an infringement on sovereignty. The economic policy regime emerged from the politics of decolonization in which the Filipino policymakers were determined to depart from the colonial economy in the midst of postwar reconstruction efforts.

CHAPTER 4

The Economic Decolonization and the Great Debate, 1951–57

Did the policy regime have any impact on Philippine economy? Considering the dominant framework of the weak state in which scholars have underestimated the capability of the Philippine government, this question sounds worth scrutinizing. This question is addressed in this chapter by revisiting the economic policy debate, which was once called the "great debate" in the 1950s. The great debate was a policy debate over fiscal and monetary policy under three successive presidents: Elpidio Quirino, Ramon Magsaysay, and Carlos P. Garcia in the 1950s (for example, Golay 1956; Roxas 1958a). Governor Cuaderno of the Central Bank argued for a tight fiscal policy and continuity in the strong currency policy, which he believed functioned as a remedy of the balance-of-payment problem as well as a vital tool for ISI. On the other hand, Salvador Araneta and some cabinet members supported a more liberal fiscal policy and a change in the currency policy that would benefit the export industry, including the politically active "sugar bloc".

At the end of the debate, Cuaderno won the confidence of President Garcia, succeeded in maintaining the strong currency policy, and was reappointed even beyond legal retirement age, although his opponents had authored bills enabling the government to conduct a more liberal fiscal policy and a barter law that was beneficial to the export industry before they resigned from the cabinet.

The debate has been understood a clash between the nationalists and the sugar bloc or the beneficiary of the colonial economic structure (Golay 1956; Soberano 1963). Cuaderno, in fact, mentioned that the sugar bloc opposed his reappointment in 1955 (Cuaderno 1964: 45). According to this understanding, the nationalists represented by the

Bank strove for industrialization in spite of the resilient political power of colonial vested interests represented by Araneta and supported by the sugar bloc.

This conventional understanding is however confusing once we put the debate into historical context. Cuaderno and Araneta, both of whom were members of the PEA, criticized American economic policy toward the Philippines and supported the idea of industrialization through import controls in the late 1940s (Araneta 1948). Araneta, in fact, abandoned his once-close relations and began to clash with Alfredo Montelibano, leader of the sugar bloc, in the 1960s (Larkin 2001: 217; Sicat 2002: 2). One cannot assume Araneta to be a stable ally of the sugar industry. Sixto K. Roxas, a former economist at the Central Bank and then at the Philippine National Bank, characterized the debate as "a struggle between two schools of [economic] thought" in an introductory note to a chapter of the compilation of Araneta's speeches (Roxas 1958a: 328). Roxas asserted Cuaderno's policy as a policy of "status quo" while summarizing Araneta's policy proposal as "a dual policy" composed of deficit financing and foreign exchange rate adjustment (ibid.). The clear distinction of two ideas does not solve the question; rather it prompts us to ask why we witness the clash of ideas only in the 1950s.

The great debate is studied here as a case study of the emerging autonomy of the economic policy regime by tracing the entire process by which Araneta gradually emerged as a key policymaker and eventually lost his influence in the government in the broader context of the politics of decolonization.[1] Considering the historical contexts in which Cuaderno and other policymakers worked for economic decolonization, we can understand that the debate emerged in response to the policy of the Bank. In this chapter, first, the emerging role of Salvador Araneta is traced. Then, as second, the politics of the great debate mainly engaged in by Cuaderno and Araneta and his allies in the administrations is revised.

[1] Hori studies changing elite structure referring to the relative autonomy of the Philippine state in the 1950s (Hori 1996), while this chapter aims at showing the role of ideas of policymakers in the political process generating the strength of a policy regime.

Changing Phase of Economic Decolonization and the Clash of Ideas

The Recovery of Private Businesses and an Alternative Policy Proposal

Salvador Araneta had been one of the leading advocates for economic nationalism since the 1930s. He joined the Philippine Economic Association (PEA) as a founding member in 1933 while organizing the NEPA with his colleagues in the Philippine Chamber of Commerce (PCC) to promote domestic manufacture and commerce in 1934. He was the most vocal advocate for economic nationalism at the Constitutional Convention that framed the 1935 Constitution (De Dios 2002). In this spirit of economic nationalism, he claimed the necessity for import substitution through favorable tariffs on local products in his testimony to the Joint Preparatory Committee on Philippine Affairs (JPCPA) in 1937 (MacIsaac 1993: 160, 232). After independence, Araneta became the vice president of the PCC, which was headed by Gil J. Puyat, and led the opposition against the Bell Trade Act of 1946. In fact, in 1946, the PCC under Puyat and Araneta's leadership, proposed to President Roxas that he introduce import controls, as the previous chapter shows.

Araneta elaborated on his import substitution idea in a speech at the Far Eastern Air Transport (FEATI) Institute of Technology on 28 April 1947, stating: "Today, it is generally admitted and no longer debated that one of the cornerstones of the edifice of a prosperous Philippines lies in industrialization" (Araneta 2000: 146). He proposed that the government amend the Bell Trade Act so that it could adopt "limited free trade" with the United States, under which the Philippines would allow the import of capital goods free of duty but impose tariffs on incoming consumer goods, while at the same time it would charge a duty on exports except sugar, coconut oil, cordage and cigars (ibid.: 148–9). Although supporters of this idea called it limited free trade, the proposed policy actually called for ISI through government trade control (Maxfield and Nolt 1990: 67). Araneta succeeded in tying his proposal for limited free trade to the PCC (Araneta 2000: 157). Araneta's policy proposal partially anticipated a subsequent policy management measure taken by the Roxas administration, because it had actually shifted its economic policy from one oriented by the Bell Trade Act to one prescribed by the Joint Philippine American Finance Commission (JPAFC), as shown in Chapter 3.

However, Araneta's proposal was not exactly the same as Roxas's economic policy, in the sense that it included a suggestion for peso devaluation. In another speech made on 6 July 1947, Araneta argued that the Philippine peso was as strong as the Mexican or Argentinian peso, and that the Philippines could encourage local production by favoring exports and hampering imports (ibid.: 153). In sum, Araneta's policy proposal straddled the free trade-oriented Bell Trade Act and the policy mix in the Roxas administration, which comprised industrialization with import controls and a strong currency.

In Araneta's search for allies—not in the administration but in Congress—he grew closer to Fernando Lopez, who expressed interest in his proposal. Lopez was a new face in national politics, having just won the senatorial election in 1947 mainly because of financial support from Eugenio Lopez, his older brother (Roces 1990; McCoy 1994b). Eugenio had established his career first as a lawyer in Manila. Then, in the 1920s, he inherited a sugar plantation, and shortly after that he expanded his business holdings to publishing and transportation (including air transportation), entertainment and a food company in Iloilo. By the 1930s, the elder Lopez had arrived as a "provincial millionaire" (Roces 1990: 90–3). The Lopez brothers helped each other: Eugenio provided financial support to Fernando, who in turn took care of the networking that promoted Eugenio's business interests (ibid.: 101).

It is important to know that Eugenio Lopez's business empire was not limited to the sugar industry, even though he was often assumed to be a leader of the sugar bloc together with Alfredo Montelibano and Oscar Ledesma, president of the National Federation of Sugar Planters (NFSP), at different times (ibid.: 105–6). In fact, Eugenio was the owner of the FEATI, which offered both local and international airline service in the Philippines, and which he sold to Philippine Airlines (PAL) in May 1947. Despite the sale, Eugenio maintained the FEATI Institute, where Araneta announced his above-mentioned policy proposal (Roces 1990: 101–2; Mendoza 2013: 88).

On 19 May 1949, Senator Lopez passed Senate Concurrent Resolution 44 to promote "selective free trade" instead of the simple free trade stipulated by the Bell Trade Act (Valdepeñas 1969: 130). In concept, selective free trade limited duty-free exports to sugar, copra and cordage and duty-free imports to only those things that could not be efficiently made in the Philippines (Valdepeñas 1969: 130). It is easy to see Araneta's influence on the resolution, considering its similarity to his proposal. Orignally, he coined his proposal "limited free trade", but later renamed it "selective free trade" in an article he published in the *Manila Daily Bulletin* on 28 March 1949, just before Lopez passed the resolution (Araneta 2000: 191).

The resolution did not become an actual law; nonetheless, Araneta gradually influenced the policy process as Lopez gained political clout in the newly organized Quirino administration, as we will see below.

Clash of Ideas

Quirino, who took over the presidency following the sudden death of President Roxas, allowed newcomers such as Lopez to climb the political ladder quickly because he did not have full command of the ruling LP. In fact, he suffered a series of power struggles within the party. First, Senate President Jose Avelino, the party president and widely regarded as the number-two man in the party next to President Roxas because of his contribution to the 1946 election campaign, was frustrated with Quirino's leadership. He even attempted to impeach the president, a first in Philippine political history. Shortly after, however, he lost his leadership in both the party and the Senate when he got involved in a scandal involving wartime surplus materials (National Historical Institute, hereafter NHI 1990: 71–161). Even after Avelino's ouster, Quirino could not, consolidate his power; instead, he seemed to expose his weakness to the other party leaders.

From the heated power struggle, party leaders chose Lopez as Quirino's running mate, although Quirino preferred Jose Yulo (Olivera 1981: 177–80; Roces 1990: 107–8). Yulo established his career not only as the son of a big sugar planter in Negros Occidental but also as a corporate lawyer. As a loyal aide to President Quezon, he became the secretary of justice and subsequently Speaker of the National Assembly in the Commonwealth government of the 1930s (Olivera 1982). Quirino preferred this established administrator to Lopez, the brother of an emerging leader in the private business sector, but he failed to convince other party leaders.

Quirino, who asserted the total economic mobilization program after his election on 14 November 1949 (Subramanian 1980: 170), still expected Yulo to lead the program's implementation. Yulo accompanied Quirino on his visit to the United States in January 1950 to seek loans to support his economic program (Olivera 1982: 181). Thereafter, Yulo was assumed to be the "top Malacañang economic advisor" (*MC* 8 March 1950: 1). On 20 March 1950 Quirino appointed him head of the Economic Survey Commission that included Finance Secretary Pio Pedrosa,

Governor Cuaderno, and National Power Corporation Chairman Filemon Rodriguez (Olivera 1981: 182). Considering the changes in the fiscal and trade situation after the economic crisis of 1949, Quirino instructed Yulo organize a commission under his leadership to revise the Cuaderno Plan. After five months, Yulo's commission drew up the revised plan for economic development and rehabilitation that would make the country self-sufficient (Olivera 1982: 183). Quirino subsequently organized the Philippine Council for US Aid (PHILCUSA) and appointed Yulo as its head (ibid.: 192).

Meanwhile, Araneta continued to propose his own economic policy. For instance, he made a study of prevailing economic conditions that he sent to the annual meeting of the PEA in April 1950 (Araneta 2000: 214–35). In this study, he juxtaposed his plan with that proposed by John W. Haussermann, a longtime American resident in Manila and a mining magnate since the 1930s (Gleeck 1977: 216). Haussermann, who was afraid of the possible condemnation of his assets by the Philippine government, had once proposed continuing US rule of the Philippines in his testimony to the JPCPA in the 1930s (MacIsaac 1993: 326). Araneta wrote that he could agree to Haussermann's plan only in terms of the scale of the investment, a five-year loan of US$1 billion from the US government (Araneta 2000: 216) proposed raising the loan locally as much as possible and using it to finance local production, while Haussermann asserted that the Philippine government should request the loan from the US government and use it only for the protection of its foreign reserve. Araneta differed here not only from Haussermann but also from President Quirino, who also wanted to seek US loans. In a broader context, however, Araneta supported the Quirino administration by proposing an industrial policy that was different from the one proposed by the prominent American businessman. Araneta must have known that Cuaderno had fought valiantly to resist pressure from American business interests in the Philippines, as the previous chapter shows.

Although Araneta opposed US economic policy toward the Philippines, he did not object to US domestic economic policy. In fact, Araneta wrote: "We must take inspiration from the New Deal measures" in the US (ibid.: 218). He argued that the Philippine government should carry out bold deficit financing in order to eradicate unemployment in the same way that the US government spent large sums to recover from the Great Depression in the 1930s. In his study, Araneta mentioned that "there are those who are afraid that such a huge public financing locally raised might lead us to inflation" (ibid.: 233), but he insisted:

> There is no choice in the matter. Either we keep our present timid policy of economic development which will increase in intensity our unemployment problem and our peace and order problem, or we courageously decide for a policy of full employment and maximum and rapid development of our land and natural resources which can only be achieved with a huge program of financing (ibid.: 234).

This argument is important to understanding the transitional phase of Philippine economic decolonization, because it reveals the fact that Araneta shifted his focus from the Bell Trade Act, a colonial legacy, to policy management by the Philippine government. His proposal was modified by the PEA and submitted to Senate President Mariano Cuenco and Speaker Perez as an "Act defining a national policy for total economic mobilization, providing the funds therefor[e] and creating a Development Authority to implement it" on 29 April 1950 (ibid.: 236). It was, however, not until Lopez gained influence within the Quirino administration that Araneta actually joined the government's policymaking process.

As the newly elected vice president in 1949, Lopez gradually demonstrated his clout in the government. Initially, President Quirino appointed Lopez as chairman of the Government Enterprises Council and several other institutions. Considering the fact that Quirino occupied the posts of secretary of finance and later foreign affairs when he served as vice president, it is easy to notice Quirino's neglect of his new vice president, who had preferred the portfolio of secretary of agriculture and natural resources. There were reports of a possible "break" between President Quirino and the Lopezes on 25 April 1950 (Roces 1990: 116). The Lopezes had launched a series of attacks charging the president with graft and corruption through columnist I.P. Soliongco of the *Manila Chronicle*, which Eugenio owned (ibid.: 108–9). "Perhaps in capitulation to all the attacks on his person", Quirino finally appointed Fernando Lopez secretary of agriculture and natural resources on 14 September 1950 (ibid.: 110).

At the same time, Quirino appointed Araneta as the secretary of economic coordination (Araneta 2000: 244). A few months after his appointment, Araneta explained his view on industrialization at a meeting of the Philippine Chamber of Industry, which was organized in 1950 by emerging businessmen to promote industrialization (Hori 1996: 43). In his speech, he reiterated his advocacy to adopt an economic policy similar to the US New Deal. For example, he proposed that the government organize the Philippine Development Authority, acting as the equivalent of the President Roosevelt's Tennessee Valley Authority (TVA), to implement the economic program (Araneta 2000: 387).

Araneta also began to challenge the Central Bank's management of economic policy and existing import controls, because he assumed that the bank and Import Control Administration, rather than his department, had played the role of economic policy coordinators (Araneta 2000: 386). Araneta publicly proclaimed the necessity for taxation and deficit financing to overcome general unemployment in a speech at the convocation ceremony for the University of the East on 22 January 1950 (ibid.: 244–9). In his speech, he criticized "the classical economists who take the traditional view that the government should reduce expenses to balance the budget to permit a reduction in taxes" and supported the views of Alvin H. Hansen of Harvard University and William Beverage, who asserted that deficit financing and taxation were the paths toward income creation (ibid.: 244–5). Hansen had promoted Keynesian theory in various books including *A Guide to Keynes*, while Beverage received notoriety for his report to the British government suggesting what became its social welfare policy (Hansen 1953). Adopting Keynesian theory, Araneta launched his fight for a bold development and finance program (Araneta 2000: 214). Influential journalist T.M. Locsin of the *Philippines Free Press* (*PFP*) introduced Araneta's idea to the public in an article entitled, "Cause for Optimism?". He summarized the policy in one phrase, "put money to work", which simplified Araneta's recommendation of government deficit spending to deal with massive unemployment (*PFP* 17 March 1951: 2).

As Araneta gradually turned the spotlight toward fiscal policy, the rivalry between Araneta and Cuaderno become apparent. Cuaderno recalled that there was an influential leader of the administration who wished to remove him from office, although he did not mention that person by name (Cuaderno 1964: 37).[2] In a speech to the PCC on 26 January 1951, Cuaderno highlighted the structural difference between the US and Philippine economies: While the former maintained "a substantial amount of unused plant facilities" that could meet the demand created by the government's deficit financing, the latter could not swiftly meet demand, which resulted in an excessive pressure on imports that only exacerbated balance-of-payments difficulties (ibid.: 130–1). He was

[2] Cuaderno mentioned the name of Salvador Araneta and existence of the "great debate" when he wrote about currency instability (Cuaderno 1964: 128–50), but did not mention any name here.

convinced that the Philippines could not adopt Keynesian theory because of the structural difference in economy.

Despite the clash with Governor Cuaderno, Secretary Araneta did not stop advocating change in the country's economic policy, and so he succeeded in changing import controls. He proposed that the government utilize control measures to develop local industries, as he did when he had advocated selected free trade in the late 1940s (*MC* 8 February 1951). On 6 March 1951, Araneta, Cornelio Balmaceda and Pio Pedrosa were appointed members of the committee to revise the conventional import control law, which had been harshly criticized by various sectors (*OG* March 1951: xx; *MC* 7, 28 March 1951). Quirino subsequently appointed new members of the Import Control Board on 2 April 1951: Alfredo Montelibano, chairman; and Alfonso Calalang and Francisco Ortigas, board members (*OG* April 1951: xxix). While Araneta and Montelibano were close to Lopez (Roces 1990: 105–6), Balmaceda and Pedrosa had been loyal to Quirino since the beginning of the president's administration (Gleeck 1993: 81). Calalang, once close to Cuaderno, eventually grew closer to the advocates of deficit financing in the 1950s (Araneta 2000: 295). The personnel affairs reflect the continuing power struggle within the Quirino administration.

The subsequent deliberations over the bill in Congress reveals an assessment on existing control measures. In the explanatory note read by congressman Ferdinand Marcos, the policymakers praised the existing law (RA 426) as having succeeded in saving the country's foreign reserves as well as encouraging the emergence of local industries, but ended up supporting the production of consumer rather than export goods (*CRHR* 10 May 1951: 1677–8). In other words, they admitted that the existing control measure had made certain achievements but pointed out that the benefits accrued mainly to the consumer goods manufacturing industry at the expense of the export industry. They claimed: "Our experience with the administration of the import control has been very sad" (ibid.: 1678). They suggested that the Import Control Administration be abolished and replaced by the Board of Trade and Industries and expected that the government would be able to abolish control measures completely within two years (ibid.: 1678). President Quirino signed the bill as RA 650, "An act to regulate imports and other purposes" that relaxed import controls on some materials, on 15 June 1951 (Valdepeñas 1969: 110).

Shortly before the enactment of RA 650, the clash of ideas between Araneta and Cuaderno became public, and the *Manila Chronicle* reported on 11 April 1951 that a businessman said he was willing to sponsor a public debate between Araneta and Cuaderno (*MC* 11 April 1951: 1). Instead of the public debate, however, Araneta submitted a letter to Cuaderno asking him whether he agreed with the idea of deficit financing, which the US government had previously carried out, and how they could "solve the unemployment problem as soon as possible without deficit spending", but he claimed that he did not receive any response from Cuaderno (Araneta 2000: 257–9).

Cuaderno repeatedly explained his ideas in speeches on various occasions. In an article published in the *Chronicle* on 21 April 1951, Cuaderno indirectly answered Araneta's questions. Cuaderno stated plainly that the Central Bank aimed to achieve economic development and that development could be accomplished only with monetary stability. He reiterated his position on the structural difference between the US and Philippine economies, and that the Philippines lacked the potential to respond to fiscal stimulations by deficit spending (*MC* 21 April 1951: 3-A). In an interview with the *PFP*, Cuaderno quoted part of a letter by M.S. Eccles, governor of the US Board of the Federal Reserve System, saying: "yours [Cuaderno's] is the most forceful statement of the differences of an environment of an underdeveloped country and that of a highly developed country like the United States.... As the experience of the South American countries demonstrates, attempts to force the rate of economic development by excessive expansion of credit produces inflation" (*PFP* 2 June 1951: 2).

Cuaderno's view clearly revealed the ideas of the Structuralist School of developmental economics. Scholars who supported this school of thought assumed that rigidities in the supply side of a developing country hindered its development, and that there were structural economic differences between developed and developing economies (Esho 1997: 12). The fact that Cuaderno learned a lot from the experience of Argentina under Raul Prebisch revealed that he was a student of the structuralist school, whose policy prescription was that ISI develop the country. Esho's explanation that the structuralist school combined classical and Keynesian economics (ibid.: 13) helps to clarify the difference between Cuaderno and Araneta, as the latter emphasized only Keynesian economics.

Facing relentless criticism by Araneta, which had "such disturbing implications", Cuaderno issued a memorandum to the Central Bank's monetary board on 1 August 1951 (Cuaderno to the monetary board 1951, *EQ*, 1). In this memo, Cuaderno strongly opposed devaluation, referring to the Bell Mission's recommendation; he even argued that devaluation at this moment "would be suicidal" because of a possible reduction in "the real income of the poor" (ibid.: 2). He explained that the exchange rate should be maintained because of the complete destruction of the export industry during WWII, and that exchange controls were necessary to constrain imports of luxury products and hinder capital flight (ibid.).

Frustrated with his failure to convince other policymakers in the administration, Araneta decided to leave the Cabinet on 18 January 1952. Araneta explained that he did so because he was dissatisfied with the government's policy on sugar exports (Araneta 2000: xxxvi). The *Chronicle* featured his dramatic departure on 19 January 1952. When Araneta went to persuade Quirino to reconsider his decision on the sale of sugar to Japan, Quirino said, "This is already a decided question. You have no discretion on the matter". Araneta replied, "In that case, Mr. President, I am resigning as of now from the government". Quirino answered, "*Esta bien* [that is good]" (*MC* 19 January 1952: 5).

Given Cuaderno's close relations with Quirino and his clash with Araneta over economic policy, it seems likely that the issue of sugar exports was not the only reason for Araneta's resignation. His relations with Quirino by then had actually become strained. His dramatic departure from the Cabinet contrasts with the resignation of Secretary Pedrosa, which Quirino had initially declined; indeed, at the end of 1950, Quirino had even expressed appreciation for Pedrosa's performance as secretary (*MC* 20 November 1950: 1). Cuaderno wrote that Araneta had resigned from the government because he could not "get the support of President Quirino to [*sic*] his 'bold' deficit financing policy" (Cuaderno 1964: 132). In his writings of 1964, Cuaderno seems sure that President Quirino had been on his side. He wrote: "Quirino recognized the importance of a Central Bank that was as free from extraneous interference as possible" (ibid.: 38).

Araneta, however, never gave up, even after his resignation. Again, he gave a speech, this one entitled "Can We Apply the New Deal Approach to our Problem?", at the graduation ceremony of San Carlos University on 6 April 1952 (Araneta 2000: 269–81). In this speech, he reminded the new graduates of the problem of unemployment, and then explained the US experience under the Roosevelt administration in which the Americans recovered from the Great Depression thanks to the New Deal policy. He asserted that "a New Deal for the Philippines is what the country sorely needs these days" (ibid.: 277).

Araneta continuously attacked the policy of the Central Bank and the Quirino administration. In a speech given on 10 April 1953, for instance, Araneta criticized the economic policies of the bank and the government, while he praised the achievement of the import control law, which he himself had helped to craft and supported to extend (ibid.: 285). Citing the example of Lopez Sugar Central, which failed to obtain sufficient credits, Araneta remarked: "I believe that a fundamental mistake committed by the Government in the past is found in its timid and too conservative monetary and credit policy. We need a more realistic and bold monetary policy that will stimulate the creation of more banking institutions in the Philippines" (ibid.: 285). He also suggested adopting multiple foreign exchange rates, instead of the single exchange rate, because he assumed that the Bell Trade Act compelled the government to maintain the official exchange rate of US$1:P2, which overvalued the peso (ibid.: 287–8).

Araneta harshly condemned the economic policies of the Central Bank as follows:

> [T]he present conservative and old-fashioned monetary policy of Monetary Board constitutes straitjacket to our economy....Unless we give our economy a more liberal credit policy, a more realistic foreign exchange policy, and a bolder deficit financing program for production, we will not be able to stimulate private initiative and the government will not be in a position to attend to the building of roads, irrigation systems, hydro-electric projects and basic industries at a rate commensurate with our ever increasing needs. (ibid.: 292)

Araneta reiterated his proposals for deficit financing, liberal credit policy and changing the foreign exchange rate over the conventional measures taken by the bank.

About one month later, on 15 May 1953, Cuaderno sent an open letter to the Manila Lions Club in reply to Araneta's speech (Cuaderno 1955: 105–30). First, he repeated his skepticism about the effect of Keynesian theory on the Philippine economy, saying that he had already "discussed the inapplicability on the Keynesian theory of deficit spending in an underdeveloped country such as the Philippines" in his short pamphlet entitled *Financing of Economic Development in Underdeveloped Countries with Particular Reference to the Philippines*, which he had prepared in order "[t]o counteract such a dangerous policy" in 1952 (Cuaderno 1955: 110; Cuaderno 1964: 130). Cuaderno reiterated his conviction that "experience in other underdeveloped countries has shown that monetary stability is a precondition for orderly economic development. The high costs which inflation generates sooner or later are bound to retard the very development that is being envisaged" (Cuaderno 1955: 111).

Besides the heated debate between these leading economists, the year 1953 was pivotal to an understanding of the subsequent policy debate. First, there was a delegation of power over import controls from the Import Control Board, which had been regarded as "a source of anomalies and abuses", to the Central Bank (Storer and de Guzman 1960: 29; Baldwin 1975: 30). The opposition NP, which had won all eight contested seats in the 1951 midterm election and consolidated the majority in the Senate, prevented the government from renewing the Import Control Act (RA 650) in 1953. Eulogio A. Rodriguez, NP president, tried to use the accusations of graft and corruption in the administration to the NP's advantage, and agitated for the removal of a hotbed of corruption—the Import Control Board—to demonstrate the party's intolerance for government dishonesty (Golay 1961: 168). Notably, the opposition party criticized the implementation of import controls but never took issue with the idea of ISI. Following the expiration of RA 650, the bank was left exclusively in charge of control policy. An economist, Amado A. Castro, argued in the 1970s that from 1953 onward, the exchange-control issues had often dominated discussions in the Bank's monetary board, which led the Bank to be "more an import-regulating body than a bank of banks" (Castro 1972: 11).

Moreover, because of the reshuffle in party politics, the Central Bank faced its opponents even within the subsequent administration of President Ramon Magsaysay, who did not necessarily share any working experience with Cuaderno. Magsaysay represented a new generation of politicians who established their political career mainly after independence. He was born in Zambales in 1907 and did not finish his university education but worked as a mechanic and subsequently a manager for a bus company before leading a guerilla force against the Japanese during WWII. He successfully mobilized his former guerilla network for his first election in 1946. In Congress, he established his career as a promoter of veterans' welfare, and subsequently he gained strong public support for his work in suppressing the Huk rebellion as defense secretary (Abueva 1971). Dissatisfied with Quirino's decision about the party's candidate for the 1953 presidential election, however, Magsaysay resigned from the LP to run for the presidency under the NP banner and won. Cuaderno therefore faced a new president with whom he had never worked.

Araneta did not miss an opportunity to find a political leader with whom he might be able to change the existing economic policy, even when Magsaysay was still the defense secretary in the Quirino administration. Araneta once said: "The present unsettled conditions cannot be met with bullet alone, as repeatedly stated by the Secretary of National Defense [Magsaysay]. It must be met with a program of social reformation and bold economic development" (Araneta 2000: 276).

Thereafter, the political developments show that Araneta successfully moved to the opposition, which had won the midterm election in November 1951 and would come into power in the presidential election in 1953. Besides, after Quirino chose Yulo as his running mate for the general election, Fernando Lopez abandoned the LP with his allies and established the Democratic Party (DP) on 21 June 1953 (Abueva 1971: 247; Quirino 1987: 174). Lopez, who failed to establish close relations with either Quirino or the LP leadership, tried to run under his own party banner but finally decided to forge an electoral alliance with the NP on 21 August 1953 (Abueva 1971: 259). Araneta therefore found his close political ally in the coming Magsaysay administration.

Continuing Clash of Ideas and the Island of State Strength

Attempt at Deficit Financing

As a result of the elections in November 1953, the Nacionalista-Democratic alliance won the presidency and a majority in Congress, which allowed Lopez and his allies to regain their influence within the administration. Magsaysay, however, did not abandon the economic policy of the previous administration entirely; rather, he attempted to resolve the clashing economic ideas within the government (Soberano 1963: 337). He actually allowed his cabinet members to engage in policy debates and then made a final decision after weighing public opinion (Abueva 1971: ch. 16). Magsaysay, for instance, requested Araneta to prepare a draft of his first State of the Nation Address (SONA), but used it only partially in his actual address (Araneta 1958: 153; Soberano 1963: 336–9).

As Araneta openly complained in a book published after death of President Magsaysay, Magsaysay discarded "the sense of urgency which runs through the draft" (Araneta 1958: 153). In his draft, which he made public in a speech given about two months after the president's

SONA, Araneta put priority on economic development using a liberal credit policy (Araneta 1953: 154–64). He began the speech by pointing out the county's increasing population and unemployment problems as well as land issues. In terms of finance, he argued, "money is just an instrument of exchange...to mobilize people and resources to create wealth" (Araneta 1953: 158). Furthermore, he emphasized the necessity of a liberal credit policy and a gradual lifting of exchange controls. He reiterated his proposal for deficit financing by saying that "economic development will be continuously stimulated by providing credit" (Araneta 1958: 161). In terms of exchange controls, he supported simple import controls and a multiple exchange-rate system.

President Magsaysay, however, began his SONA [on 24 January] with the security issue posed by the Huk rebellion (*OG* 1954: 81–9). He then moved on to the issue of land, farmers and laborers, pointing out the need for economic planning and cooperation between government and private enterprise. Here, he mentioned: "My administration is pledged to the eventual elimination of controls"; but he also emphasized the need for economic development as a condition for their elimination (ibid.: 85). In terms of finance, Magsaysay confirmed the government's constricted fiscal conditions, mentioned the need for strict tax collection, and proposed that "ordinary expenses should never exceed the total revenues in any fiscal year" (ibid.: 87), a view that hewed closely to the opinion of Cuaderno.

President Magsaysay heeded the advice of Filemon Rodriguez, who was regarded as close to Cuaderno, in completing the portion of the SONA devoted to economic issues (Soberano 1963: 337). Magsaysay eventually asked Rodriguez to lead the NEC as its acting chairman, and Rodriguez took the lead in crafting the administration's socioeconomic program. In an address before the Manila Rotary Club on 4 February 1954, Rodriguez explained the principal elements of the socioeconomic program and enumerated six points as its bases, namely, industrialization; the proper role of private enterprise; a balance between production and employment; a balance between consumption and investment; the modernization of productive facilities; and the development of rural communities (Rodriguez 1967: 147, 152). Rodriguez shifted the emphasis of the program back from agriculture to industry (Storer and de Guzman 1960: 16). Magsaysay adopted the Rodriguez Plan as his administration's economic plan on 20 March 1954 (Storer and de Guzman 1960: 16).

Cuaderno continued to emphasize the need to maintain the country's strong currency policy, citing the possibly harmful effects of devaluation. In his remarks at the annual convention of the Philippine Coconut Planters Association on 6 March 1954, Cuaderno argued that the government did not need to devaluate the currency vis-à-vis the US dollar (Cuaderno 1955: 201–7). He asserted that "both [the] volume and value of copra exports of the Philippines increased tremendously during the postwar period" in spite of the highly appreciating peso, and argued that devaluation would be harmful to the Philippine economy, because it would increase the price of essential imported consumer goods such as milk, flour and medicines (ibid.: 202).

He also warned that devaluation would increase the cost of imported machinery, equipment and raw materials and would turn the Philippine economy back into a colonial economy, saying:

> Unfortunately, a few shortsighted individuals think of economic development only in terms of their particular interests and not that of the entire nation. At the present time we have already achieved some improvement over the colonial economy of the prewar period.... Devaluation at this time would mean the surrender of all these gains and a return to the export economy of the past. (ibid.: 207)

Cuaderno was determined to support ISI even in front of the representatives of the export industry, which would become devaluation's beneficiary.

President Magsaysay, however, never neglected those who were close to the sugar industry, for two reasons. First, it was said that, as a candidate of the NP-DP coalition, he was grateful for the sugar bloc's financial support, and that he aimed at highlighting a change from the previous Quirino administration in which Cuaderno had played a major role in economic policymaking (Liang 1971: 347; Soberano 1963: 336). Second, in suppressing the Huk rebellion, Magsaysay became convinced that the government needed to improve socioeconomic conditions rather than resort merely to arms, which led to his support of deficit financing (Cuaderno 1964: 142). Magsaysay replaced the president of the Philippine National Bank, Pio Pedrosa, who had worked with Governor Cuaderno in the Roxas and Quirino administrations, with Arsenio J. Jison, who would oppose Cuaderno's monetary and credit policy (ibid.: 145). Moreover, Magsaysay appointed Araneta as secretary of agriculture and natural resources, Alfredo Montelibano as the administrator of the office of economic coordination, and Oscar Ledesma as secretary of commerce and industry. All of these men were close to Fernando Lopez, who won a seat in the Senate in the 1953 election (Golay 1956).

Araneta and his allies gradually gained influence within the Magsaysay administration. For instance, they dominated the newly created cabinet committee on employment and production in April 1955. When establishing the committee, President Magsaysay asked them to examine the feasibility of the New Deal measures in the Philippines (Soberano 1963: 340). Within a month, the committee submitted a memorandum asserting the need for and viability of bolder deficit financing by issuing government bonds (ibid.: 340–1). Once the congressional commission of appointments failed to approve the appointment of Rodriguez as NEC chairman, Magsaysay appointed Montelibano instead on 13 August 1955. An article in the *PFP* implied that Montelibano's remarks in a radio program, criticizing Rodriguez for exploiting a public position for his private business, prompted the commission to bypass Rodriguez's appointment (Ty 1955: 4, 73). Magsaysay then instructed the Montelibano-led NEC to revise the Rodriguez Plan, and to draft a strategy to, among other things, implement devaluation, abolish exchange controls, enhance agricultural production and carry out bolder deficit financing (Soberano 1963: 343). Araneta and his allies apparently succeeded in winning the support of President Magsaysay.

In addition to the struggle over key government positions, Araneta and his allies steadily undertook legislative activities that brought them into conflict with the Central Bank over several economic policies. In the case of Senate Bill (SB) 167, for example, the NEC and the bank's monetary board "[did] not seem to see eye to eye" (*MC* 14 May 1954: 1). SB 167, patterned after West Germany's import rights system, would allow exporters to sell their dollars on the free market at a higher rate than the bank's official rate (Araneta 1958: 338–9). Araneta strongly supported SB 167, which embodied his own ideas (Roxas 1958a: 329). In a speech on 22 July 1954, he criticized the bank's conventional monetary policy and expressed the need for devaluation, saying, "the existence of the black market at about three pesos to one US dollar is an evidence [*sic*] of the overvaluation of our peso" (Araneta 1958: 334–41). He claimed that the continuity of exchange controls for more than four years and the existence of mass unemployment as well as the unfavorable balance-of-trade were evidence of fundamental disequilibrium, and then advocated the devaluation of the peso through SB 167 as a remedy, which the Senate passed on 17 May 1954 (Araneta 1958: 335–6, 338–9).

SB 167 called for a partial devaluation to would help the export industry, which Cuaderno could not accept. Cuaderno and his deputy governor, Andres Castillo, strongly opposed the bill, which Araneta argued would never devalue the peso in general but instead encourage exporters directly, and all producers indirectly, to increase their production (*MC* 19 May 1954: 1). The Lower House suspended discussions on the bill in the midst of the clash between key policymakers and Magsaysay's opposition to the bill (Roxas 1958a: 329).

The first major accomplishment of Araneta and his allies was RA 1000, passed on 12 June 1954, which allowed the government to carry out deficit financing through bond issuance. Through RA 1000, the Magsaysay administration departed from the conservative monetary and fiscal policy that the previous administration had maintained (Golay 1961: 90; Soberano 1963: 345). Before the passage of RA 1000, only the bank had been allowed to issue bonds, albeit with the restriction of not more than P200 million (Golay 1956: 258).

In addition to the legislative initiative, Araneta and his allies attacked the Central Bank itself. On 20 July 1955, they succeeded in convincing Senators Puyat and Edmundo B. Cea to urge a "general reorganization" of the bank in response to reported irregularities in dollar allocations (Soberano 1963: 344–5). President Magsaysay established the Central Bank Survey Commission to investigate the bank's performance. Cuaderno was upset when he found out about the creation of the commission through newspaper articles (Cuaderno 1964: 50). Thereafter, the bank became a fragile target of investigation rather than a stable policymaking body (Soberano 1963: 345).

Araneta submitted a memorandum to the survey commission in August 1955 (Araneta 1958: 384–90). In the memorandum he clarified his ideas on Philippine economic development. After enumerating three objectives of the Bank—maintenance of monetary stability; preservation of the international value of the peso and its convertibility into other currencies; and promotion of a rising level of production, employment and real income—he argued that the first and second objectives were a means to achieve the third objective. As for exchange controls, Araneta pointed out that Governor Cuaderno had once written that the bank would impose foreign-exchange controls as a temporal measure in case of temporal disequilibria. He argued that, if the government needed to impose exchange control continuously, the free convertibility of the peso would be preferable to maintaining the rate of exchange supported by continuous controls.

Araneta and his allies did not stop trying to take the lead in changing Philippine economic policy. President Magsaysay issued a directive to the NEC on 5 September 1955 asking them to examine the possibility of eliminating exchange controls as soon as possible (Roxas 1958a: 300). Araneta and his allies also urged Congress on 10 September 1955 to enact a bill calling for a so-called "No-Dollar Import Law", or RA 1410. Under RA 1410, exporters, authorized by the secretary of commerce and industry, would be able to engage in the barter trade outside the exchange-control system (Golay 1956: 259). The advocates, who had failed to alter the system of exchange controls through SB 167, changed their strategy and aimed at creating a loophole in the existing control system through RA 1410. Governor Cuaderno sent President Magsaysay a memorandum on 26 August 1955, in which he expressed concern about the inflationary tendency that would be caused by the bill and recommended that Magsaysay veto it (Cuaderno 1964: 50).

Cuaderno was greatly surprised by the newspaper article reporting President Magsaysay's decision to allow the bill to become law (Cuaderno 1964: 51). Later, Cuaderno recalled that he had become "the unfortunate victim of intrigue" and remembered thinking at the time that he had finally lost presidential support. He offered the president his resignation, but Magsaysay did not accept it (ibid.: 49, 51–2).

Decline of the Sugar Bloc

In the middle of the storm of criticism against the Central Bank, President Magsaysay extended Cuaderno's appointment for another year, even though he would reach the retirement age of 65 (*MC* 12 December 1955: 1). Before Cuaderno's reappointment, Magsaysay suddenly ordered the justice secretary to study the charges levied against the special investigator for the Central Bank's case. The investigator had been accused of illegal garlic trade and thus lost his credibility (Golay 1956: 262). Although it took about a year for the congressional committee to accept the reappointment, senators Jose P. Laurel, Lorenzo Tañada and Gil Puyat strongly supported Cuaderno's reappointment (Hori 1997: 267). Laurel worked with Cuaderno when the Philippine government negotiated with the US government to replace the agreement for the Bell Trade Act with the Laurel-Langley Agreement.[3]

[3] The agreement stipulated the gradual elimination of mutual tariff preferences and admitted the right of the Philippine government to decide on monetary and exchange policies. It was widely understood as an improvement in economic relations with the United States (Doronila 1992: 56–7).

Cuaderno maintained his conviction about a balanced budget even under siege. He urged the government to adopt the measures necessary to check inflationary tendencies in a speech before members of the Manila Rotary Club on 17 November 1955 (*MC* 18 November 1955: 1, 11). In this speech, he said that "the recessionary conditions which the government tried to check with easy money and easy credit policies during last few years have come to an end" (ibid.). On 5 January 1956, Cuaderno sent a long memorandum to the Montelibano-led NEC emphasizing that "inflationary pressure had emerged during the last few months of 1955", and that without reconsideration of the additional bond issues the government would have to cease deficit financing (Cuaderno 1960: 140). As a result of the split between Governor Cuaderno and the other members of NEC, the Central Bank and NEC presented different documents to President Magsaysay regarding the economic situation and related policies (Soberano 1963: 353).

In January 1956, the *PFP* featured a two-part series on the two different views of the Philippine economy. First, the *PFP* introduced the view of NEC chairman Montelibano, which he delivered in a public speech in Baguio (*PFP* 7 January 1956: 2, 47). He mentioned how the fast-growing population and almost static productivity aggravated unemployment, and distinguished two approaches to the problem of production—conservative and liberal. He argued that the government had maintained the conservative approach for the past ten years and yet failed to solve the problem, and warned that the Philippines would be in chaos if the government stuck to the same policy.

In the second installment, the *PFP* summarized Cuaderno's idea, even as Cuaderno tried to avoid any public debate among government officers (*PFP* 14 January 1956: 3, 54–5).[4] Cuaderno pointed out that there were those who criticized the Central Bank for the government's spending, borrowing and taxation, but he forgot the fact that these fiscal measures were beyond the bank's purview. He added that the bank was not in charge of production, and pointed out his skepticism about the adaptability of economic theory in the developed countries to their underdeveloped counterparts, referring to the Keynesian theory advocated by Araneta.

---

[4] The *PFP* summarized Cuaderno's thought on the public debate. According to the article, Cuaderno thought the debate should be conducted at the cabinet level in a closed-door session; otherwise it would result in panic or confusion.

In the last section of their article, the *PFP* took a position that was more sympathetic to Cuaderno (ibid.). While the Central Bank continued to perform well and supported industrialization through foreign-exchange allocation to new industries, the NEC could hardly contribute to an increase in production. Although the *PFP* admitted that previous attempts at industrialization remained inadequate, it also recognized the need for industrialization and the bank's singular achievement in providing the necessary loans to some extent.

President Magsaysay had slowly recognized inflation as a threat to the lives of Filipinos and thus appreciated Cuaderno's argument (Soberano 1963: 354–62). At the end of January, even the NEC admitted the seriousness of price hikes, though it endorsed the plan to establish a price control board rather than abandon deficit financing (*MC* 21 January 1956: 1). In his message to Congress about the budget on 7 February 1956, President Magsaysay said: "the most significant feature of the current economic status has been our success in maintaining monetary stability in the face of public borrowings for development and extensions of liberal credit for private enterprise" (Soberano 1963: 361). In a speech at the business awards dinner sponsored by the business writers' association on 20 February, Magsaysay was unequivocal when he said that he "came out strongly against public borrowing, devaluation of the peso, and relaxation of exchange and import controls" (*MC* 21 February 1956: 1). Montelibano and Araneta subsequently resigned from the cabinet on 22 and 23 February respectively (Roxas 1958a: 328). Meanwhile, on 24 March, Cuaderno returned from a mission to the United States to ask for a credit line for the bank and a loan from US banks (Golay 1956: 263).

The Central Bank survey commission submitted the results of its investigation following months of research. It concluded that bank policy headed generally "in the right direction" although it found some points for improvement (*Manila Times* 20 May 1956; LM, *Central Bank*, 1–2). The commission supported the exchange controls and rejected ideas such as devaluation. Although the commission suggested that the monetary board be enhanced to engage in fiscal policymaking, it opposed the idea that the bank should share the role of monetary policymaking with the NEC. The commission concluded that the bank's independence should be respected. Obviously, the commission supported Governor Cuaderno and opposed the suggestions made by Montelibano or Araneta. Cuaderno, in his memoir, confirmed: "I finally won Magsaysay to my side in the so-called 'Great Debate' on fiscal and monetary policy" (Cuaderno 1960: 55).

The debate over SB 167 was rehashed, however, after President Magsaysay's sudden death on 16 March 1957 (Roxas 1958a: 329). Carlos P. Garcia, who took over the presidency, belonged to the elder generation of Laurel and Recto. Born in Bohol in 1896, Garcia studied at the National University, passed the bar exam and was elected congressman and governor of the NP. He was not at all vocal about almost any issue, however. The record of an interview with Garcia reveals only that he was loyal to Quezon during the colonial period and then closer to Laurel after independence, although he was a guerrilla leader in Visayas (Gleeck 1993: 210–1). It would be safe to assume that the Garcia administration was run by members of the old guard of the NP such as Laurel.

Legislators close to the sugar bloc brought SB 167 back and succeeded in passing it through Congress. Thereafter, they fought with the Central Bank over the approval or veto of President Garcia, who was also pressed to consider the influence of the sugar bloc, which would receive huge profits from the implementation of the bill, in the upcoming presidential election at the end of the year (*PFP* 15 June 1957: 3, 83). Cuaderno warned that if the bill became law, the country would face grave economic and social dangers and would "return to a colonial economic pattern" (Ty 1957: 4–5).

Meanwhile, Montelibano reiterated his support for the bill, stressing that without it, the country would face economic doom marked by a high unemployment rate, rising daily costs, and an unbalanced foreign trade owing to the control policy. He even asserted that those who opposed to the bill, some of whom were aliens, constituted a small minority in the country, and that the bill would encourage exports, increase production and employment and improve the balance-of-payments (ibid.: 81).

President Garcia vetoed the bill on 22 June 1957, explaining his decision in his message. He said that it would cause inflation and profit the prosperous at the expense of the masses, and that it would lead to the adoption of multiple currency practices, which was prohibited by the IMF agreement. He even stated that it would violate the constitution, which forbade any single law from containing more than one issue (*Official Gazette* 1957: 3734–5). The fact that President Garcia, a generally quiet man, decided against a bill that would benefit the sugar bloc while winning the general election in the same year reveals a retrenchment in the country's strong vested interests.

A great debate emerged when the Philippine government created the economic policy regime with which it attempted to change the colonial economic structure. Before this debate, two leading economists collaborated with each other in the Constitutional Convention in the 1930s, shared similar critical views toward the Bell Trade Act in the 1940s, and supported the establishment of a central bank and imposition of import controls even under pressure from several private sector, which included American businesses. After the establishment of the Central Bank and import controls in the 1950s, they abandoned their common goals and began to clash with each other.

The debate constituted a clash of policymakers' ideas. First, Cuaderno was skeptical about the feasibility of adopting an economic theory created from the experiences of developed countries, and he assumed that a stable currency was a precondition for economic development, while Araneta believed in the utility of Keynesian economics and expected the government to adopt a more active role. Second, Cuaderno emphasized the need for a tight monetary policy to curb inflationary tendencies and a high peso value to allow imports of essential materials for the industrialization of local economy, whereas Araneta advocated a bold fiscal policy to respond to the unemployment problem and suggested a devaluation of the peso to increase the profits of the export industry.

The results of the great debate reveal the role of the Central Bank as the island of state strength. The debate was a clash among policymakers, which was usually settled once the president clarified his position. The president, in fact, could decide unilaterally in spite of opposition from the pressure groups that had emerged since the colonial period. Under the Quirino administration, Cuaderno was appointed governor of the Bank, and under his watch the Central Bank maintained tight monetary policy and foreign-exchange controls. Under the Magsaysay administration, Cuaderno failed to prevent Araneta and his allies from enacting RA 1000, which enabled the government to conduct a more liberal fiscal policy, and RA 1410, which allowed the export industry to engage in trade outside exchange controls to a certain degree. But Cuaderno did not budge, and ultimately he won the president's confidence. He succeeded in maintaining the foreign-exchange rate and in convincing President Garcia to veto SB 167 despite strong pressure from the sugar bloc during the election year. The bank maintained its autonomy in the midst of a power struggle with special-interest groups.

It is, however, important to note a certain limitation faced by the Central Bank in the 1950s. The bank was not up against foreign or neocolonial pressure, however, throughout the great debate it faced a challenge from Filipino capitalists. In other words, the strength of the Central Bank did not come from nationalism in society but from the particular ideas of policymakers who believed that industrialization was the way to achieve decolonization, or rather, from nationalism within the government. The bank's increasingly isolated position will be revealed when we study the complex political process that attended the Filipino First campaign in the next chapter.

CHAPTER 5

The Central Bank and Economic Nationalism, 1958–61

The Central Bank won the great debate in the end. What is missing in my explanation so far is the reason why it took years for policymakers to win the fight against colonial vested interests. One may ask who could have sustained Cuaderno's ideas in private business if the export industry supported that of Araneta. This chapter tackles this question by tracing the political process of a nationalist economic policy under the Garcia administration (1957–61).

"Filipino First" has been remembered as a battle cry in the era of the Garcia administration (Abinales and Amoroso 2005: 182; Sicat 2008: 9). The National Economic Council (NEC) proclaimed Resolution 204 to encourage the growth of Filipino businesses through favorable foreign exchange allocations on 21 August 1958 (Golay 1961: 332). NEC Chairman Jose Locsin acknowledged President Garcia's endorsement of Filipino First in his SONA of January 1960 (J.C. Locsin 1960: 152). Industrialization underpinned by economic nationalism was supposedly a goal of the Filipino First policy (Hawes 1987: 36). Economists asserted that the Philippine Chamber of Commerce (PCC) and the Philippine Chamber of Industry (PCI) were the locomotives driving the Filipino First policy (Sicat 2002: 16), and maintained that "the influence of exporting interests, which had traditionally dominated economic policymaking, declined as competing interest groups benefited from policies of *Filipinism* and acquired political power" (Golay 1969: 33).

Frank H. Golay defines *Filipinism* as "structures of policies and institutions created to transform the racial dimensions of the colonial-type economies" and deemed beneficial to the Filipino people (Golay et al. 1969: 9). Data from Table 5.1 seem to support this assertion of economic transformation from a racial dimension.

Table 5.1 Composition of Imports by Nationality of Importers (%)

	Filipinos	*Americans*	*Chinese*
1948	23	28	39
1949	23	29	37
1950	28	32	31
1951	37	30	27
1952	34	30	28
1953	40	28	25
1954	42	26	24
1955	47	24	22
1956	48	28	15
1957	54	24	14

Source: Golay 1968: 318.

Table 5.1 shows the decline in the Chinese share of businesses and the rise in Filipino enterprises, while Americans, who were protected by the parity clause of the Bell Trade Act (and subsequent Laurel-Langley Agreement), maintained their shares.[1]

The political process of Filipino First, however, leaves several questions unanswered. First, no study has yet been done to scrutinize the complex chronological developments in the politics of Filipino First. Why did the NEC announce the Filipino First policy only in 1958, even though the preceding administrations had already been carrying out ISI since 1949? Table 5.1 shows that the change had begun long before the NEC's proclamation in 1958. Nick Cullather stated that "the Filipino First movement" was only a statement of the policy that the Philippine government had implemented for a decade (Cullather 1994: 163). In terms of the influence of interest groups, the PCC organized the NEPA and began to advocate ISI starting in 1934 (Purugganan 1959). Why did the PCC not urge the government to call the battle cry much earlier? Moreover, we still do not know why President Garcia finally articulated Filipino First in his SONA in 1960 instead of 1959 or right after its proclamation by the NEC in August 1958. Those who highlight the rise of nationalism as a background to the politics of Filipino First (Cullather 1994; Golay 1961) have failed to explain the rapid decline in the policy's

[1] Carol Hau aptly points out that anti-American sentiments were displaced by anti-Chinese sentiments (Hau 2000: ch. 4).

advocacy by the Philippine government after the Garcia administration ended. In order to know the actual process in creating Filipino First, which burst into life in 1958 and faded away with the Garcia administration in 1961, we need to trace the chronological development of its politics.

Besides these questions of chronological dynamics, we still do not know the exact role played by the Central Bank, which was expected to implement the Filipino First policy. Governor Cuaderno, in his informative memoir, did not mention Filipino First at all, other than to briefly state that "there was the policy of giving Filipinos every opportunity to have a larger share in the country's economic activities" in the chapter on his work in the Garcia administration (Cuaderno 1964: 81). Remembering that he plainly exposed the existence of the great debate, one cannot say that his silence on Filipino First reflects his decision not to expose any dispute within the government. Rather, Cuaderno's silence on the matter in his memoir simply seems to reflect his indifference toward the policy. Jose Romero, for example, profusely praised Cuaderno's achievements as an exception within the corrupt Garcia administration and criticized the Filipino First policy (Romero 2008: 78). Besides the Filipino First slogan, the Garcia administration is best known for graft and corruption alongside discrimination against foreign businesses (for example, see Gleeck 1993: 249–51; Cullather 1994: 154–80). According to those who emphasize graft and corruption in the Garcia administration, the politics of Filipino First turned into a symbol of the oligarchic state whose analytical problem was discussed in the Introduction.

It would be inappropriate, however, to assume that the Central Bank had nothing to do with the politics of Filipino First. Cuaderno's indifference did not necessarily mean that the bank was completely disengaged from the policy. If Cuaderno was seemingly indifferent to it, we should ask why Cuaderno agreed to head the implementing authority of a policy that did not much interest him, and what was his work during that period.

In Cuaderno's book, the chapter on the Garcia administration seems to be a collection of various ideas and interests among policymakers on fiscal as well as currency policy (Cuaderno 1964: 56–85). In terms of fiscal policy, the Central Bank under Cuaderno was always concerned about excessive government expenditure, while private businesses and most politicians favored deficit financing (ibid.: 127–54). In the case of the currency policy, there were three different positions. First, the Bank worked continuously to maintain its strong currency policy in the early

1950s but decided to lift exchange controls gradually later in the decade (ibid.: 71). Second, the PCC and PCI, both of which comprised companies that mainly worked for the domestic market and depended on imports for their primary products and capital stock, supported the strong currency policy and exchange controls. Third, the sugar bloc spearheaded by Alfredo Montelibano, who had opposed Cuaderno since the early 1950s, favored devaluation in order to maximize their peso-value profit. In addition to all these positions, the US government, from which the bank expected to receive a necessary loan to finance gradual decontrol, supported immediate devaluation in the late 1950s (ibid.: 72). In this context, the Central Bank inevitably had to negotiate with the various actors in order to carry out its economic policies.

The actual political process that the Central Bank followed in managing its economic policy is analyzed in the following three sections. First, a review of the policy agenda before the proclamation of the Filipino First policy clarifies the main actors, their ideas and their interests. The second section traces the actual political dynamics of Filipino First from 1958 to 1959, and studies the role and limitation of the PCC. The third section examines the consequence of the politics of Filipino First from 1960 to 1961. The significance of Filipino First in the context of the Philippine political economy is considered at the end of this chapter.

Economic Policy Before Filipino First

The Garcia Administration's Agenda and the Central Bank

President Garcia appealed not for Filipino First but for austerity in his inaugural address on 30 December 1957 (Golay 1961: 96; Malaya and Malaya 2004: 184). Referring to the depletion of the country's international reserve, Garcia said: "reality now constrains us to restore the correct proportion between dollar reserves and industrialization, and also between these reserves and bond issues and other forms of public borrowing. To achieve this end, it behooves us to submit temporarily to measures of austerity, self-discipline, and self-denial" (Garcia 2000: 190). He attributed the critical situation of the international reserve to the rapid industrialization program and the liberal credit policy under the Magsaysay administration, and tried to deal with it by appealing for austerity.

Garcia's remark was a de facto endorsement of the economic policy that the Central Bank had implemented after it prevailed over the pressure of the sugar bloc under the Magsaysay administration. Before

Garcia's inaugural address in 1957, the Bank had tried to constrain inflationary pressure through a series of disinflationary policies, raising the rediscount rate from 1.5 per cent to 2 per cent on 2 April and then from 2 per cent to 4.5 per cent on 2 September, and approving Circular 79 on 9 December to increase the rate for imports from the reserve fund (*Central Bank Annual Report*, hereafter, *CBAR* 1957: 113–7; Golay 1961: 96, 235). The Bank sought to curtail excessive loans to businesses by increasing the rediscount rate and aiming to constrain immoderate imports through a restrictive policy on the letters of credit for the import trade. In his first SONA in 1958, President Garcia introduced the policies of the Central Bank as ways to implement the austerity program (*Congressional Record House of Representatives*, hereafter, *CRHR* 1958: 22).

In terms of currency policy, in January 1958 Cuaderno held a consultation with Central Bank economists to consider whether the Philippines should change the exchange rate of the peso to the US dollar (Cuaderno 1964: 69). After the Philippine government introduced the tariff policy on 22 June 1957 (Valdepeñas 1969: 153), Cuaderno began to consider the possibility of lifting the exchange controls. Cuaderno (1964: 69) and his fellow economists concluded that "a straight devaluation of the peso was not the solution to our immediate problem, which was excessive aggregate demand induced by inflation" and recommended adopting a stabilization program composed of restrictive fiscal and monetary policies and a 25 per cent tax on the sale of foreign exchange. The bank's conservative fiscal policy and gradual decontrol of foreign-exchange controls were the economic policies the Garcia administration first pursued.

Clash over the Exchange Policy

But the Central Bank faced difficulty in mobilizing support for its currency policy, especially from the US, whose financial support the bank sought in order to carry out its gradual decontrol. The US government shifted the emphasis of its economic policy from one that accepted foreign-exchange controls imposed by other countries to one that encouraged free trade by other countries, because of the overall balance-of-payment deficit and a gold drain from 1957 (Tadokoro 2001: 79). In fact, Cuaderno noted that the staff of the International Monetary Fund (IMF) suggested that the Philippine government should devalue its currency referring to the example of France which had devalued its currency (1964: 71).

When Cuaderno began negotiations for his stabilization program with the IMF and requested a certain amount for the stabilization loan, the organization turned him down. Cuaderno argued that devaluation without fiscal and monetary restraints would not remedy the balance-of-payments crisis. He felt, however, that the US government at the time preferred to remove exchange controls and devalue the peso in the Philippines (Cuaderno 1964: 71).[2] Cuaderno was disappointed that the IMF officers decided to suspend discussions after they learned that the US State Department did not favor Cuaderno's program (Cuaderno 1964: 72). With regret, he recorded: "Considering the critical situation [of the balance-of-payments] which existed at that time, I could not but feel frustrated in the efforts I had made in preparing the memorandum and in enlisting the support of a ranking official of the International Monetary Fund in Washington to the stabilization plan I suggested therein" (Cuaderno 1964: 59).

In addition to the unyielding IMF, Cuaderno was also frustrated over the persistently uncooperative voices coming from private businesses in the Philippines. The opposition against Cuaderno's policy continuously attacked the strong currency policy. Its leading opponent was still Alfredo Montelibano, who had resigned from the NEC and become president of the Chamber of Agriculture and National Resources of the Philippines, over which the sugar bloc wielded significant influence. The agro-export industry opposed the Central Bank's exchange rate policy because the industry has suffered from the country's overvalued peso (*Manila Bulletin*, hereafter, *MB* 31 July 1958, A).

The controversy over economic controls was so intense that Speaker Daniel Z. Romualdez organized a special team with Majority Floor Leader Jose Aldeguer and Congressman Jose J. Roy, chairman of the House ways and means committee, to evaluate the existing control measures (*MB* 2 August 1958: 1). Both Aldeguer and Roy were members of the Democratic Party organized by Senator Lopez and his allies from

[2] The following analysis of US currency policy is helpful, although it is directed mainly toward European countries and does not directly address the Philippines. According to Tadokoro, the US government shifted the emphasis of its economic policy from accepting foreign-exchange controls by other countries to encouraging free trade by other countries, because of the overall balance-of-payments deficit and a gold drain beginning in 1957 (Tadokoro 2001: 79). Cuaderno, in fact, recorded that the IMF staff suggested that the Philippine government devalue its currency, citing the example of France, which had devalued its currency (Cuaderno 1964: 71).

the sugar bloc, including Montelibano (Abueva 1971: 477). Aldeguer belonged to the minority faction within the Democratic Party, which was hostile to the existing Garcia administration, while Roy was believed to be Aldeguer's rival within the Democratic Party (Abueva 1971: 477; *MB* 23 August 1958: 1).

Within a week, Aldeguer presented to the team a concrete program to lift exchange controls. He suggested that the government open "a partial free exchange market beginning 1 January 1959" to achieve the full elimination of exchange controls by 1 January 1962 (*MB* 7 August 1958, A). He said that "the gradual creation of a free-exchange market is the basic remedy to our existing [economic] ills.... It is also [the] only way to establish a truly realistic rate of exchange" (ibid.). Aldeguer's program lift the exchange controls, which meant a devaluation of the peso, constituted a counter proposal to Cuaderno's policy that sought a more gradual implementation of decontrol.

President Garcia said that he favored the moderate adjustment of Philippine currency policy in a press conference on 2 August 1958, but added that it was up to Congress whether or not to rescind the controls (*Official Gazette*, hereafter *OG* 1958: cccviii). President Garcia's cautious remark might reflect the opinion of his economic advisers, including Cuaderno. At the time, Cuaderno was in Washington for the preparatory negotiation for the loan from the United States, along with budget commissioner Dominador Aytona and Eduardo Romualdez, chairman of the Rehabilitation Finance Corporation. While there, they sent a joint cablegram to President Garcia, warning him that any talk implying a possible devaluation in the Philippines might adversely affect the ongoing negotiations (*OG* 1958: cccviii).

Cuaderno and others set up economic decolonization as a policy goal. In fact, they argued that these might not be desirable as an economic policy but were needed nonetheless as a step away from the colonial economy and a step toward achieving industrialization (*OG* 1958: cccxxviii–cccxxix; *MB* 12 August 1958: 1, 12). The last point reflects their belief in industrialization not only for economic development but also for economic decolonization.

The opponents of Aldeguer's program pooled their influence in cooperation with private sector organizations such as the PCI and PCC. In a memorandum to Speaker Romualdez, the PCI argued that decontrol without proper preparations would cause devaluation as well as inflation. Instead of immediate decontrol, the chamber suggested a total abolition of controls "from 1968, or ten years from now" (*MB* 20 August 1958,

A, B). On 20 August, acting Central Bank Governor Andres Castillo, PNB manager Arsenio Jison, new PCC president Marcelo Balatbat, and PCI president Fernando E.V. Sison urged Speaker Romualdez in a meeting not to take such drastic measures as Aldeguer's decontrol program in a meeting (*MB* 21 August 1958: 1, 13).

President Garcia finally decided to abandon Aldeguer's program, although he stuck to his cautious style to avoid creating any sensation. After mentioning the congressional move to study possible decontrol, Garcia remarked: "I have confidence in the sound opinion of Congressman Roy who is a conservative economist" (*OG* 1958: cccxxviii). Considering that Roy was a leader of Aldeguer's rival group in Congress (*MB* 23 August 1958: 1), this articulation can be understood as Garcia making public his opposition to Aldeguer's program. Roy was not a layperson in the field of financial policy making. As Chapter 3 shows, he played a significant role in passing the Central Bank bill when he was a chair of the committee on banks and corporations in the 1940s. Garcia put his faith not only in Roy but also in Cuaderno, and continued to support Cuaderno's governorship despite the fact that Cuaderno, who was already 67 years old in 1957, was beyond the official retirement age. Generally speaking, Cuaderno's retention in office was "believed to be an official endorsement of his non-devaluation policy" (*MB* 4 July 1958: 20). The process of the clash over the currency policy reveals, however, that Cuaderno could barely maintain Garcia's confidence amidst a complicated political power struggle.

Clash Over the Austerity Program

The Central Bank bore the brunt of the criticism of the austerity program from the beginning of its implementation, because the bank failed to convince the private sector about the existence of inflation. The private sector expected the government to stimulate economic growth through expansive fiscal and monetary policy. For instance, PCC President Primitivo Lovina blamed the bank's rediscount rate policy, saying that it was motivated by a "morbid fear of inflation" (Cuaderno 1964: 147). Lovina accused the government's austerity policy of leading the country to the collapse of its economic and social structure. In addition, Salvador Araneta, longtime advocate of bold deficit financing, criticized the Central Bank's Circular 79 and its general monetary policy. He asserted that the circular would not discourage but rather encourage inflation, because it would curtail production and eventually raise the prices of remaining products (*Manila Times* 20 January 1958, LM, *S. Araneta*). He even described the Central Bank's policies as "un-patriotic and 'foreign-inspired'" (*Manila Times* 20 January 1958, LM, *S. Araneta*). The last statement attempted to highlight the image of the bank as an institution influenced by foreign interests. In fact, it was not the first time that the Central Bank was accused of operating under possible foreign influence. The bank was once criticized for its employment of American advisers in the midst of the great debate in 1955 (*Manila Times* 13 March 1955, LM, *Central Bank*). Araneta's criticism pushed the bank to claim something nationalistic in addition to continuously arguing the policy's validity.

The toughest battle the Central Bank faced was not with its opponents in the private business sector but on its own monetary board. This is because certain private businesses succeeded in making their interests known through their representatives in the monetary board. Gaudencio Antonino, who engaged in lumber export and was the founding president of the Producers and Exporters Association of the Philippines, was appointed member of the monetary board together with Roberto Villanueva, a member of the PCI and the "right-hand man" of the Lopezes in business (*MB* 20 October 1958, A, C; Roces 1990: 127). When they were appointed to the monetary board, Antonino declared that "[their appointment] had ended a period of non-consultation with business elements by the Bank" (*MB* 20 October 1958, A). While Antonino was an ally of Montelibano and Araneta in their attack on Cuaderno's currency policy under the Magsaysay administration (Subramanian 1980: 209, 283), Villanueva was a member of the PCI, which supported the bank's exchange controls. While the new appointees did not share their views on exchange controls, they reflected the consolidated voice of the private-business sector, which did not favor the austerity program. This new mix in the monetary board's membership soon led it into controversy.

In his memoir, Cuaderno recorded an incident that occurred on 27 November 1958, when he was at home recovering from a surgical operation. He recalled: "Deputy Governor Castillo informed me by telephone that the Monetary Board had approved the Government's request for the issue of five-year Treasury notes, in the amount of P75 million; also an overdraft line of P80 million" (Cuaderno 1964: 61). Cuaderno was very much upset about the board's decision because he had already reiterated his strong opposition to deficit financing on various occasions, including in letters to Secretary Jaime Hernandez of Finance and to

President Garcia. In a confidential letter to President Garcia dated 22 November, the governor revealed that "our free reserves...will be around $3 million only", and he appealed to Garcia for fiscal, monetary and credit restraints in order to avoid "*a forced* [*sic*] devaluation of the peso [which] will bring chaos to the country" (ibid.: 182–3). Cuaderno then sent a memorandum to the monetary board, through Castilllo, reminding its members of "the critical position of the peso due to the rising aggregate demand" (ibid.: 61).

Faced with Cuaderno's objection to the immediate implementation of the monetary board's resolution, board members Jaime Velasquez and Roberto Villanueva visited Cuaderno at his home at around 9 PM on the same day, together with Auditor General Pedro Gimenez, Budget Commissioner Dominador Aytona, Deputy Governor Castillo and Central Bank lawyer Natalio Balboa (ibid.: 62–3). Cuaderno reiterated his objection and argued that the bank was not allowed to certify the issue and acquisition of the treasury notes based on Section 128 of the bank's charter, because it would have an adverse effect on the money supply, the price level and the balance-of-payments. Simply put, he asserted, the execution of the monetary board's plan under these circumstances would constitute "an illegal act" (ibid.: 183).

Failing to convince Cuaderno otherwise, the board members and their supporters called on President Garcia on 11 December 1958; once again, they were rejected. Garcia explained that while he agreed with the observations about inflation expressed by the other members of the monetary board—something with which Cuaderno disagreed—he was convinced that Cuaderno had the right to exercise his responsibility as governor of the Central Bank (ibid.: 64). In other words, Garcia was not so convinced by Cuaderno's claim that the Philippine economy suffered from devastating inflation, but he nonetheless believed that the governor's legal position should be respected. Without Cuaderno's legal knowledge, President Garcia might have decided differently.

Cuaderno may have barely won Garcia's confidence, and he gladly reproduced the president's birthday message to him dated 12 December 1958 in his memoir. "[M]ay our people continue to profit from your valuable services as we also wish you continued success, good health, and prosperity in the coming years", he wrote (ibid.: 65). The incident, however, provided only a foretaste of the emerging influence of private-business interests over the monetary board and within the Garcia administration.

The Politics of Filipino First

The NEC, Central Bank and Philippine Chamber of Commerce

Amidst controversy over fiscal policy, the NEC, led by its new chairman, Jose C. Locsin, proved uncooperative with the Central Bank. For instance, Locsin openly expressed his dissatisfaction over the existing system of dollar allocation, asserting that the miserable performance of ISI resulted in the development of a mere packaging industry rather than that of a manufacturing industry (*MB* 3 July 1958, A).

Responding to criticism from Locsin on a variety of sectors, the bank emphasized ISI's achievements. Acting Bank Governor Andres Castillo came to the defense of ISI, arguing, "the Central Bank has succeeded in shifting emphasis of importation from consumer to producer goods in the face of ever-increasing opposition of importers, especially established firms" (*MB* 21 July 1958, A). He pointed out that "whereas capital goods made up 53 percent of our imports in 1949,...they made up 78 percent of aggregate imports in 1957" (ibid.). Castillo highlighted the changes in the composition of imports in order to demonstrate the success of industrialization, but he failed to convince Locsin.

The NEC approved Resolution 204 and proclaimed the enactment of the Filipino First policy on 21 August 1958 (*MB* 22 August 1958: 1, 13). The resolution aimed to "encourage Filipinos to engage in enterprises and industries vital to the economic growth, stability and security of the courtiers" (NEC 1974: 371). In order to achieve this goal, the NEC recognized that "the allocation of the foreign exchange is now the most effective instrument by which the above objective can be realized" (ibid.). On 28 August 1958, or within days of proclaiming Resolution 204, the NEC approved Resolution 206 to support the joint Filipino-Gulf Oil Company refinery by limiting the foreign-dominated oil company's allocation to its 1957 level (Golay 1961: 333). When Locsin talked with officials of the foreign oil companies about the Filipino First policy, he explained that he basically agreed with the idea of free enterprise but also recognized its limits under the system of dollar allocations (*MB* Supplement 11 September 1958, A). The NEC began its campaign to promote Filipino First, but the real driving forces behind it were not so clear at the time.

Locsin, a partisan politician of the NP as well as a wealthy sugar plantation owner, expected a certain return for his dedication to the party in the election in 1957. Locsin was not so excited about exercising leadership in the NEC because, he confessed in a private letter to party president Eulogio Rodriguez, he had sought a higher position than that (Yoshikawa 1987: 60). In fact, Locsin revealed that Senator Gil Puyat, an NEC member and the presiding officer before Locsin's appointment (Puyat 1960: 66), had taken the initiative in crafting the resolutions (*MB* 23 August 1958, C). Puyat had been the PCC's president from 1945 to 1949 and had supported import controls before he was elected senator in 1951, as seen in Chapter 3.

The subsequent development of the politics of Filipino First reflected the strong support of the PCC, then led by Marcelo S. Balatbat. Balatbat, born in Bulacan in 1908, started his professional career in the Bureau of Commerce and then moved to the Bureau of Banking in the 1930s. He built a career in private business as a successful realtor before he was elected president of the PCC (Jacinto 1957: 78). In his inaugural address before the PCC on 18 August 1958, he said:

> While the Philippines is no longer a colony, a pattern of the obnoxious colonialism still runs through some of the government's economic policies and regulations. It is time we took stock of the present conditions of Filipinos in business and discharged our duty to our fellow countrymen. It behooves the government and all of us to adopt economic policies that would really promote and protect the interests of the Filipinos. That is the only way to encourage greater participation of Filipinos in business in this country. (*MB* Supplement 30 January 1959: 1)

Balatbat urged the government to adopt a bolder economic policy that would be more beneficial to Filipino businesses. A day after the NEC announced its Filipino First policy, Balatbat argued: "Filipinos will never be able to increase their participation in commerce and industry unless they are given a fair deal in the allocation and use of dollars" (*MB* 23 August 1958, A). He complained that the previous pattern of foreign-exchange allocations and scarce credit for Filipino businesses were "the two stumbling blocks" preventing Filipinos from expanding their economic activity (*MB* Supplement 30 January 1959: 1). Almost a month after the NEC's proclamation, Balatbat openly claimed that the PCC had encouraged the government to adopt the Filipino First policy, saying: "Fortunately, in response to persistent clamors from the Chamber [of Commerce], the National Economic Council adopted recently what is now known as the 'Filipino First Policy'" (Balatbat 1959: 61).[3] It is

[3] Balatbat's speech was first printed in *Commerce* in October 1958 (Balatbat 1959).

important to confirm that the chamber encouraged the government to modify its foreign-exchange allocation but never called for the complete abolition of exchange controls, unlike the sugar bloc or foreign firms that directly opposed the bank's policy.

Meanwhile, foreign firms grew afraid of the possible imposition of a ceiling on their production. A.V.H. Hartendorp, editor of the *American Chamber of Commerce Journal* (*ACCJ*), the voice of American businesses in the Philippines, opposed the Filipino First policy. He argued: "the slogan is not inspired by an honest nationalism, let alone patriotism, but by greed and cupidity" (Hartendorp 1961: 367). Hartendorp accused the Filipino First policy of discriminatory and noncompetitive tendencies. As a result of his harsh criticism, Hartendorp was branded as "anti-Filipino" (Gleeck 1993: 249).

Responding to Hartendorp's criticism, Balatbat said: "it is clear from the ... editorial [of the *ACCJ*] that some American interests resent the aspirations of Filipinos who wish to engage in business" (*MB* 22 October 1958, C). In response to the Americans who publicly expressed their concern about the Filipino First policy, Balatbat argued that their sentiments would have been justified under the American colonial occupation, "but certainly not today when they are no longer masters, but merely guests" (ibid.). He strongly supported the Filipino First policy by pleading for the abolition of "this pernicious alien-first policy" (ibid.). From the viewpoint of Balatbat, who believed that Philippine economic policies before the Filipino First policy had discriminated against Filipino businesses, the Filipino First policy proved a valid claim for Filipinos.

Balatbat even argued that the government should reexamine the effects of the parity rights clause and the Laurel-Langley Agreement in order to reevaluate whether they promoted Filipino interests (*MB* 28 October 1958, A). Although the government did not take action on this issue, it is worth noting that a prominent supporter of the Filipino First policy aired his skepticism about existing Philippine-US economic relations as maintained by previous administrations.

In contrast to the chamber's bold criticism of American business privileges, the NEC responded to the American complaint and moderately toned down its advocacy about a month after its proclamation. Locsin even reiterated that the Filipino First policy never intended to deprive American businesses of their economic gains in the country, since that was protected by the revised constitution and the Laurel-Langley Agreement (*MB* 24 September 1958, B). He said that such a reaction was "understandable" coming from American businesses, but confirmed that the NEC would nonetheless implement the policy (*MB* 23 October 1958, A). The NEC's moderate reaction portended the council's lukewarm attitude to the Filipino First policy thereafter. Instead of the NEC, it was the Central Bank that was gradually drawn into the politics of Filipino First.

Implementation by the Central Bank

On 5 January 1959, a few months after the proclamation of Filipino First by the NEC and less than a month after the fiscal-policy controversy among the Central Bank's monetary board, the bank approved Resolution 12, which reduced foreign exchange allocations for all aliens except Americans, whose rights were protected by the parity clause of the Laurel-Langley Agreement (Golay 1961: 321). It was reported that "the Central Bank is expected to help implement the 'Filipino First' policy of the National Economic Council" (*MB* 6 January 1959, A). The bank made the resolution effective on 15 January (*MB* 21 February 1959: 7) and set provisions to reduce foreign-exchange allocation gradually, with a 50 per cent reduction in the first quarter of 1959 compared with the allocation for the last quarter of 1958, a 25 per cent reduction in the second and third quarters, and a further 25 per cent reduction in the fourth quarter (*CBAR* 1959: 153). The bank would have virtually eliminated all foreign-exchange allocations to aliens except to the Americans by the end of 1959, had it completely implemented the resolution.

While Balatbat expressed his support for the resolution (*MB* 23 January 1959, A), congressional leaders did not take an aggressive position on the Filipino First policy, saying that they had no intention of impairing Chinese interests in the country, which would be substantially affected by the bank's resolution (*MB* 21 January 1959: 1, 16). Senators Pedro Sabido and Edmundo Cea expressed their concern about the Bank's Filipino First policy, saying that they were not entirely opposed to the idea but favored a more moderate implementation. Congressional leaders thus asked President Garcia to urge the Central Bank to reconsider the resolution.

In this context, Garcia delivered his SONA on 26 January 1959. It is revealing that while he mentioned the policy agenda set by the Central Bank in 1957, he avoided referring to the Filipino First policy (*CRHR* 1959: 5–14). The president attributed the economic crisis to deficit financing under the previous Magsaysay administration and warned against the existence of inflationary pressure on the economy (ibid.: 6).

He clarified: "I am definitely against the devaluation of the peso"; nonetheless, he kept silent about the Filipino First policy (ibid.: 11).

Without support from President Garcia, the Filipino First policy drew much flak from the foreign-business sector in the Philippines. On 17 February 1959, the diplomatic corps met with Foreign Affairs Secretary Felixberto M. Serrano to ask the Philippine government to reconsider the Central Bank's resolution (*MB* 18 February 1959: 1, 13). In a conference, the British ambassador who headed the corps, George L. Clutton, subsequently handed President Garcia a resolution against Filipino First from the Board of Governors of the Philippine national committee of the International Chamber of Commerce (*MB* 21 February 1959: 1, 7).

Responding to the protests, Garcia directed the Monetary Board to reexamine and slow the implementation of Filipino First (ibid.). Shortly after this incident, the president's office appears to have distanced itself from the issue. When Monetary Board members met with Serrano, they decided to hold a series of meetings between the monetary board and the foreigners (*MB* 26 February 1959: 1, 11). The NEC and the president's office also avoided being reeled in the controversy. Some NEC officials reportedly even denied any relationship between the NEC's Filipino First policy and the bank's resolutions (*MB* 25 February 1959, A, C). Regarding the query posted by the Philippine embassy in London, NEC officials said that most of the council's members favored a moderate implementation of the Filipino First policy.

In contrast to the virtual neglect of the president's office and the NEC, the PCC supported the Central Bank's resolution. Balatbat, who was already recognized as the "advocate of the 'Filipino First' policy", harshly criticized the moves of the foreign-business sector (*MB* 1 April 1959, A, C). He even insinuated that the president's office ordered the bank to reconsider the resolution because several foreign businessmen had corrupted public officials. A few days after Balatbat's assertion, Deputy Governor Castillo explained that the bank adopted the resolution in order to change the country's economic structures from one dominated by foreigners to one handled by Filipinos (*MB* 7 April 1959, C). Although he mentioned a certain influence exerted by European and American businesses, he reportedly emphasized his skepticism about the dominance of Chinese businesses in the Philippine economy. Lewis Gleeck, an American diplomat and a longtime observer of Philippine politics, asserted that Castillo was a proponent of the policy (Gleeck 1993: 205).

Although there is hardly any further evidence to support Gleeck's assertion, some foreign businesses were seriously concerned about the development of the Filipino First policy. Sensing a growing clamor for the Filipino First policy, foreign firms began to consider abandoning their businesses in the Philippines (Hartendorp 1961: 351). In his book, Hartendorp mentions the case of the firm Smith, Bell & Co., established in Manila in 1846, 91 per cent of whose capital stocks were British-owned. On 10 April 1959, a 100 per cent Filipino-owned company name Aboitiz & Co. acquired 60 per cent of the firm's capital stock. Hartendorp, a foursquare believer in free enterprise, associated Filipino First with the WWII-era Japanese propaganda "Asia for the Asians" when he accused President Garcia of having succumbed to a "fascist slogan" as well as grown dependent on economic controls (ibid.: 366–7). In response to complaints from American businesses in the Philippines, the US State Department formally sent a letter of protest to the Philippine ambassador in Washington. Visiting Manila, the US assistant secretary of commerce made a direct appeal to several cabinet members to revise the Filipino First policy (Cullather 1994: 174).

In the midst of controversy, the policymakers worked hard to clarify the purpose of Filipino First. However, Foreign Secretary Serrano and Governor Cuaderno responded to the American protests by claiming, "the compelling needs to reduce the excessive alien control of business justified Filipino First policies" (ibid.). In addition, Antonino of the Central Bank's monetary board organized a forum to determine how best to implement the Filipino First policy (*MB* 23 June 1959: 1, 11). One of the guest speakers was Leonides Virata, former head of the bank's research department and now both president of the Commonwealth and Philippine Food Corporations and director of the Chamber of Commerce. According to Virata, the nationalism movement merely reflected "a new middle-class mentality" that was growing, and which found "a rallying point in the concept of 'Filipino First'" (ibid.). Based on this perspective, Virata suggested that the government pass a law breaking up the monopoly to expand business opportunities for the emerging middle class.

It would be misleading to assume that there was a consensus among the policymakers to promote Filipino First. First, the above-mentioned remark by Deputy Governor Castillo definitely sounded anti-Chinese, but it was a remark he made only in 1959. Castillo, as we have seen in the previous chapters, had maintained several key positions in the government since the 1930s but had not taken any initiative to oppose the

Chinese in the Philippines. His remark should be understood in the context of the Central Bank's need for support from the PCC and PCI to implement the government's austerity policy and maintain its currency policy, both of which had been generally unpopular. Second, the above-mentioned response by Cuaderno and Serrano should be understood as a legitimate reaction expressed simply to clarify sovereignty over the government's economic policy management. As we see in Chapter 3, Cuaderno often claimed autonomy in economic policymaking and condemned pressure from other countries attempting to influence it. Third, Virata's assertion could be understood as a proposal to recommend de-emphasis on the ethnic aspect in economic policymaking in favor of highlighting economic development.

In fact, the Central Bank suspended the implementation of the Resolution 12 and maintained the country's foreign-exchange allocation at the level of the first quarter of 1959, which was a 50 per cent reduction from the quota imposed during the last quarter of 1958 (*CBAR* 1959: 153). There is no evidence that directly shows the reason for this suspension, but the above-mentioned pressure and apparent indifference of Governor Cuaderno could be factors that led to it. Professor Amado Castro of the University of the Philippines, who held the policy of Cuaderno in high esteem (see, for example, Castro 1974), assumed that Cuaderno might have known that Filipino First constituted a selfish strategy emanating from the private-business sector, although he admitted that he did not know exactly what Cuaderno had in mind.[4]

Meanwhile, the PCC gradually realized that neither the NEC nor the Central Bank could vigorously carry out Filipino First, and thus shifted its focus to electoral politics, which would ultimately twist the goal of the Filipino First policy.

Filipino First and Electoral Politics

After the sudden death of Ramon Magsaysay in March 1957, two political parties emerged, adding to the existing parties, the NP, LP and the DP (Liang 1971: 358–78). While the ruling coalition of the NP and DP remained in the conservative center of the political spectrum under the leadership of Magsaysay, who could mobilize general support from the

[4] Interview with Professor Amado Castro in Ortigas City, Metro Manila on 4 February 2012. The writer appreciates the help of Mr Martin Galan, who kindly set up the meeting and shared his time with us.

people, three opposition parties aimed at differentiating themselves from the ruling parties. The LP, led by young politicians such as Diosdado Macapagal, Ferdinand Marcos and Cornelio Villareal, sharpened its criticism of the NP over the logic of the Cold War, in which the LP tried to associate nationalism with communism. Meanwhile, emerging parties such as the Progressive Party of the Philippines (PPP) and the Nationalist-Citizens Party (NCP) sought to build popular support in different ways. While the PPP was established by close aides of the late President Magsaysay to promote the reformism championed by the late president, the NCP led by Senator Claro M. Recto, who bolted from the NP due to his dissatisfaction with President Magsaysay, promoted nationalism aimed at achieving independence from the influence of the US government. In this context, the DP, a small ally of the NP's ruling coalition, split into two factions—one remained in alliance with the ruling NP, while the other joined the NCP (Abueva 1971: 477). When votes from the general election of 1957 came in, the NP maintained the presidency and its majority in both chambers of the House, while the LP won only the vice presidency for Macapagal. However, it tried to further consolidate its power by approaching the NCP, which without Magsaysay's close aides became similar to the original NP, having recognized Recto as one of the party's leaders.

Within the newly formed NP-NCP coalition, Recto attempted to enhance his influence in policymaking and found in Filipino First an agenda he would like to promote. Recto enjoyed fame as a leading nationalist politician in the 1950s (Constantino 1969). It is, however, important to remember that he mainly aimed at a revision of Philippine relations with the United States, which for him was a diplomatic or security issue rather than an economic issue. Since the beginning of his career, Recto proved a determined opposition leader rather than a policymaker and thus left no significant policy legacy aside from his sharp criticism of the Magsaysay administration. Therefore, he did not create but did support the Filipino First policy of the Garcia administration. Nationalist historian and Recto supporter, Renato Constantino, recorded that Recto "was even more enthusiastic in his support of Garcia's 'Filipino First' policy", referring to Recto's letter to Jose Y. Orosa, one of the prominent figures in the PCC and the one who introduced Balatbat to Recto (ibid.: 283, 311).

Recto's approach to the Filipino First policy had a lot to do with his agenda for revising Philippine-American relations. Recto's public remark about Filipino First was, in fact, triggered by an article in *U.S. News & World Report* entitled "An Ally Angry at U.S.", written by Robert P. Martin, an American correspondent in Manila. Martin warned that communists, taking advantage of the Filipino First policy, had found a chance to make a comeback in the Philippines. Martin wrote that Recto opposed the US bases in the Philippines, favored recognition of and trade with "Red China" and the Soviet Union, was a powerful friend of the communists and was a major supporter of Filipino First. Although Martin recognized that the Filipino First policy had so far yet to make a dent in American business in the Philippines, he warned that the policy could not but eventually affect it, even before the Laurel-Langley Agreement expired in 1974 (Martin 1959: 68–70). The article was published and broadcast in the Philippine local media (*MB* 24 February 1959: 1, 12).

Recto refuted Martin's article in a public speech and argued that the source of the article was "a clever admixture of truth, half-truth, honest error, and deliberate falsehoods", and that "the magazine represented the most conservative and even reactionary group in the United States" (*MB* 5 March 1959: 5). Recto reiterated his support for the Filipino First policy, explained the background of Filipino First in reference to Filipino nationalism, and clarified the relationship of the Philippines and the United States. For example, he emphasized the difference between Philippine First and Filipino First, warning that the Philippine First policy would not promote the welfare of the nation but rather that of foreign capitalists in the country (ibid.: A, B). Recto used this idea of Philippine First to clarify his position in support of Filipino First only. In other words, Recto revealed his own ideas on Filipino First instead of explaining or supporting the existing Filipino First policy of the Garcia administration.

The gap between Recto's ideas and the position of the Garcia administration is striking, especially because Recto related Filipino First to his proposal on foreign policy. He explained that because of the parity rights stipulated by the Philippine Trade Act in 1947, which the Laurel-Langley Agreement in 1954 had left untouched, the Filipinos were forced to assume the position of second-class citizens in their own country. Furthermore he claimed that resentment against such a position resulted in the adoption of Filipino First by nationalists (*MB* 5 March 1959: 5). Recto even advocated the repeal of parity rights for American businesses, which would expand the coverage of the Filipino First policy, although

President Garcia denied the possibility of repealing those rights the day after Recto's remark (*MB* 7 March 1959: 1). Recto supported Filipino First but did not necessarily adhere to the existing diplomatic policy of the Garcia administration, which maintained the status quo in its relationship with the United States.

As the midterm election of 1959 approached, Recto requested NP leaders to consider incumbent Senator Lorenzo Tañada and Marcelo Balatbat as candidates for the NCP-NP coalition (*MB* 1 January 1959: 15; 28 July 1959: 1). While Tañada had been his running mate in the 1957 presidential election, Recto first met Balatbat through an introduction by Orosa and afterwards grew closer to him, because he was impressed by Balatbat's nationalism (Constantino 1969: 284).

Meanwhile, the NP leaders did not yield to Recto and accepted only Tañada as a candidate of the NP-NCP coalition. The NCP's Tañada argued that the economic emancipation of the Filipinos from the "selfish aliens" would lead to industrialization (*MB* 8 September 1959: 5). Tañada appealed for industrialization based on nationalism as a means to emancipate the people from agriculture (*MB* 17 September 1959: 2). He also clarified that the NCP had decided to collaborate with the NP because it had adopted Filipino First (Constantino 1969: 285). The NP finally put out the slogan of "Filipino First" in the advertisement proclaiming its candidates (*MB* 12 September 1959: 8).

Even though Recto failed to make Balatbat a candidate of the NP-NCP coalition, he and Balatbat continued to advocate for the Filipino First movement. Recto justified the NCP's coalition with the NP on account of the latter's support for the NCP platform of "complete independence in the field of foreign policy and Filipino First in the sphere of economy" (*MB* 21 September 1959: 14). Balatbat continued to work on strengthening and hastening the Filipinization of the country's economy. In this context, the PCC supported the activity of the National Economic Protectionism Association (NEPA) and published a book to celebrate its silver anniversary entitled *NEPA Silver Anniversary Handbook* (Purugganan 1959). He continuously proposed possible economic policies meant to enhance economic nationalism. For example, he called attention to Indonesia's nationalistic policy and argued that the Philippines should adopt a similar one (*MB* 3 October 1959, A). While the Indonesian government nationalized "the large chunks of foreign private enterprise (Dutch and Kuomintang Chinese)" (Anspach 1969: 125), the Philippine government did not have any intention to nationalize its private enterprises. Recto and Balatbat thus proposed policies that went beyond the original scope of the NEC's Filipino First policy.

While Recto and Balatbat vigorously advocated and deepened the scope of Filipino First, President Garcia maintained his distance from the policy. For instance, during the electoral campaign, Garcia delivered an address in a meeting with the Junior Chamber of Commerce, which was a representative of ISI beneficiaries (Castro 1974: 18; *MB* 16 October 1959: 1, 14). In this address, he emphasized the achievement of the Central Bank's foreign-exchange control policy. According to him, the Filipino business sector had increased its share of dollar allocation from 39 per cent in 1953 to 44 per cent in 1958 and to 51 per cent in the first semester of 1959 (*MB* 16 October 1959: 14). He cited the changing share of American businesses as follows: From 26 per cent in 1953 to 36 per cent in 1958 and 34 per cent in the first semester of 1959, alongside a similarly declining share of Chinese businesses from 20 per cent to 10 per cent to 7.5 per cent for the same period (ibid.). Interestingly, President Garcia emphasized the achievements of the Central Bank's control policy, which had been implemented by the Magsaysay administration, but avoided mentioning the NEC's Filipino First policy that was being implemented under his administration. Moreover, he also missed mentioning Filipino First in his contribution to the NEPA's commemorative publication, which should have offered one of his best opportunities to affirm his commitment to Filipino First (Garcia 1959).

When the LP began a full-scale campaign in September, it reiterated its criticism against graft and corruption and tried to relate the Filipino First policy to the spread of communism (*MB* 2 September 1959: 19). In a press statement, Macapagal questioned President Garcia regarding the NP's definition of nationalism, implying a possible relationship between the NP's slogan and Stalin and Lenin (*MB* 7 October 1959: 2; 12 October 1959: 1). In a paid advertisement published in the *Manila Bulletin* entitled "Macapagal Warns against Use of Nationalism by Communists", the LP raised the specter of communism within the NP (*MB* 23 October 1959: 2). Macapagal also continuously cautioned audiences that nationalism was being used as a tool by the government to divert voters' attention away from graft and corruption, and that it was also being utilized by the communists to promote their goals (ibid.).

The NP-NCP coalition refuted charges by the LP on various occasions. Recto, for instance, accused the opposition of resorting to McCarthyism in an effort to put down the nationalist movement in the country (*MB* 21 October 1959: 1, 17). In their defense, the NP published a paid advertisement entitled "Wanted, for Anti-Filipinism" (*MB* 31 October 1959: 2). In this advertisement, after pointing out Macapagal's opposition to the nationalist agenda, the NP emphasized his pro-US tendencies, such as the priority he gave to strengthening economic relations with the United States while neglecting Filipino sovereignty over US bases in the country. In other advertisements, the NP appealed to voters for support by arguing that a vote for the NP was a vote for nationalism and a vote for the opposition was a vote for colonialism and the status quo (*MB* 9 November 1959: 10). Regarding the LP's charges on communist influence, the NP countered by saying that nationalism was communism's worst enemy, and that the NP would create better relations with the United States based on mutual esteem (*MB* 10 November 1959: 3). The NP-NCP coalition stuck to the slogan of Filipino First throughout the election, but it was embroiled in vicious electoral politics that spilled beyond Filipino First as a domestic economic policy.

When the election results were in, the NP-NCP coalition won five seats, while the LP won three (Comelec n.d.). After the election, President Garcia said that "for the first time since the Philippines became independent, 'nationalism became a burning issue at the polls'" (Hartendorp 1961: 369). In his 1960 SONA, Garcia stated that "the Filipino First policy of this administration received a resounding popular [e]ndorsement in the last election" (*CRHR* 1960: 6). It was the first time he acknowledged Filipino First as a policy of the administration.

The leading journalist Teodoro Locsin's candid observation of the electoral outcome in 1959 differed from Garcia's evaluation. Locsin mentioned that two close aides of President Garcia, Juan C. Pajo and Sofronio Quimson, had lost, and argued that "the people may be for nationalism, but they are against graft" (T. Locsin 1960: 2). Locsin added that people had cast their votes based on their judgment not only on the nationalist slogan of the NP-NCP coalition but also on the LP's appeal for clean government. Considering the early developmental phase of Filipino First as well as Locsin's comment, it is not unlikely that the Office of the President had become a symbol of graft and corruption rather than one of economic nationalism in the electoral competition.

Thus it was the NEC rather than the president that was identified as the main advocate of the Filipino First policy. On 6 February 1960, NEC Chairman Jose Locsin was featured as the "father of the 'Filipino First' policy" in a lead article of the *Philippine Free Press* (Ty 1960: 4–5,

57). He explained the policy by referring to the case of the Filipino-owned Filoil Refinery Company, which received substantial support from the NEC. Locsin said the policy was "dictated by common sense" that was inspired by neither anti-foreign nor anti-American sentiments (ibid.: 4). The fact that he never mentioned any endorsement of Filipino First by the Central Bank at the very least suggests that there was hardly any coordination or cooperation among government agencies on this issue.

Gradual Decontrol by the Central Bank and the End of Filipino First

Governor Cuaderno did not publicly support the Filipino First policy; instead, he took advantage of the policy proposal to encourage support for the policy agenda that he believed to be more important. Cuaderno asserted that only the gradual lifting of exchange controls, or its gradual decontrol, could help the government avoid the rise of the cost of living, the disturbance of operations in infant industries, and the disruption of support to Filipino businesses (Cuaderno 1964: 83). As the last point reveals, Cuaderno did recognize the policy of Filipino First but used it as one of his arguments for the adoption of the gradual decontrol program.

While Recto and Balatbat were busy proposing various economic and foreign policies, Cuaderno spent 1959 hard at work implementing the gradual decontrol program (ibid.: 80–3). He submitted the stabilization program to carry out gradual decontrol in March of that year. His program was more moderate than the program suggested by Congressman Aldeguer two years before. While Aldeguer had suggested eliminating exchange controls beginning in January 1959 and completing the decontrol program by 1961, Cuaderno designed his program to be implemented from April 1960 to 1964 (Baldwin 1975: 50–2). Cuaderno stated in his memoir: "Perhaps the most dangerous substitute for the gradual decontrol that had been suggested by the influential group was the immediate lifting of controls" (Cuaderno 1964: 83).

The Central Bank began to carry out Cuaderno's program through circulars 105 and 106 on 22 and 25 April 1960, respectively, which differed in content from both Aldeguer's program and the policy prescriptions of both the US government and the IMF (Cuaderno 1964: 69–83; Payer 1973: 60). With Cuaderno's program, the bank maintained its prerogative to regulate the pace of decontrol; in fact, it resorted to reversing the pace of devaluation in September 1960 (Baldwin 1975: 50–2). Satisfied with the implementation of his decontrol program, Cuaderno decided it was time to retire from the bank on 7 June 1960, finishing his term on 31 December 1960 at the age of 70 (Cuaderno 1964: 84).

Cuaderno had not actively supported the Filipino First policy, but that did not mean he was indifferent to industrialization. Once, after retiring from the Central Bank, Cuaderno worked for the Lopez brothers, who had become close to Senator Recto (Abueva 1971: 477). In October 1961, at the height of the Filipino First policy, the Lopezes expanded their business beyond the sugar industry and succeeded in acquiring a major electric company, the Manila Electric Company (Meralco), from an American firm through the support of Cuaderno, who had already resigned from the bank and had become engaged in the private-business sector (Roces 1990: 127–8). In line with this, the Lopezes had been widely regarded as one of the prime beneficiaries of Filipino First (McCoy 1994b: 503). However, we should not underestimate the government's contribution to the change in the portfolio of a leader of the sugar bloc to accelerate industrialization. Cuaderno had, in fact, taken a position against the Lopezes when he was involved in the great debate, as seen in Chapter 4.

By this time, the advocates of Filipino First had lost momentum. On 2 October 1960, Senator Recto suffered a fatal heart attack and passed away while on his way to Spain as the Philippines' newly appointed ambassador (Constantino 1969: 296). Balatbat thus lost a provocative ally in the Senate. While President Garcia reiterated his support for the Filipino First policy, he did not vigorously advocate it on his own. In an address delivered at a meeting of the PCC, Garcia remarked, "the Filipino First movement which you are spearheading is of tremendous significance to our life as a people" (Garcia 1961: 36). Subsequently, he emphasized the achievements of his administration, which he enumerated in his SONA about two months earlier. After saying that "we touched a few peaks in the progress highway in 1959", the president pointed out the country's self-sufficiency in some food staples, favorable balance-of-payments, increase in dollar reserves and stabilization of the financial and monetary system, but never mentioned any concrete achievement by the NEC or the Central Bank with regard to Filipino First (ibid.: 41). Interestingly, President Garcia labeled Filipino First not as a policy but as a "movement". He even stated that the PCC had spearheaded this movement, as if he didn't want to have anything to do with it.

Although the NP attempted to advocate Filipino First as its agenda for the 1961 general election, the party seems to have failed to convince voters that it was serious about implementing it (Meadows 1962). For example, in 1961 journalists Adrian and Rene Cristobal published a booklet entitled *Filipino First, an Approach to the "Filipino First" Policy and Selected Readings to Support the Filipino First Policy*, in which they reiterated that "the fundamental purpose of the 'Filipino First' policy is to effect the transfer of economic control from foreign into native hands" (Cristobal and Cristobal 1961: 20). The opposition LP, however, continuously accused the NP of graft and corruption and of possible links with communists. Meadows, a contemporary observer concluded that "much more important than the issue of government controls was that of graft and corruption in [the] government" (Meadows 1962: 263). As a consequence, Filipino First completely disappeared with the election of the LP's Diosdado Macapagal. Upon assuming the presidency, Macapagal abandoned Cuaderno's decontrol measure and abolished exchange controls on 27 January 1962.

By tracing the entire political process guiding the Filipino First, we have recognized the Central Bank's significance in economic policy making. The bank shouldered the dual charge of underpinning both the government's fiscal policy and also its foreign exchange controls. Prior to the NEC's proclamation of the Filipino First policy, most policymakers in the Garcia administration did not discuss economic nationalism. They were more concerned with the emergent balance-of-payment crisis or the validity of the existing currency policy. After defeating the influence of the sugar bloc inside the government and implementing a tariff on imports in 1957, the Central Bank decided to lift the exchange controls with minimal fluctuations of the peso's value and, at the same time, to compel the government to carry out an austerity program to curtail inflation. The policymakers, therefore, had to promote the unpopular austerity program and deal with politically complicated issues such as the elimination of foreign exchange controls.

In this context, the NEC and Central Bank engaged in the politics of Filipino First. The NEC proposed the policy of Filipino First based on the exchange controls managed by the bank, and the latter shaped the NEC's proposal by adopting its resolution. While the private sector failed to compel the government to enforce bolder implementation of the policy, the Central Bank won the confidence of the president in its effort to curtail deficit financing and to implement a moderate decontrol program. The implementation of the gradual decontrol program saw the end of the industrialization policy through foreign exchange controls, which meant the disappearance of the very policy tool that the advocates of Filipino First had relied upon. The advocacy for Filipino First reflected the emergence of private-sector economic interests produced by the bank's policy, while the Central Bank's decision marked the end of Filipino First politics.

Under Cuaderno, the Central Bank was interested in industrialization. During the 1950s, the bank worked for ISI through foreign exchange controls. The industrialization the bank sought is apparently similar but in fact different from the private sector's plea of economic nationalism. While the bank favored a structural shift from a colonial agricultural economy to an industrial economy, it was not interested in a change in the racial share of the economic pie. In other words, the type of nationalism policymakers had in mind consciously adopted a national economic structure with a certain shape that could be reformed independently of international and domestic pressures. Considering the nature of the policymakers' kind of nationalism, we can see that the Central Bank worked consciously for its policy goal, namely, economic decolonization.

CHAPTER 6

New Generation and New Policy: Decontrol, 1962–64

"NATION DECONTROL!"

Thus the front-page headline of *The Manila Times* announced President Diosdado Macapagal's decision to eliminate foreign-exchange controls on 21 January 1962 (*The Manila Times*, hereafter *MT*, 22 January 1962: 1). He did so within a month after his inauguration on 30 December 1961. If it were indeed the case that the Central Bank led by Cuaderno would already have carried out the decontrol program, why then did the new president's decision become such news? It seems that Macapagal's decontrol is different from Cuaderno's decontrol. This chapter traces the process of political reform under the Macapagal administration, which changed the economic policy regime previously shaped by Cuaderno and his contemporaries, and examines the process in which young Filipino policymakers with different policy goals created a new policy regime in the 1960s.

In addition to decontrol, the Macapagal administration carried out a series of socioeconomic and administrative reforms utilizing the economists who were called technocrats (for example, Ocampo 1971; Broad 1988; Dubsky 1993). It organized a group of economists to draft a five-year socioeconomic development program, and then established the Program Implementation Agency (PIA) in August 1962 to carry out the program. Sixto K. Roxas, the first director-general of the PIA, represents the "rise of technocrats" (Ocampo 1971: 32) or "the advent of technocrats" (Dubsky 1993: 64) in the Philippine government in the 1960s. In fact, Roxas actually had a vision to organize an "economic developmental administration" composed of several policies and institutions (Roxas 1964, *SKR*, i).

Some scholars have also argued that the year 1962 marks the beginning of liberalization heavily supported by international financial institutions such as the International Monetary Fund (IMF) and the World Bank (Bello et al. 1982: 131; Broad 1988: 33–4, 61, 82). Other scholars, meanwhile, assume that the Macapagal administration portends a failed attempt to create a developmental regime, due to unsettled disputes between "the vested interests of the political classes" and reformism for "more professional and technical solutions" (Raquiza 2012: 69–75). Roxas resigned from the cabinet before the end of Macapagal's term. What did the president's administration seek?

Considering the autonomy of the policymakers in the 1950s, we cannot dismiss the case of Roxas's resignation as one of a weak state captured by "the vested interests of the political classes". Rather, we should ask why Roxas could not enjoy close working relations with politicians, unlike predecessors such as Cuaderno. Moreover, previous administrations had already utilized the expertise of economists in policymaking, and the Garcia administration had already implemented gradual decontrol. We need, therefore, to study what really changed under the Macapagal administration.

A study of the political process in which Sixto Roxas once played a pivotal role in economic policymaking but later left in resignation allows us to trace a shifting phase of Philippine state building that occurs with the new economic policy regime. Considering the fact that the previous policy regime was composed of exchange controls run by the Central Bank, the decision to lift the controls and establish a new institution to carry out the development program was done in order to change the policy regime. This chapter, therefore, examines the process by which policymakers stopped using the Central Bank as the island of state strength and attempted to create a new policy regime.

It is worth mentioning that several existing works mention a clash between President Macapagal, who believed in minimal government intervention into the private sector, and Roxas, who was more familiar with active intervention by the government in order to coordinate the national economy (Doronila 1992: 135). A contemporary observation by a leading banker and future governor of the Central Bank, Jose B. Fernandez, reveals that President Macapagal and Governor Castillo favored more liberal management of economic policy than did former governor Miguel Cuaderno (Hutchcroft 1998: 88). Moreover, one of the early studies of technocracy in the Philippines argues that the early technocrats represented by Roxas were influenced by "French-style planning", which expected government to actively utilize the resources of a particular economy (Ocampo 1971: 32; Roxas 2013: 74, 80). This chapter therefore sets out to trace the changing phase of state building with a focus on the ideas of the government's policymakers.

First, we focus on a new generation of policymakers with new ideas. We trace the process in which policymakers worked together to lift foreign-exchange controls using different rationales. Second, we study the political process of change in the policy regime in order to clarify what the president actually thought about and how he framed his policy in the midst of domestic power struggles as well as negotiations with international financial institutions. In the end, we briefly discuss the mechanism of policy regime change and the changing role of the Central Bank in the 1960s.

New Ideas, New Generation

Changing Ideas and Generations

Exchange controls was an issue over which the country's major parties clashed in the 1961 election. It is worth remembering that the LP accused the NP of graft and corruption as well as communistic tendencies. The LP, led by young politicians such as Diosdado Macapagal, Ferdinand Marcos and Cornelio Villareal, sharpened criticism of the NP over the logic of the Cold War. In other words, they associated the exchange controls with the Cold War more than they did with sovereignty or economic decolonization. Their view reflected a generational change among policy leaders led by Macapagal.

Born in Lubao, Pampanga, in 1910, Diosdado Macapagal launched his government career in the Office of the President under Manuel Quezon in 1941 (Gwekoh 1962: 33). After working as an underground intelligence agent during the war, he joined the restored government as a chief of the law division in the DFA and then at the Philippine Embassy in Washington, DC, both on the advice of Vice President and Foreign Secretary Elpidio Quirino (ibid.: 34). Macapagal belonged to Magsaysay's generation, which experienced Japanese occupation and guerrilla activities while waiting for liberation by the US army.

He ran for Congress in 1949, during which he experienced a unique electoral contest because of his opponent (ibid.: 38–43). He fought the congressional race against Amado Yuzon of the Democratic Alliance, which was allied with the NP but was heavily supported by the Huk

(Gwekoh 1962: 39–41; Kerkvliet 2002), while most of his colleagues in the LP were up against NP candidates. Macapagal recognized the influence of the socialists or communists in his district when he was in high school, but he declined to join them because he regarded them as oriented toward violence (Macapagal 1968: 83–4). When he ran for Congress, he was supported by landlords rather than peasants or agricultural laborers. Former governor Sotero Baluyut of Pampanga, who was "an enemy of the peasant movement from as far back as the 1930s", supported Macapagal's candidacy over Yuzon's (Gwekoh 1962: 41; Kerkvliet 2002: 211). Throughout the electoral campaign Macapagal experienced a heavy battle against a strong opponent supported by peasants and agricultural laborers, but he nonetheless won the seat.

In Congress, he was appointed the chair of the House committee on foreign affairs, and he worked hard for the Mutual Defense Treaty between the Philippines and the United States (Gwekoh 1962: 44). After the LP lost the election of 1953 and subsequently a lot of its stalwarts with it, Macapagal emerged gradually as a young leader of the LP along with Marcos and Villareal (Gwekoh 1962: 75; Macapagal 1968: 356). It is interesting to know that Villareal had gained his clout when he led the committee on anti-Filipino activity, the powerful committee created not only to investigate but also ascertain that politicians close to the Huk were communists as well as anti-Americans (Takagi 2009: 28–31).

The LP depended on the new party leaders, who leaned toward aggressive anticommunism in the context of the Cold War. The members of this new generation, who shared a middle-class background, established their careers mainly as leaders in the anti-Japanese guerrilla movement, and mostly were supported by the United States during WWII (Doronila 1992: 92). Three presidents, in fact, belonged to this generation: Ramon Magsaysay (1954–57), Diosdado Macapagal (1962–65) and Ferdinand Marcos (1965–86), though Magsaysay left the LP for the NP before the election. Because of their experience during WWII, the younger generation was positively impressed by the US military, which had played the role of liberator in the Philippines; this generation would eventually be called "America's boys" (Nakano 2007: 127–8). The American influence on them was politico-military rather than economic, unlike predecessors such as Roxas and Quirino.

Macapagal joined with several congressional colleagues in 1955 in the foundation of the Free Enterprise Society of the Philippines, which advocated "minimum interference by the government in private business" and opposed the Central Bank's exchange controls (Gwekoh 1962: 94).[1] The society promoted an idea that differed from the idea that had predominated among policymakers since the 1930s. As the previous chapters reveal, most of the leading policymakers at the time took it for granted that the government should play a certain role in economic development and associated the idea of free enterprise with the colonial economy. In contrast, members of the Free Enterprise Society had totally different ideas.

It was also important to know that the Free Enterprise Society was composed mainly of politicians and businessmen, unlike the PEA, which was a mixture of politicians, bureaucrats and economists. The society's ideas were therefore shaped by the political context in which the member-politicians operated to distinguish themselves from their counterparts in the government. For example, Congressman Benedicto Padilla, a founding member of the society, even asserted that the government should abolish the Central Bank and return the Philippines to the gold standard, because he believed that the abolition of the gold standard and the prevailing managed-currency system signalled a victory of communism over democracy (*CRHR* 29 February 1960: 858). Padilla's idea was obviously influenced by the logic of the Cold War rather than inspired by the historical context of economic decolonization.

Although not as extreme as Padilla, Macapagal still believed in the abolition of economic controls. In his memoir, he records his observation of rapid economic recovery and growth under free enterprise in West Germany, while at the same time he remained unconvinced by the economic performance of India, whose economic policy he discussed with close aides of Prime Minister Jawaharlal Nehru (Macapagal 1968: 55). He states: "it had been my view since I was a congressman that the suitable economic system for Filipino was free enterprise....[T]he Filipinos are freedom-loving; they are at their best when they are free" (ibid.: 56). The idea of free enterprise was suited not only to those who opposed communism in accord with a Cold War worldview but also to those who opposed existing exchange controls imposed by the government (ibid.: 54).

[1] The other founding members were Benedicto Padilla, Jose W. Diokno, Lorenzo Sumulong and Jose Ma. Hernandez (Gwekoh 1962: 94).

Abolition of the Gradual Decontrol of Cuaderno

The Macapagal administration faced a divided government in which the administration might choose compromise over radical change. In the election the LP won the presidency and the vice presidency, but 13 of the 24 members of the Senate belonged to the Nacionalistas, as were 74 of the 104 in the Lower House (Macapagal 1968: 393). Confident in their remaining strength, the Nacionalista leaders in Congress tried to prevent the incoming administration from running the country smoothly down to its last moments. President Garcia had appointed Dominador Aytona as Central Bank governor on 30 December 1960, or the very last day of his term, after talking with Nacionalista congressional leaders, including Senate President Eulogio Rodriguez and Speaker Daniel Romualdez (*OG* 1 January 1962: vi). Macapagal began his administration facing a hostile Congress dominated by the opposition.

The Macapagal administration was nonetheless determined to scrap the gradual decontrol program designed by former bank governor Cuaderno. Macapagal stated his intention in his inaugural address on 30 December 1961, in which he set up the following as his administration's mission: the eradication of graft and corruption, the attainment of self-sufficiency in rice and corn, the creation of conditions for income enhancement, and the establishment of a socioeconomic development program (Malacañang Press Office hereafter, MPO 1962: 2–3). In this message, Macapagal promised that he would present his socioeconomic program in his first SONA in January 1962. Although he did not directly mention the possibility of decontrol in his inaugural message, he reiterated: "the program will call for a return to free and private enterprise" (MPO 1962: 3).

On 1 January 1962, President Macapagal changed his key policy-maker by appointing Andres Castillo as Central Bank governor (*OG* 8 January 1962: xvi). He did this in order to carry out his program (ibid.), reversing President Garcia's appointment of Aytona, which Macapagal had criticized as "a transparent act of sabotage of the new administration", even as Aytona claimed that President Garcia had appointed him specifically to direct the final phase of the decontrol program, "which was initiated by the Nacionalista Party" (ibid.: xvii–xx). Macapagal argued that Aytona was "a rabid Nacionalista partisan", and that his appointment as governor placed "a roadblock to the success of my administration's economic program in disregard of the welfare of the people" (ibid.: xvii). After asserting that Castillo was "not a politician but 'a highly respected and eminently qualified career official'", Macapagal concluded that he could not neglect the fact that Aytona had tried to maintain the gradual decontrol program of the defeated administration, and reiterated the necessity to appoint a career official rather than a Nacionalista partisan (ibid.: xvii–xxi).

The decontrol program was, however, not a single policy that the government could carry out on its own. The administration needed to prepare for a development program so that it could arrange for "sufficient reserves and standby foreign credits to support the peso in a free foreign-exchange market" (Roxas 2000: 56). The administration, therefore, needed to negotiate with the IMF and World Bank. Macapagal chose Sixto Roxas as his adviser on economic affairs and assigned him to present "the administration's economic and financial program" (ibid.).

Roxas was a newly educated economist who graduated from top American universities in the 1950s (Dubsky 1993: 64–5). He was born in Batangas in 1927, graduated from Ateneo de Manila University and the graduate school of Fordham University in New York. After returning to the Philippines, Roxas joined the Central Bank but soon moved to the PNB headed by Arsenio Jison, which had a historical tie with the sugar industry (cf. Nagano 1986, 2003, 2015). As an economist at the PNB, Roxas began to publish policy proposals and criticize Cuaderno's currency policy. For instance, he submitted his policy proposal on the multiple exchange-rate system to the Senate committee on banks, corporations and franchises on 14 March 1957 (Roxas 1957). In the memorandum, he proposed that the government adopt the multiple exchange system, which comprised fixed and free-market exchange rates depending on the trade commodities. He argued that the existing measures managed by the bank have "in effect imposed a tax on exportation and bestowed a subsidy to importation" (ibid.: 7). By proposing a free-exchange rate for certain trades, Roxas suggested a partial devaluation, although he denied a general devaluation out of concern over inflation. His proposal supported Araneta's SB 167 which, according to Roxas, aimed at breaking through the "status quo" (Roxas 1958a: 328), though Araneta's proposal was finally vetoed by President Garcia, as Chapter 4 shows. By supporting Araneta and opposing Cuaderno, Roxas took a position close to that of President Macapagal in the context of the policy debate over foreign-exchange controls.

Besides, Sixto Roxas was no stranger to the world of development programs. He had been among the young economists who participated in the creation of the Magsaysay administration's development program. Alfredo Montelibano, NEC chairman, who had resigned as a result of a clash with the Central Bank, had begun to craft another development program in May 1956 in consultation with a panel of economists that included Roxas and Armand Fabella, another key figure whom we shall examine below (NEC 1956, *SKR*). In October 1956, the NEC and its panel of economists completed a five-year economic and social development program that covered the period between 1957 and 1961 (Romualdez to Roxas 26 October 1956, *SKR*). A private letter from Fabella to Roxas reveals that there had been "heterogeneous thoughts" among the panel members that were not necessarily reflected in the final version of the program (Fabella to Roxas 27 May 1957, *SKR*). Thus, Roxas was acquainted with leading economists even before he was conscripted by President Macapagal.

However, Roxas was not a member of Macapagal's Free Enterprise Society. When the president approached him, in fact, he was an executive of the Filoil Refinery Corporation, established in 1958, the first joint-venture oil refinery in the Philippines heavily supported by the government (Rodriguez 1967: 249). In addition, Roxas had pointed out the uselessness of the idea of free enterprise before he joined the Macapagal administration, saying:

> The concept of free enterprise in the mind of the public is rather vague and it would be hazardous to attempt to pin it down in definite propositions. The statement most often repeated is, "The government should stay out of business." It is perhaps more precise to say that the belief is that the economy of the Philippines should be strictly a private enterprise economy.... As for freedom of enterprise, the predominant attitude appears to be that free and unbridled competition in the market is a condition not suited to a poor nation which is just starting out on the road to development. (Roxas 1958b: 7)

Roxas made clear that he could not agree to the existing economic policy, but he did not ally himself with the Free Enterprise Society.

Collaboration to Change the Status Quo

However, because of the control measures, Roxas could still work under Macapagal. Since the late 1950s, Roxas made public through his policy proposals that he was critical of the Central Bank's currency policy (Roxas 1958b). He wrote that he had caught Macapagal's attention as a chief economist of the Philippine National Bank and columnist for the *Manila Chronicle* appealing for the necessity of decontrol (Roxas

2000: 55). After President Macapagal organized an economic advisory committee—"composed of Fernando E.V. Sison, who [was former PCI president and] later would join his [Macapagal's] Cabinet as secretary of finance, Manuel Marquez, the president of the Bankers Association, and Andres V. Castillo, then governor of the Central Bank"—he asked Roxas and some other economists to draft an economic program, which became a section of both Macapagal's 1962 SONA and his administration's five-year socioeconomic program (ibid.).

President Macapagal needed to arrange for a fund to carry out decontrol, for which he collaborated with the IMF and the World Bank. After reading the report of the World Bank's mission to the Philippines, Macapagal and Finance Secretary Sison invited Dragoslav Avramovic, who had headed the mission, to discuss the report and economic conditions for about one hour on 9 January 1962 (*OG* 15 January 1962: xxxi; Broad 1988: 33–4). After the meeting on the same day, Sison and his technical mission left for Washington for what the *Official Gazette* described as a "routine consultation with the International Monetary Fund" (*OG* 15 January 1962: xxxi). It was not routine, however, but instead a special consultation between the Philippine government and the IMF. The Philippine mission succeeded in receiving the stand-by credit they sought to prepare for decontrol (Roxas 2000: 56).

On 21 January 1962, President Macapagal declared the decontrol of foreign-exchange transactions by approving Central Bank Circular 133, which the bank's monetary board adopted (MPO 1962: 50). Macapagal claimed that his administration, by lifting the exchange controls, had restored the principle of free enterprise in the Philippines (Macapagal 1968: 54). Roxas wrote in an article published in April the same year that the implementation of Circular 133 "marked the end of a system of allocating foreign exchange" and "the beginning of a new system of exchange operations ... a system of floating exchange rates" (Roxas 1962: 183). In the article, he distinguishes the Macapagal's administration of the decontrol program from Cuaderno's existing gradual decontrol program in his judgment that President Garcia's program did not constitute a genuine decontrol program but rather "a new control system" (ibid.: 186). Furthermore, he says that Circular 133 "established a genuine free market for foreign exchange" and "transferred the function of allocating exchange for most categories of payments" from the Central Bank to the free market (ibid.: 187).

This marks the beginning not the end of the change in policy regime. As part of the preparation for decontrol, Roxas elaborated on his ideas in a draft of the development program and also prepared a document entitled, "The Integrated Economic Program of his Excellency President Diosdado Macapagal" (hereafter, "the Program"), which formed the basis of the administration's socioeconomic program (Roxas 1965: 366; Macapagal 1962, *SKR*). The Program informs us that the development program was designed to address two salient economic problems the Philippines faced at that time. In the introduction, Roxas and his colleagues argued that the government should remove the uncertainty caused by the Central Bank's existing gradual decontrol program and that the government needed to "set clear directions for overall economic, monetary, fiscal and commercial policies and for government investment programs" (Macapagal 1962, *SKR*, 2–3). In other words, the policymakers believed that the gradual decontrol program generated a "speculative atmosphere" in the business sector and prevented private businesses from making decisions over long-term investment, and that decontrol would remove the speculative atmosphere (ibid.).

On 22 January 1962, a day after the announcement of decontrol, President Macapagal delivered his SONA to Congress. As a part of his address, he submitted his five-year integrated socioeconomic program, in which he summarized three of its objectives: "(1) immediate [restoration of] economic stability, (2) alleviating the plight of the common man, and (3) establishing a dynamic basis for future growth" (MPO 1962: 49). While these points were, at best, vague, he went on to point out three ways his government would seek to restore economic stability. First, the administration was carrying out decontrol. On a separate occasion, Macapagal said that the government initiated decontrol in order to shift "from the corruption-breeding system of controls to the free market economy to release the energies of the people and bring about vigorous economic growth" (ibid.: 73). Second, the government would implement "a set of complementary measures to protect Philippine and Filipino industry and agriculture from undue foreign competition at their 'infant stages'" (ibid.: 49). The president intended to clarify that his administration encouraged foreign capital investment in the Philippines by stating that the administration would protect both Philippine and Filipino industry. Third, the government would therefore establish policies to encourage foreign investment and joint ventures between Philippine and foreign firms (ibid.).

In the historical context, we can see that the focus of Macapagal's program was administrative reform, as the second point clearly reveals that the administration would continue the existing policy of import substation industrialization not through exchange controls but through tariffs. The policymakers wished to lift exchange controls based not on their opposition toward ISI but rather because of the speculative atmosphere that kept the business sector from allocating its resources to long-term investments. The third point—to invite foreign investments as much as possible—had been the long-term agenda for previous administrations. Even the Garcia administration had recognized necessity to invite foreign investments and declined Recto and Balatbat's proposal to repeal the Laurel-Langley Agreement with the United States as shown in Chapter 5.

On 28 January 1962, within a week after the declaration of decontrol and the SONA, President Macapagal delivered a message before the national directorate of the LP, in which he emphasized decontrol as "our most potent advance in the brief space of less than one month" before Congress convened (MPO 1962: 14). He asserted that he was determined to "uplift the masses from poverty and blaze a new trail of progress for the Filipino people" (*OG* 5 February 1965: lxv). The president reiterated that decontrol was "not only the way for the restoration of the health of the national economy but also as a major step in the eradication of corruption" (MPO 1962: 14). He had consistently emphasized that decontrol represented a change not only in economic policy but also in politics, given its aim at stamping out graft and corruption.

While it is true that Macapagal and Sixto Roxas were not fully in agreement with regard to the purpose of decontrol, it is also true that Roxas led the opposition party, which changed economic policy. Macapagal's rapid and determined move to lift controls succeeded in getting rid of most of the speculation caused by the unclear exchange rate policy of the previous administration (Wurfel 1962: 35). Without conflicts between the two major parties over economic policy and the change in government from the NP to the LP, we could not have understood the substantial change in the government's currency policy in January 1962.

The Politics of Administrative Reform

A Divided Government and the Macapagal Administration

The power struggle between the president and legislators reveals another face of the politics of the Macapagal administration, in which the president was determined to clash with the political representatives of the export industry that supposedly was the beneficiary of the decontrol.

President Macapagal did not hide his antagonism against Congress, once he failed to gain support from the NP through bipartisan arrangements (Macapagal 1968: ch. 52; Emmer 1983: 52–4). Macapagal declared:

> I cannot countenance the imposition of congressional dictatorship over the Executive, as desired by certain congressional leaders, without forsaking the well-being of the people who gave me a clear mandate to solve the economic problems of the country...it is the aim of the present NP leaders to win the elections in 1963 and 1965 regardless of what happens to the people, while it is our aim to serve the people regardless of what happens to us, politically, in 1963 and 1965 [on 5 January 1962]. (*OG* 8 January 1962: xxiv)

Within a week, Macapagal bluntly said in a statement dated 7 January 1962, that the people voted for president "with an eye to national policies", while they voted for congressmen "primarily motivated not by national policies but by the personality, record and local problems related to congressional candidates, including pork barrel allotments" (MPO 1962: 159).

Macapagal, however, did not hesitate to use pork barrel allotments whittle down the opposition, at least in the Lower House. During the harsh struggle for the speakership, rumors had been rife that Nacionalista politicians sympathetic to the Liberal aspirant, Cornelio Villareal, were given a hundred thousand pesos each. That issue drew so much attention from the public that the president himself was compelled to clarify "that he had absolutely no knowledge" about it (*OG* 15 January 1962: xxxvii).

While we cannot confirm whether the LP actually bribed its NP counterparts, we know that President Garcia attempted to cut down the opposition. As Soliven argues, the Philippine president was regarded as a "powerful president to be found in a working democracy" (Soliven 1962: 22). Because of his control over the allocation of the public works fund that was the vital source of pork-barrel politics and appointive power, the president could get a firm grip on running the government (ibid.). He had vetoed a part of the congressional budget for the first time in Philippine political history, breaking with the "tradition" of approval in previous administrations (Macapagal 1968: 231). On 9 March 1962, Villareal at last won the speakership of the Lower House, with 25 supporters from the NP, with whom the LP created the chamber's Allied Majority (MPO 1962: 11).

In addition to the battle for the speakership, the LP sought the majority on the joint commission on appointments, which was composed of members of both the Senate and House. This is because the party needed the concurrence of the commission with the president's appointments to several key government positions, including the governorship of the Central Bank (*MT* 2, 4 January 1962). It was not enough for the Allied Majority members to support the LP as a dissident Nacionalista, because the constitution stipulated that the members of the joint commission on appointments should be elected on the basis of proportional representation among the political parties in Congress. The remaining Nacionalistas questioned the legitimacy of the Allied Majority members' position and the controversy went to litigation. The Supreme Court ruled that the actions of the commission on appointments composed of Liberal and Allied Majority members were null and void (*MT* 11 May 1962).

The day after the Supreme Court's decision, the Allied Majority members completely switched their affiliations to the LP (*MT* 12 May 1962). On 17 May 1962, President Macapagal issued a statement entitled "a crucial and historic meeting" after a breakfast meeting with members of the Allied Majority who had belonged to the NP but had made a pledge to support the president (MPO 1962: 161–4). Macapagal said that he needed the Allied Majority to fulfill his administration's implementation of decontrol measures. Considering the significant role of Governor Castillo, the creation of the Allied Majority in the Lower House had a lot to do with the power struggle over who was in charge of economic policy.

President Macapagal had barely diminished the opposition in the Lower House, but he failed to achieve the same in the Senate, where his most relentless opponents resided. Among them, he targeted the sugar bloc as the main opponent against his administration. In his address before the Ninth National Congress of the Philippine Sugar Industry on 13 February 1962, Macapagal declared that "the President of the Republic owes to the people for the national welfare, it is your duty to the country to refrain from engaging in organized power politics as a means of promoting the welfare of the sugar industry" (MPO 1962: 145). Although he said "that is history", he reminded his audience that he recalled how the leaders of the sugar bloc had supported the NP during the 1961 elections (ibid.: 139, 145).

On 19 February 1962, about one week after his address, President Macapagal declared open hostilities against the sugar bloc at a breakfast meeting with the congressional reporters club (*OG* 26 February 1962: civ). Before journalists of the local dailies, he said:

> I judge others by what they do, and not by what they say. I am not ready to accept the present offer of cooperation by the present congressional leaders as evidence of their good intention while they are moving to place both Houses of Congress in the control of the so-called sugar bloc led by Sen. Fernando Lopez in the Senate, and Rep. Jose M. Aldeguer, Francisco Ortega, and Ramon Mitra in the House.... It would harm the nation's interests and the people's welfare to place both Houses of Congress in the control of vested interests. (ibid.: civ)

Macapagal noted that "efforts would be made to weaken politically the opposition candidate for the Senate Presidency, President Pro-tempore Fernando Lopez" (Macapagal 1968: 401). He claimed that his fight against the sugar bloc was part of the realization of free enterprise, "which should make available to everyone to all businessmen and to all citizens equal and fair opportunity to advance not through unfair tactics but according to the merits of everyone" (Roces 1990: 130). The power struggle between the president and the sugar bloc had become public knowledge.

President Macapagal did not let up. In a June 1962 radio and TV broadcast, he condemned Congressman Lorenzo Tevez by name for opposing measures to accomplish the full decontrol program, which included carrying out the socioeconomic plan (MPO 1962: 155). Singling out Tevez as "one of the leaders of the Lopez sugar bloc in the House of Representatives", Macapagal condemned him and his group for not wanting "to give up any part of the benefits that they have derived from the institution of decontrol" (ibid.). The president then challenged the Lopez brothers by flexing political muscle on their business activities: The administration demanded that the Meralco directors remove Eugenio from their board and charged the Lopez-owned company with export violations (McCoy 1994b: 505). The Macapagal administration would keep up its attack against the Lopez brothers until Macapagal lost in the 1965 elections (ibid.: 506).

Establishment of the Program Implementation Agency

In the midst of a power struggle over legislative leadership, President Macapagal began to accelerate the implementation of his five-year socioeconomic program. When the World Bank mission led by Avramovic came to Manila in June 1962, it issued a memorandum recommending "the immediate formation of a full-time economic staff to energize the various economic arms of the Executive Branch, coordinate programs, remove bottlenecks and see to the transparent and efficient implementation of projects" (Roxas 2000: 56).

In late July 1962, Macapagal called on Sixto Roxas late in July to ask him to form his economic staff, and on 1 August he appointed him assistant executive secretary for economic affairs (ibid.). Roxas promptly prepared a document that specified the responsibilities and functions of the assistant secretary (Roxas to the President, 31 July 1962, *SKR*). In this memorandum, Roxas argues that the secretary's most important responsibility is to organize an implementing agency for the five-year socioeconomic program that would coordinate several related agencies. Roxas believed that the government needed to establish a new institution because the National Economic Council (NEC), which had designed several programs but failed to implement them, by the late 1950s had ended up as a political institution through which politicians sought shares of the war reparations from Japan.[2]

On 24 August 1962, the President issued Executive Order 17 creating the Program Implementation Agency (PIA) to oversee the administration's socioeconomic program and appointed Roxas as its director-general (*OG* 17 September 1962: 6077–8; Roxas 2000: 56). The PIA was directly responsible to the president, and its director-general held Cabinet rank (EO 17, *SKR*). It was expected to liaise with the NEC and other implementing economic agencies (ibid.: 2). Considering that the administration had already established the program, whose implementation should have been the NEC's responsibility before, the PIA grew to play the administration's most substantial role in implementing the economic policy. From then on, Roxas played a pivotal role in economic policymaking and would be later called the administration's "mega-technocrat" (Serrano 2005: 50).

Roxas actively recruited his fellow professionals to the PIA, which he later remembered as "[a] critical mass of technocrats" (Roxas 2000: 87). He explained the concept of technocracy as having developed from two different schools of thought (ibid.: 84–5). First, the "managerial revolution in the Western industrial countries" created "a class of professionals" who made use of scientific knowledge in management of government. Second, both the Marxist and Keynesian revolutions "created a new field of macroeconomic management". In the Philippines, Roxas explained, this created new kinds of professionals that first gathered in the Central Bank and later the PIA (ibid.: 86–7). Roxas's distinction

[2] Interview with Dr Sixto K. Roxas on 24 February 2007.

between the technocrats at the Central Bank and those at the PIA reflects his sense of a generational change among the government's technocrats from Cuaderno's generation to his own.

In fact, the early 1960s marks a time when a new generation of economists emerged in not only the government but also the university. As the Philippine Economic Association, underpinned by colonial economic bureaucrats, gradually disappeared, the Philippine Economic Society (PES), organized by young professional economists recently graduated from top universities in the United States emerged in its place. Organized in August 1962, the PES sought "to foster and encourage professional and social relations among economists and to improve the standards of economic research and instruction in the country".[3] In this context, Roxas, who was also a founding member of the PES, said that the University of the Philippines became one of the two incubators for leading technocrats under the administration of Ferdinand Marcos (1965–86), producing such figures as Rafael Salas, Cesar Virata, O.D. Corpus and Jaime Laya (Roxas 2000: 87; Sicat 2008).

The Program Implementation Agency became another incubator for these new economists or technocrats. Roxas claimed: "Out of here [the PIA], came some of the principal technocrats that served in the Marcos government—Armand Fabella, Placido Mapa Jr., Vicente Paterno" (Roxas 2000: 87). Table 6.1 profiles these technocrats, including Roxas himself.

Table 6.1 Selected Members of the PIA

	Birth Year	*Education*	*Affiliation*
Sixto K. Roxas	1927	Fordham U. (MA), Ateneo de Manila U. (AB)	Filoil, Central Bank and Philippine National Bank
Armand Fabella	1930	Jose Rizal College (MA), Harvard U. (AB)	Jose Rizal College
Placido Mapa Jr.	1932	Harvard U. (PhD), St. Luis U. (MA), Ateneo de Manila U. (AB)	Private banks in the United States
Vicente Paterno	1927	Harvard (MBA), UP (BSME)	Philippine Investment Management Consultants

Sources: Roxas 2000: 87; Ocampo 1971: 42–3.

[3] PES website available at http://pes.org.ph/ [accessed 5 July 2013].

Comparing these technocrats in the 1960s with PEA members in the 1930s, we find several differences. First, these younger technocrats established their professional careers after independence or the period when the Philippine government carried out ISI through the Central Bank's exchange controls. In his memoir, remembering the days when he returned from the US, Roxas recalled: "In the Philippines, Ramon Magsaysay had been elected President and a whole new spirit of reform was in the air" (Roxas 2014: 57). It was, therefore, natural for Roxas to assume that the Central Bank was responsible for the "status quo", while the bank's opponent, Araneta, had been bold enough to break through the status quo in the 1950s (Roxas 1958a).

Second, in terms of membership, the technocrats did not include among them politicians, while the PEA had been organized under the leadership of a politician, Elpidio Quirino. Macapagal's Free Enterprise Society had almost nothing to do with the PES. The president had instructed Roxas to organize the PIA but was apparently not as actively involved in recruiting staff as Quirino had been in the 1930s. The working experience of the members in these two organizations also differed. While most PEA members were well experienced colonial bureaucrats with education abroad, PES members were fresh graduates of top US universities with little working experience. While Cuaderno was the same age as presidents Roxas and Quirino and established his professional career in both the colonial bureaucracy and the banking business, most of the technocrats belonged to Sixto Roxas's generation, which was younger than Macapagal by almost 20 years. In other words, PIA members were more or less junior partners to the leading politicians of the time.

The first two reports prepared by the PIA provide to understanding the agency's focus and position within the government (PIA 1962, 1963, *SKR*). The first progress report reveals that the PIA did not have enough data to examine, and thus it states: "The immediate task requested of the government agencies now is to supply the PIA with all the data that it needs" (PIA 1962, *SKR*, 6). No wonder then that other government agencies cooperated so little with the PIA, considering that the latter was mandated to search for "the bottlenecks existing in the decision-making and administrative machinery in the government" (ibid.: 11–2). The PIA, which directly reported to the president, could play the role of supervisor over all related government agencies, although it was only recently established and staffed with relatively young government outsiders. In addition to its supervising role, the PIA was expected to be a guiding agency leading the private sector toward economic development.

These two reports also reveal an uneasy situation for PIA, which ended up being in charge of two different sets of policies at the very outset: It dealt with the ad hoc economic agenda and long-term development policymaking. For instance, in September 1962, Director-General Roxas had to leave the country for Washington, DC to join an attempt to organize the Private Development Corporation, which would request loans from the World Bank and US government, and stayed there until the middle of October (PIA 1963: 4). Roxas worked hard to obtain loans to deal with economic uncertainties on the heels of decontrol, which made it difficult for firms to accept long-term investments at least until the market exchange rate had stabilized.

Meanwhile, in the Philippines, PIA Deputy Director-General Fabella drew up the organization's first progress report, including several policy proposals, in September while Roxas was still in the United States (PIA 1963: 4–5). The PIA focused on liquidity tightness in the economy, due to decontrol and the consequently uncertain exchange market, and searched for a remedy (PIA 1962: 65). The agency suggested that instead of tapping the cautious private sector, the government should provide market liquidity through expenditure on public works and adopt a more liberal credit policy. The PIA emphasized government roles in the economy and focused on public works as one of its tools.

The eight-page annual report, which was prepared after Roxas returned to the Philippines, was short compared with the more than one hundred-page first report, but it sharply reveals the focus of its study. The report states that the PIA revised all of the public works and power projects that the government had suspended since January when the agency was formed (PIA 1963: 3). In his memoir, Macapagal asserted: "Our Administration viewed public works not in the concept of the pork barrel but as a vital segment of the Socio-Economic Program", knowing fully what the pork barrel signified for politicians (Macapagal 1968: 122). However, he admitted: "the pork barrel questions became academic because the non-cooperation of the Senate with the President extended to public works. No public works bill was passed for 1963, 1964, and 1965" (ibid.: 123). The PIA's attempt to change the economic policy was too critical for a government that faced a hostile Congress.

Shouldering a broad and heavy responsibility with little bureaucratic support, the PIA clearly needed Macapagal's strong and stable backing. But such critical support was hard to get from a president who faced a hostile Congress, as the previous section of this chapter shows. Roxas had indeed needed to work at his former office in the Filoil Refinery building before moving in to a space in the Philippine National Bank building—not on the strength of a Macapagal directive but because of a kind offer by the PNB president at the time (PIA 1963: 2). It was only after Roxas returned with Avramovic and four other economists from the World Bank that the PIA finally found him a permanent office, which still needed renovation, and even then only on 24 November 1962, more than three months after his appointment. Comparing the close collaboration between presidents Roxas and Quirino with Cuaderno in various international negotiations with a solitary battle of Sixto Roxas, it is easy to anticipate a dismal future for him at the PIA.

Clash of Ideas

While the PIA was struggling to establish its authority within the government, Roxas was instructed by President Macapagal to address the issue of land reform. Macapagal had organized a presidential committee on land reform on 13 January 1963 (Roxas 1965: 394), although he had never shown interest in the issue before that year (Putzel 1992: 114). Roxas wrote that the PIA, which was assigned to support the committee with the technical perspective, aimed to seize the opportunity "for a fundamental revision in overall agricultural policy in the country and a realignment of some of the most important agencies dealing with agriculture" (Roxas 1965: 394). Learning from the experience in Taiwan, he actually envisioned the possible expansion of the country's domestic market through land reform (Roxas 2013: 77–8).

However, the Macapagal administration did not carry out land reform vigorously. In fact, Congress defanged the bill with more than 200 amendments (Putzel 1992: 116–7). In addition to opposition from politicians who were huge landowners or were supported by them, reform also faced opposition from prominent nationalist politicians such as Lorenzo Tañada, a close ally of Claro Recto in the 1950s. Nationalist politicians opposed Macapagal's land reform proposal because they considered it an intervention by the US government which, from their perspective, prevented the Philippines from industrializing its economy and left it a colonial agricultural economy (ibid.: 95–6). Only after substantial revision did Congress pass the bill on 12 July, and the Land Reform Act went into effect on 8 August 1963 (Roxas 1965: 394–5).

Another important reason for the failure of land reform has to do with the passive attitude of President Macapagal himself. As the previous section shows, Macapagal had not been active in land reform. In fact, as a politician supported by landlords, he once opposed the land reform proposal that Robert S. Hardie, an American agricultural specialist, prepared in 1952; ruling LP leaders labelled the proposal as un-Filipino and communistic (Putzel 1992: 85–91, 114; Gleeck 1993: 112). In a comprehensive study of land reform in the Philippines, Sixto Roxas revealed his view that Macapagal had attempted to show any seriousness about land reform only for the purpose of elections (Putzel 1992: 117).

One of the reasons for Roxas's harsh evaluation came from his bitter fight with a close aide of Macapagal, Rufino Hechanova, who had been in the advertisement industry and was in charge of public relations for the LP in the 1959 and 1961 elections (Macapagal 1968: 26; Gleeck 1993: 262). The Philippines witnessed the rise of the advertising and marketing industry, especially through the diffusion of radio in the 1960s (Hedman 2006: 82). Hechanova was so close to Macapagal that the president even invited him to the vice president's cottage in Baguio to outline a platform for the 1961 elections (Reynolds and Bocca 1965: 159–64). The author of a biography of Macapagal called Roxas a "mega-technocrat" and dubbed Hechanova a "super secretary" because the latter was appointed press secretary, executive secretary, secretary of commerce and industry and then secretary of finance over the course of Macapagal's administration (Serrano 2005: 50). Hechanova was not at all an economist, and presently he began to clash with Roxas on various occasions (Gleeck 1993: 300–1, 304–5).

In February 1963, there was an initial broadcast about an internal dispute between PIA Director-General Roxas and Commerce Secretary Hechanova (*The Far Eastern Economic Review*, hereafter *FEER*, 7 February 1963: 271). The dispute emerged over the issue of foreign investments in the fertilizer industry, when ESSO Standard Philippines announced its plan to construct a fertilizer plant to utilize the waste product and byproducts from its petroleum refinery. The plant would be the largest fertilizer plant in the Philippines and cover up to 80 per cent of the country's local industry. ESSO's proposal, however, had an adverse effect on another proposal to establish a fertilizer plant by Jesus Cabarrus, a Filipino industrialist (Macapagal 1968: 109). Compared with the huge scale of ESSO's proposal, Cabarrus's proposal was modest, and it would be abandoned.

While Roxas argued that the government should regulate new entries to avoid a possible overcrowding of the local fertilizer industry and proposed that the government ask ESSO reduce the scale of its plant, Hechanova differed, saying that the government, by encouraging a free-enterprise economy, should not regulate the industry but rather encourage foreign capital to enter the market (*FEER* 7 February 1963: 271; Macapagal 1968: 110). Although Hechanova said that he didn't deny the necessity of regulation in the future and emphasized that he differed with Roxas only on the issue of timing, the clash between him and Roxas was picked up by local newspapers and described as an internal dispute among policymakers (*FEER* 7 February 1963: 271).

President Macapagal supported Hechanova's position, saying, "it is of the essence of free enterprise not to impose restrictions on the establishment of business ventures other than on the basis of sound public policy" (Macapagal 1968: 110). Macapagal even visited the site of the ESSO plant on 27 April 1963, before the plant initiated production in 1965. Although Macapagal could not convince Congress to pass the business incentive bill during his term, he did encourage foreign investments (ibid.: 283–9). The Macapagal administration, for example, reached an agreement with Dole on establishing a huge pineapple plantation in Mindanao (Hawes 1990: 109–11).

While Hechanova consolidated his influence, Roxas became increasingly isolated within the administration (Gleeck 1993: 300–1, 304–5). Among the Sixto K. Roxas papers donated by Roxas to the University of the Philippines, a news clipping indirectly demonstrates Roxas's difficult position within the government. Adelardo A. Codero, a businessman and president of the Free Enterprise Society, heavily criticized the socioeconomic program of the administration and even said that "the World Bank is regarded as the source of the communist-sounding five-year plan" (*Sunday Chronicle* 12 August 1962, *SKR*, 1). Although the article did not mention Roxas or the PIA, it was as clear as day that the Free Enterprise Society was hostile to Roxas and the PIA, as the person and agency in charge of the plan were known associates of the World Bank.

Two months after his clash with Hechanova, Roxas was appointed NEC chairman. Roxas wrote an eight-page letter to President Macapagal to convey his dismay over this decision, and went on to submit a set of proposals for administrative reform. The letter is worth considering here because it helps us understand the following: First, it confirms the clash between Hechanova and Roxas. Roxas, who had once believed that he should be concurrently appointed as both the NEC chair and PIA governor-general for empowerment's sake, claims in the letter:

> Last night, Mr. President, you mentioned that it was Secretary Hechanova who had suggested Mr. Fabella for the position. I hope

> Your Excellency will forgive me for saying that it seemed a bit irregular that he should be the one consulted on a replacement for PIA. (Roxas to the President 30 June 1963, *SKR*, 3)

Although Roxas did not write anything further, he clearly expressed his dismay that Macapagal took the lead from Hechanova.

Second, the letter pointed out problems with what seemed to have become standard practice in economic policymaking. Roxas reminded the President that "the crying need was to establish a machinery in the government for the substantive and systematic programming of government's resources among projects…." (ibid.: 1). Roxas believed that he had convinced Macapagal to establish an implementing agency of the development program and assumed that the PIA would be precisely that agency. As a condition to move from the PIA to the NEC, he, however, suggested that the government strengthen the NEC in order to supervise "the programming of government funds for infrastructure projects, development services and external funds" (ibid.: 4). He subsequently asserted that it was easy to strengthen the NEC because what the President should do is to transfer related staff from the PIA to the NEC headed by Roxas (ibid.: 4). Recalling that the PIA touched upon the revision of the implementing system of public works from the very beginning, we could understand Roxas's attempt to do so under his supervision.

Third, the letter showed the problems PIA faced in its formative period. In the latter part of the letter, Roxas further suggested that the strengthened NEC shoulder the responsibility for long-term development policy, while the PIA focus on "ad hoc" problems in the day-to-day implementation of the policies (ibid.: 6). In other words, the PIA had been hobbled by ad hoc problems, leaving it little time or energy to supervise and coordinate the relevant government agencies.

Roxas's proposal, however, was somewhat neglected by Macapagal, although there had been no record of any response from the president. Roxas told this writer in an interview that he was "kicked out" to the NEC,[4] leaving Hechanova free to solidify his position as the closest aide of Macapagal after he succeeded in gathering support from American

---

[4] Although this author refers to Gleeck's writings to describe the power struggle between Hechanova and Roxas, he uses the expression "kick out" based on his own interview. It was a demotion for Dr Roxas, who had recognized the limitation of the NEC and was determined to set up the PIA, to be appointed as the Chairman of the NEC. Interview with Dr Sixto K. Roxas, Manila, Philippines, on 24 February 2007.

businesses interested in the Philippine market in early 1964 (Gleeck 1993: 290–91, 304–5).

Writing to Macapagal that "there is a basic conflict between the political need for visible display of accomplishment ... and the requirements of sound, long-range planning", Roxas at last resigned from all of his government posts on 1 March 1964 (Roxas 2000: 58). Roxas submitted a terminal report entitled "Review of Progress and Definition of Future Imperatives" (Roxas 1964, *SKR*). He had prepared the documents not only to provide a review of the economic situations but also "for organizing the government for economic development administration" (Roxas 1964, *SKR*, i). Roxas's terminal report is, therefore, a view from an administration insider on the consequence of reforms in the Macapagal administration and its lingering problems.

Roxas began his report with a review of the economic situation before decontrol. He claimed: "The years 1959, 1960, and 1961 were, for the most part, a period dominated by a speculative atmosphere" that was caused by "the uncertainty of the exchange policy of the government" (Roxas 1964, *SKR*, i–ii). Because of the Central Bank's gradual decontrol program, "businessmen engaged in speculative inventory build-ups of imported products and accumulation of foreign exchange balances" instead of making long-term plans (ibid.: ii). Roxas argued that in order to deal with the speculative atmosphere, which resulted in a lack of consideration for long-term development, the Macapagal administration lifted the foreign exchange controls and set up the five-year socioeconomic program.

With the socioeconomic program, the administration had aimed at rehabilitating industries impaired by decontrol as well as expanding and diversifying industrial and agricultural productivity (ibid.: iii). The administration increased tariff protection for these affected industries, even as it continuously promoted basic and intermediate industries. At the same time, the administration had attempted to increase income levels in the countryside so that the Philippines would develop a domestic market for its own industries (ibid.: iii). From these points it is clear that Roxas had basically followed the ISI line, although he preferred tariffs to the previously used exchange controls as a tool to realize industrialization. The more innovative character of Roxas's attempt, therefore, could be found in the field of administrative reform.

Roxas, in fact, reiterated the significance of administrative reform, which he had undertaken with the establishment of the PIA. Simply put, it aimed at emphasizing "concrete planning" in contrast to "the broad and aggregative planning done habitually by the government during the past decade, which had resulted in plans that had no operational significance" (ibid.: viii). In other words, Roxas asserted that decision-making should be centralized rather than diffused among various agencies.

To be sure, Roxas sympathized with the idea of a coordinated economy headed by the government. Decontrol could be the only and last agenda under which Roxas could work with Macapagal, and the subsequent economic policies had failed to consolidate their working relationship, which deteriorated even further. Roxas was not convinced that President Macapagal fully comprehended his economic idea. In a book he published almost 40 years after his resignation, Roxas revealed his dissatisfaction with the Macapagal administration:

> When I resigned in February 1964, I said in my letter that it was clear that the next two years until the presidential election would be even more political than the previous two. I pointed out that the last thing the President needed would be an "economic conscience", and that it would be better for me to resign early rather than late, lest my resignation be interpreted as having any political motives or implications. (Roxas 2000: 55)

Considering that Hechanova was the former campaign manager of the LP and that Roxas was an economist working in the financial sector, it seems that Macapagal had chosen an aide who would help him win elections rather than one with an economic conscience who joined the administration only after the election.

Setting aside Macapagal's conviction about the necessity of decontrol based on an adherence to his idea of free enterprise, a rational appreciation of the political process at work in the administration is, at best, elusive in two ways. First, Macapagal did not integrate power struggle and policymaking. He did not hesitate to implement immediate decontrol, although he had known that decontrol benefitted the sugar industry. Had he concentrated only on his fight against the Lopezes from the very beginning, he would not have lifted the exchange controls. Macapagal had decided to carry it out, although he assumed that "it [the decision] was disadvantageous and probably political suicide", because "it would provide increased profits to our main political adversaries who were in the exporter's groups" (Macapagal 1968: 57, 55). Second, if Macapagal had lifted the exchange controls because of international pressure from the IMF and World Bank, he would have supported Roxas's work in the PIA because Roxas maintained good relations with the international financial organizations. The fact that President Macapagal chose Hechanova at a late stage in his administration reveals that the Philippine president did not necessarily follow the advice of the IMF and World Bank.

From these points we can conclude that the president's ideas, rather than international or domestic structures, make or unmake change in the Philippine policy regime. While President Macapagal believed in free enterprise—notably a more political than economic idea—shaped in the context of the Cold War, his economic adviser Sixto Roxas did not assume the idea of free enterprise as a valid policy idea and attempted to centralize the decision making process of economic policy. Macapagal ultimately went with his own ideas and let Roxas resign from his administration.

In the broader context of Philippine state building, the Macapagal administration represents the changing and evolving ideas among policymakers. In earlier administrations, the policy regime had been run by policymakers who established their careers during the American colonial period and who experienced the cumulative efforts made toward economic decolonization in the post-independence era. They aimed at expanding autonomy in economic policymaking and structural change in the Philippine economy, which had depended heavily on the market of the country's former colonial master, the United States. Meanwhile, the policymakers of the Macapagal administration had established their careers in the midst of economic decolonization. They believed that the efforts made by senior policymakers were merely attempts to stick to the status quo and therefore were determined to change the situation even though they had no consensus on the direction of the reform.

President Macapagal, who had believed in the idea of free enterprise in the context of the Cold War, ultimately chose to liberalize the Philippine economy and change the policy regime so that the government played little or no role in intervening in or coordinating the economy. Technocrats who took over Roxas's position in subsequent administrations could not establish such close ties with their respective presidents as had the economic bureaucrats led by Cuaderno. The rise of technocracy beginning in the 1960s paradoxically accompanied the decline in the influence of economic bureaucrats in the government. The Philippine government lost the autonomy it had established in the 1950s, not because the social forces against it had been strong but because the government ultimately opted for a policy regime that eased its role in the regulation of private business. The Philippines witnessed rise of a new policy regime based on new ideas in the 1960s.

CONCLUSION

Policymakers have played certain roles in shaping the dynamics of Philippine political economy. They enjoyed a level of autonomy that allowed them to maximally make use of internationally floating ideas to create policy proposals that were not induced from the existing colonial interest structure. They advocated the creation of a central bank despite opposition from American colonial officers and neglect by Filipino elites who had already established their power base in the 1930s. They strove for autonomous economic policymaking in the midst of their struggle to reconstruct the country after WWII. Because of Filipino participation in colonial economy, however, the policymakers could not be embedded through cooperative relations with an active private sector. Instead, they clashed with leaders of private businesses during the 1950s. While they succeeded in making the Central Bank the island of state strength, they could not work closely enough with private sector to create embedded autonomy. The policymakers did work toward industrialization, but they were not so enthusiastic about the racial dimension of economy. The island of state strength's role changed beginning in the 1960s, not because of social pressure or international intervention but instead because of a decision by policymakers.

The process tracing of emergence of the island of state strength sheds new light on Philippine politics in three ways. First, the Philippine state, which has been regarded as a patrimonial state, can be understood as at least an intermediate state with an island of state strength, if not a developmental state. Plunder, graft and corruption have always been present in Philippine political history, but it is not entirely true that the Philippine state has been always a predatory or oligarchic state to the same extent as most patrimonial states. We can say that the predatory or patrimonial phenomenon that allows social forces to exploit national resources might be found especially under the authoritarian regime that controlled the country from 1972 to 1986 (Hutchcroft 1998). The state is built by political actors who emerge from particular contexts surrounding their activities but who may attempt to change the existing structure with particular ideas. Such policymakers strove for particular policy goals within particular historical contexts.

The policymakers making the island of state strength arose in the 1930s when they worked hard to establish an independent state based on their own definitions of nationalism. These policymakers differed from their predecessors insofar as their awareness of the significance of economic decolonization was concerned. In the contexts of the politics of independence triggered by the economic crisis and the US government's monetary policy change, Filipino policymakers assumed that creating a central bank was a part of state building. They were convinced that the Philippines needed to establish a central bank in order to manage its own economy. Once established, the Central Bank took charge of the country's industrial policy through exchange controls. The bank established its autonomy which the government used to fend off remaining American colonial interests and resist pressure from Filipino agro-export industries. When it faced the Filipino manufacturing industry over the government's deficit financing, the bank once again succeeded in withstanding pressure from the private sector and pursued its policy goal of gradual decontrol through its own prerogatives to manage the exchange market. Filipino policymakers in the 1950s were determined to achieve economic decolonization of the country, which until then had maintained its colonial structure.

The second contribution of this study is a deepening of our understanding of the shifting nature of the Philippine state and role of ideas among Filipino policymakers. In fact, the changing nature of the Philippine state demonstrates the significance of ideas, rather than various structural constraints, in understanding the dynamics of Philippine politics. Filipino policymakers emerged in the 1930s despite a consolidation of the colonial economic structure. They adopted the idea to make a central bank that could evolved internationally, away from domestic politico-economic structures. Relying on nationalism, these policymakers countered pressure from American businesses that attempted to impose neocolonial trade relations. Once they established the policy regime sustained by the bank, however, they clashed with each other over differences in policy ideas, namely conservative and Keynesian. When their successors dismantled the existing policy regime in the 1960s, they again clashed with each other over whether they believed in the utility of managed economy or in full-bloom free enterprise. A focus on ideas helps us to understand the dynamic face of Philippine political economy.

Third, these ideas could be shared among policymakers who comprised a particular generation. A certain generation emerged when some of its members succeeded in projecting a new agenda that had a lot to do with the life of the Filipino nation as a whole. This emerges not from the existing institutions or structures but from the critical assessment of them. In other words, a new generation emerged when its members could locate their significance through policy proposals to a certain historical context in which the Filipino people were looking for change in politics.

Interestingly, successful political leaders have emerged with new policy ideas since the Philippine revolution. The revolutionary fought for independence from Spain that had ruled the Philippine Islands for more than two centuries. After the country's new colonial master, the United States, clashed with its militant revolutionaries, Manuel Quezon and Sergio Osmeña challenged the Federal Party, which had collaborated with the Americans. Quezon's generation advanced the agenda for immediate and absolute independence. Although they were accused of entering into a compromise with the American colonial authority, they were different from their predecessors, who had asserted Philippine annexation by the United States, at least for a while. In the 1930s, policymakers like Manuel Roxas and Elpidio Quirino enjoyed Quezon's support, but at the same time they continually searched for opportunities to get out from under the Commonwealth president's shadow. Manuel Roxas's generation, by comparison, ushered in economic ideas about how the government could best manage the national economy and carry out economic decolonization. Early in their careers, Ramon Magsaysay and Diosdado Macapagal enjoyed Quirino's support, even as the Magsaysay directly challenged the leadership of Quirino's generation in the early 1950s. They differed from their seniors in the sense that they had established their careers after independence and lived in the age of the Cold War. Magsaysay first tried to change the orientation of Philippine economic policy, although Cuaderno and other members of the elder generation in his administration finally prevailed over him. Macapagal was the first president who did not have close relations with the earlier generation of Manuel Roxas and Quirino, and so he ultimately dismantled the existing policy regime.

A consideration of the changing generations of political leaders has revealed a different face of power struggles among politicians. While the power struggle has been typically regarded as a clash among politicians without consideration for national interests, the power struggle described in this study has revealed the opportunity for the younger generation to challenge the established generation with innovative policy ideas that attack existing institutions and structures. The political power struggle has never allowed particular groups of policymakers to dominate Philippine politics. Leaders of a particular generation have emerged once they could develop their ideas into particular policies and present themselves as engines for change.

Having said that, there is no need to glorify the attempts of policymakers. What has been revealed is the fact that the individual policymakers profiled in this study bear greater responsibility for the consequences of Philippine politics than do structures or institutions. The nationalism they had in their minds, for instance, faced certain limitations. The generation of Manuel Roxas did not accommodate the voice of peasants, fisherfolk and agricultural or manufacturing laborers seeking various social reforms including land reform, although its members must have been familiar with the recurrent peasant uprisings in their country, especially those of the 1930s or late 1940s. Even self-conscious nationalist politicians like Claro Recto did not take bold actions to carry out land reform, which Recto had considered a Washington agenda. Taking this into consideration, some may say that nationalism as analyzed in this study is indeed elite-oriented. In any case, a contested nature of policymaking has been revealed, which we cannot understand as long as we assume the monolithic interest of the elite exists.

In terms of industrial policy, it is far more critical to see that Filipino policymakers could create an island of state strength but fail to create embedded autonomy for the government. They succeeded in building an autonomous Central Bank as the island of state strength but could not establish cooperative relations with private businesses. These policymakers faced stiff opposition from Filipino entrepreneurs in the export industry, while at the same time they failed to work with domestic industry, highlighting the racial dimension of the Philippine economic structure.

Nonetheless, Filipino policymakers could have gone beyond the structural constraints they faced, as this study reveals. In addition to attacking structural constraints, we should evaluate both the efforts and limitations of those who are striving to change them.

BIBLIOGRAPHY

Private Papers

AMD: Amando M. Dalisay Papers. University of the Philippines.

Cuaderno to Quirino. 1948. "Report on the Negotiations with the International Bank for Reconstruction and Development for a Loan for Waterpower Development and Fertilizer Plant, Nov. 16, 1948". Box No. 1.

EQ: Elpidio Quirino Papers. Filipiniana Heritage Library.

Araneta, Salvador. 1951. "Speech Delivered by the Honorable Salvador Araneta, Administrator of Economic Coordination, Before the Graduating Class of the Jose Rizal College in Mandaluyong, Rizal, on Sunday Evening, 24 June, 1951". File 001, Folder Code B35F2 (Central Bank of the Philippines, 1952), Box No. 35 (Government Financing Institutions: Central Bank of the Philippines).

Balmaceda to Cabinet. 1950. "Memo from Cornelio Balmaceda for the Cabinet. re. Report of priorities in the allocation of foreign exchange, Feb. 15, 1950". File 004, Folder Code B10F1 (Commerce and Industry), Box No. 10 (Department of Commerce and Industry).

Cuaderno to Quirino. 1949a. "Confidential letter from M. Cuaderno to the President re. Devaluation of world currencies, Oct. 10, 1949". File 010, Folder Code B 34F1 (Central Bank of the Philippines [1949]), Box No. 34 (Government Financing Institutions: Central Bank of the Philippines).

Cuaderno to Quirino. 1949b. "Personal and confidential letter from Mike to President, Dec. 30, 1949". File 001, Folder Code B 34F1 (Central Bank of the Philippines, 1949), Box No. 34 (Government Financing Institutions: Central Bank of the Philippines).

Cuaderno to Quirino. 1950. "Top secret letter from Mike to the President. Re. anomalous position in which Ambassador Cowen and the high officials of the National City Bank have been trying to place the Central Bank, Dec. 4, 1950". File 001, Folder Code B 34F3 (Central Bank of the Philippines, 1950), Box No. 34 (Government Financing Institutions: Central Bank of the Philippines).

Cuaderno to the Monetary Board. 1951. "Memorandum for the Monetary Board, Aug. 1, 1951". File 001, Folder Code B35F2 (Central Bank of the

Philippines, 1952), Box No. 35 (Government Financing Institutions: Central Bank of the Philippines).
Dalisay to Quirino. 1948. "Memorandum for Vice President, Proposed Import Control Bill, Apr. 3, 1948". File 004, Folder Code B38F3 (National Economic Council), Box No. 38 (Philippine National Bank, Commission on Election, General Auditing Office, National Economic Council and Surplus Property Commission).
Mapa to Quirino. 1948. "Copy for the Vice President, Jan. 30, 1948". File 002, Folder Code B38F3 (National Economic Council), Box No. 38 (Philippine National Bank, Commission on Election, General Auditing Office, National Economic Council and Surplus Property Commission).
Virata to Dalisay. 1948. "Memorandum to the Executive Secretary NEC, Subject: Import Control Bill, 2 April, 1948". File 004, Folder Code B38F3 (National Economic Council), Box No. 38 (Philippine National Bank, Commission on Election, General Auditing Office, National Economic Council and Surplus Property Commission).

JWJ: J. Weldon Jones Papers, Harry S. Truman Library, United States of America.

Luna, J.L. and B. Soliven. 1937. "Bill No. 2444: Explanatory Note". In Jones to Coy, 1937, "Memorandum for Mr. Coy, Subject, National Assembly Bill, No. 2444, Nov. 4, 1937", Folder (Currency, 1933–37), Box No. 5.
Singson-Encarnacion to Governor-General. 1933. "Memorandum for his Excellency, the Governor-General, Subject: Amendment to the Provisions of Section 1611 of the Administrative Code, 6 July, 1933". Folder (Currency, 1933–37), Box No. 5.
Jones to High Commissioner. 1939. "Memorandum for the High Commissioner, Subject Commonwealth Act No. 458, Nov. 27, 1939". Folder (Currency Reserve), Box No. 5.
Quirino to Governor-General. 1935. "Memorandum for His Excellency, the Governor-General: Subject: Independent Philippine Currency System, Jan. 13, 1935". Folder (Currency, 1933–37), Box No. 5.
Jones to Coy. 1937. "Memorandum for Mr. Coy, Subject, National Assembly Bill. No. 2444, Nov. 4, 1937". Folder (Currency, 1933–37), Box No. 5.
"Excerpt from Quarterly Report of H.C. For quarter ended 30 September, 1937". Folder (Currency, 1933–37), Box No. 5.

MAR: Manual A. Roxas Papers, Main Library, University of the Philippines.

Cuaderno to Alas. 1944. "Memorandum for Minister Alas, 23 June, 1944". Folder (Central Bank of the Philippines, 1944–48), Box No. 7 (Cabinet—Central, 1938–48), Series No. IV (General Miscellany).

Cuaderno to Roxas. 1947. "Memorandum for His Excellency, The President of the Philippines, re: Draft of Report of the Joint Finance Commission, 27 May, 1948". Folder (Joint Philippine American Finance Commission 1947), Box No. 22. Series IV (General Miscellany, 1916–48).

National Economic Council (NEC). 1948. "Report of the Chairman on the Activities of the National Economic Council, Jan. 12, 1948", Folder (National Economic Council 1948), Box No. 29, Series IV, General Miscellany (National Economic Council, 1936–48).

NEC, National Economic Council. Various years. *Annual Report.* Folder (National Economic Council 1948), Box No. 29, Series IV (General Miscellany "National Economic Council, 1936–48).

MLQ: Manuel L. Quezon Papers, National Library, Republic of the Philippines.

Press Conference. 1937. "Press Conference at Malacañang, 6 October, 1937". Box No. 15, Series No. III.

SKR: Sixto Roxas Paper, Digital Archives, Main Library, University of the Philippines.

EO. Executive Order No. 17, "Creating the program implementation agency for carrying out the socio-economic program".

Roxas to the President. "July 31, 1962. Responsibilities of the assistant executive secretary for economic affairs".

Roxas to the President. 30 June 1963. "Dear Mr. President".

Executive Order No. 17, "Creating the program implementation agency for carrying out the socio-economic program".

Macapagal, D. 1962. "The integrated economic program of his excellency President Diosdado Macapagal".

NEC. 1956. "Minutes of the first meeting of the panel of economists held in the NEC conference room on Friday, 18 May 1956".

Romualdez to Roxas. 26 October 1956. "Dear Mr. Roxas".

Fabella to Roxas. 27 May 1957. "Dear Mr. Roxas".

PIA. 1962. "First Progress Report".

PIA. 1963. "Program Implementation Agency Year-End Report for the President ending December 31, 1962".[1]

[1] The author changed the publication year from 1962 to 1963, although the original document is dated 2 January 1962. Otherwise the PIA would have published an annual report for a year when the agency did not yet exist.

Periodicals

ACCJ. American Chamber of Commerce Journal.
CBAR. Central Bank Annual Report. Manila: Bureau of Printing.
CRHR. Congressional Record: House of Representatives. Manila: Bureau of Printing.
FRUS. Foreign Relations of the United States. Washington: US Govt. Printing Office.
MB. Manila Bulletin.
MC. Manila Chronicle.
OG. Official Gazette. Manila: Bureau of Printing.
PFP. Philippines Free Press.
PFR. Philippine Finance Review.
RPC. Report of the Philippine Commission. Washington: US Govt. Printing Office.
Tribune.

Other Sources

Abinales, P.N. 2000. *Making Mindanao: Cotabato and Davao in the Formation of the Philippine Nation-state*. Quezon City: Ateneo de Manila University Press.

———. 2005a. "Progressive-Machine Conflict in Early-Twentieth-Century US Politics and Colonial-State Building in the Philippines". In *The American Colonial State in the Philippines: Global Perspective*, ed. J. Go and A.L. Foster, pp. 148–81. Pasig: Anvil Publishing.

———. 2005b. "Governing the Philippines in the Early 21st Century". In *After the Crisis: Hegemony, Technocracy and Governance in Southeast Asia*, ed. T. Shiraishi and P.N. Abinales, pp. 134–55. Kyoto: Kyoto University Press.

Abinales, P.N. and D.J. Amoroso, 2005. *State and Society in the Philippines*. Lanham: Rowman & Littlefield.

Abrami, R. and R.F. Doner. 2008. "Southeast Asia and the Political Economy of Development". In *Southeast Asia in Political Science*, ed. E.M. Kuhonta, D. Slater, and T. Vu, pp. 227–51. Stanford: Stanford University Press.

Abueva, J.V. 1971. *Ramon Magsaysay: A Political Biography*. Manila: Solidaridad Publishing House.

Adachi, S. 安達誠司. 2006. *Datsu defure no rekishi bunseki: "seisaku regimu" tenkan de tadoru kindai nihon,* 脱デフレの歴史分析–「政策レジーム」転換でたどる近代日本 [Historical Analysis on Reflation: Modern Japan in the Context of "Policy Regime" Shift]. Tokyo: Fujiwara Shoten 藤原書店.

Agoncillo, T.A. 1974. *Filipino Nationalism 1872–1970*. Quezon City: R.P. Garcia.

———. 1996. *The Revolt of the Masses: The Story of Bonifacio and the Katipunan*. Quezon City: University of the Philippines Press. First published 1956.

———. 1997. *Malolos: The Crisis of the Republic*. Quezon City: University of the Philippines Press.

Agoncillo, T.A. and O.M. Alfonso. 1961. *A Short History of the Filipino People.* Quezon City: University of the Philippines Press.

Aguilar, F.V. 2000. "The Republic of Negros". *Philippine Studies* 48, 1: 26–52.

Anderson, B. 1972. *Java in a Time of Revolution: Occupation and Resistance, 1944–1946*. Ithaca: Cornell University Press.

———. 1988. "Cacique Democracy in the Philippines: Origins and Dreams". *New Left Review* 169: 3–31.

———. 1991. *Imagined Communities: Reflections on the Origin and Spread of Nationalism*, rev. ed. London: Verso.

———. 1998. *The Specter of Comparisons: Nationalism, Southeast Asia and the World.* London: Verso.

———. 2006. *Under Three Flags: Anarchism and the Anti-colonial Imagination.* Pasig: Anvil.

Anspach, R. 1969. "Indonesia". In *Underdevelopment and Economic Nationalism in Southeast Asia*, ed. F.H. Golay et al., pp. 111–201. Ithaca: Cornell University Press.

Araneta, S. 1948. "Basic Problems of Philippine Economic Development". *Pacific Affairs* 21: 280–85.

———. 1958. *Christian Democracy for the Philippines: A Re-examination of Attitudes and Views*. Rizal: Araneta University Press.

———. 2000. *Economic Re-examination of the Philippines: A Review of Economic Policies Dictated by Washington*. Manila: Sahara Heritage Foundation.

Aruego, J.M. 1937. *The Framing of the Philippine Constitution*, vol. 2. Manila: University Publishing Co.

Awano, G. 粟野原. 1943. *Senzen hitou ni okeru chuoho ginko setsuritsu mondai,* 戦前比島に於ける中央銀行設立問題 [An Issue of Central Bank Making in the Philippines Before the War]. Tokyo: Research Division, Southern Development Bank.

Balatbat, M.S. 1959. "Protectionism". In *NEPA Silver Anniversary Handbook 1934–1959*, ed. T. Purugganan, pp. 58–61. Manila: National Economic Protectionism Association.

Baldwin, R.E. 1975. *Foreign Trade Regimes and Economic Development: the Philippines*. New York and London: Columbia University Press.

Bangko Sentral ng Pilipinas. 1998. *50 Years of Central Banking in the Philippines.* Manila: Central Bank of the Philippines (hereafter, BSP).

———. 2003. *Money and Banking in the Philippines*. Manila: BSP.

Batalla, E.V.C. 1999. "Zaibatsu Development in the Philippines: The Ayala Model". *Southeast Asian Studies* 37: 18–49.

Beland, D. and R.H. Cox. 2011. "Introduction: Ideas and Politics". In *Ideas and Politics in Social Science Research*, ed. D. Beland and R.H. Cox, pp. 3–20. Oxford: Oxford University Press.

Bello, W., D. Kinley, and E. Ellison. 1982. *Development Debacle: The World Bank in the Philippines*. San Francisco: Institute for Food and Development Policy.

Bello, W. et al. 2004. *The Anti-developmental State: The Political Economy of Permanent Crisis in the Philippines*. Quezon City: Department of Sociology, College of Social Sciences and Philosophy, University of the Philippines Diliman.

Blyth, M. 2002. *Great Transformations: Economic Ideas and Constitutional Change in the Twentieth Century*. New York: Cambridge University Press.

Boncan, C.P. 2000. "The Philippine Assembly 1907–1916". In *Philippine Legislature, 100 Years*, ed. C.P. Pobre, pp. 63–88. Quezon City: Philippine Historical Association.

Brazil, H. 1961. "The Conflict of Political and Economic Pressures in Philippine Economic Development". PhD diss., Ohio State University.

Broad, R. 1988. *Unequal Alliance, 1979–1986: The World Bank, the International Monetary Fund, and the Philippines*. Quezon City: Ateneo de Manila University Press.

Bureau of Banking. Various years. *Annual Report of the Bank Commissioner of the Philippine Islands*. Manila: Bureau of Printing.

Cabildo, J.A. 1953. *Appraisals: Sketches of Outstanding Personalities*. Manila: Bureau of Printing.

Castillo, A.V. 1934. "Economics and Economists in the Philippines". *Tribune*, 13 May.

______. 1935. "Economic Partnership with America". *Tribune*, 3 March.

______. 1943. *Philippine Economic Readjustment under the New Order with Special Reference to the Greater East Asia Co-prosperity Sphere*. Manila: n.p.

______. 1949a. *Principles of Economics*. Manila: University Publishing.

______. 1949b. *Philippine Economics*. Manila: n.p.

Castro, A. 1972. *The Central Bank of the Philippines*. UPSE Discussion Paper 72–13. Quezon City: Institute of Economic Development and Research, School of Economics, University of the Philippines.

______. 1974. *Import Substitution in the Philippines, 1954–1961: A Historical Interpretation*. UPSE Discussion Paper 74–21. Quezon City: Institute of Economic Development and Research, School of Economics, University of the Philippines.

Chu, R.T. 2010. *Chinese and Chinese Mestizos of Manila: Family, Identity, and Culture, 1860s–1930s*. Mandaluyong: Anvil.

Comelec, Commission on Elections. n.d. *Consolidated List of Candidates for President, Vice-President, Senators and Members of the House of Representatives Provincial/City Officials with their Perspective Votes and Party Affiliations 1946–1965 Elections*. Manila: Bureau of Printing.

Constantino, R. 1969. *The Making of a Filipino: A Story of Philippine Colonial Politics*. Quezon City: Renato Constantino.

Constantino, R. and L.R. Constantino. 1975. *The Philippines: A Past Revisited*. Quezon City: The Foundation for Nationalist Studies.

———. 1978. *The Philippines: The Continuing Past*. Quezon City: The Foundation for Nationalist Studies.

Corpuz, O.D. 1957. *The Bureaucracy in the Philippines*. Manila: Institute of Public Administration, University of the Philippines.

———. 1989. *The Roots of the Filipino Nation*. 2 vols. Quezon City: Aklahi Foundation.

———. 1997. *An Economic History of the Philippines*. Quezon City: University of the Philippines Press.

Cornejo, M.R. 1939. *Cornejo's Commonwealth Directory of the Philippines*. Manila: M.R. Cornejo.

Christobal, A. and R. Christobal. 1961. *Filipino First: An Approach to the "Filipino First" Policy and Selected Readings*. Manila: n.p.

Cuaderno, M.P. 1937. *The Framing of the Constitution of the Philippines*. Manila: Philippine Education.

———. 1949. *Central Bank of the Philippines: A Monograph*. Manila: Central Bank of the Philippines.

———. 1952. "The Bell Trade Act and the Philippine Economy". *Pacific Affairs* 25: 323–33.

———. 1955. *Guideposts to Economic Stability and Progress: A Selection of the Speeches and Articles of Miguel Cuaderno*. Manila: Central Bank of the Philippines.

———. 1964. *Problems of Economic Development (The Philippines: A Case Study)*. Manila: n.p.

Cullather, N. 1992. "The United States, American Business, and the Origins of the Philippine Central Bank". *Bulletin of the American Historical Collection* 20 (4): 80–99.

———. 1994. *Illusions of Influence: The Political Economy of United States–Philippines Relations, 1946–1960*. Stanford: Stanford University Press.

Cullinane, M. 2003. *Ilustrado Politics: Filipino Elite Responses to American Rule, 1898–1908*. Quezon City: Ateneo de Manila University Press.

Dacy, D.C. 1986. *Foreign Aid, War and Economic Development: South Vietnam, 1955–1975*. Cambridge: Cambridge University Press.

Doner, R. and A. Ramsay. 1997. "Competitive Clientelism and Economic Governance: The Case of Thailand". In *Business and the State in Developing Countries*, ed. S. Maxfield and B.R. Schneider, pp. 237–76. Ithaca: Cornell University Press.

de Dios, E.S. 2002. *Welfare and Nationalism in the 1935 Philippine Constitution*. UPSE Discussion Paper 2002–03. Quezon City: School of Economics, University of the Philippines.

de Dios, E.S. and P.D. Hutchcroft. 2003. "Political Economy". In *The Philippine Economy: Development, Policies, and Changes*, ed. A. Balisacan and H. Hill, pp. 45–73. Quezon City: Ateneo de Manila University Press.

Doeppers, D.F. 1984. *Manila, 1900–1941: Social Change in a Late Colonial Metropolis*. Monograph Series No. 27. New Haven: Yale University Southeast Asia Studies.

Doner, R.F., B.K. Ritchie and D. Slater. 2005. "Systemic Vulnerability and the Origin of Developmental States: Northeast and Southeast Asia in Comparative Perspective". *International Organization* 59: 327–61.

Doronila, A. 1992. *The State, Economic Transformation, and Political Change in the Philippines, 1946–1972*. Singapore: Oxford University Press.

Dubsky, R. 1993. *Technocracy and Development in the Philippines*, Quezon City: University of the Philippines Press.

Eckstein, H. 1975. "Case Study and Theory in Political Science". In *Handbook of Political Science*, vol. 7, ed. F.I. Greenstein and N.W. Polsby, pp. 79–138. Reading: Addison-Wesley.

Eichengreen, B. 1992. *Golden Fetters: The Gold Standard and the Great Depression*. New York: Oxford University Press.

Eisner, M.A. 1993. *Regulatory Politics in Transition*. Baltimore: John Hopkins University Press.

Encarnacion-Tadem, T.S. 2005. "The Philippine Technocracy and US-led Capitalism". In *After the Crisis: Hegemony, Technocracy and Governance in Southeast Asia*, ed. T. Shiraishi and P.N. Abinales, pp. 85–104. Kyoto: Kyoto University Press.

Esho, H. 絵所秀紀. 1997. *Kaihatsu no Seiji Keizai Gaku*, 開発の政治経済学 [The Political Economy of Development]. Tokyo: Nihon Hyoronsha.

Espinosa-Robles, R. 1990. *To Fight without End: The Story of a Misunderstood President*. Makati: Ayala Foundation.

Evans, P. 1995. *Embedded Autonomy: States and Industrial Transformation*. Princeton: Princeton University Press.

Evans, P., B.D. Rueschemeyer and T. Skocpol, eds. 1985. *Bringing the State Back In*. Cambridge: Cambridge University Press.

Fegan, Brian. 1982. "The Social History of a Central Luzon Barrio". In *Philippine Social History: Global Trade and Local Transformations*, ed. Alfred W. McCoy and Ed. C. de Jesus, pp. 91–129. Quezon City: Ateneo de Manila University Press.

Flaviano, D.F. 1950. *Business Leaders and Executives: Inspiring Biographies of Men and Women Who Became Successful*. Manila: Fal Service and Trading.

Forbes, W.C. 1928. *The Philippine Islands*. Boston: Houghton Mifflin.

Friend, T. 1963. "The Philippine Sugar Industry and the Politics of Independence, 1929–1935". *The Journal of Asian Studies* 22: 179–92.

______. 1965. *Between Two Empires: The Ordeal of the Philippines, 1929–1946*. New Haven: Yale University Press.

Fukushima, S. 福島慎太郎, ed. 1969. *Hitou nikki: Murata Shozo ikou*, 比島日記—村田省蔵遺稿 [Diary in the Philippines: Remains of Shozo Murata]. Tokyo: Hara Shobo.

Galang, Z.M. 1932. *Leaders of the Philippines: Inspiring Biographies of Successful Men and Women of the Philippines*. Manila: National Publishing.

Garcia C.P. 1959. "Message". In *NEPA Silver Anniversary Handbook 1934–1959*, ed. T. Purugganan, n.p. Manila: National Economic Protectionism Association.

———. 1961. "The Filipino First Movement". In *Filipino First: An Approach to the "Filipino First" Policy and Selected Readings*, ed. A. Cristobal and R. Cristobal, pp. 36–44. Manila, n.p.

———. 2004. "Inaugural Address". In *So Help Us God: The Presidents of the Philippines and Their Inaugural Addresses*, ed. E. Malaya and J. Malaya, pp. 188–95. Manila: Anvil.

Giesecke, L.F. 1987. *History of American Economic Policy in the Philippines during the American Colonial Period 1900–1935*. New York and London: Garland.

Gleeck, L.E. 1977. *The Manila Americans (1901–1964)*. Manila: Carmelo & Bauermann.

———. 1993. *The Third Republic 1946–1972*. Quezon City: New Day Publishers.

Go, J. 2005. "Introduction: Global Perspectives on the U.S. Colonial State in the Philippines". In *The American Colonial State in the Philippines: Global Perspectives*, ed. J. Go and A.L. Foster, pp. 1–42. Pasig: Anvil Publishing.

———. 2008. *American Empire and the Politics of Meaning: Elite Political Cultures in the Philippines and Puerto Rico during U.S. Colonialism*. Durham: Duke University Press.

Golay, F.H. 1956. "Philippine Monetary Policy Debate". *Pacific Affairs* 29: 253–64.

———. 1961. *The Philippines: Public Policy and National Economic Development*. Ithaca: Cornell University Press.

———. 1969. "The Philippines". In *Underdevelopment and Economic Nationalism in Southeast Asia*, ed. F.H. Golay et al., pp. 21–109. Ithaca: Cornell University Press.

———. 1997. *Face of Empire: United States–Philippine Relations, 1898–1946*. Quezon City: Ateneo de Manila University Press.

Golay, F.H. et al. 1969. *Underdevelopment and Economic Nationalism in Southeast Asia*. Ithaca: Cornell University Press.

Green, J.C. 2001. "The Politics of Ideas: Introduction". In *The Politics of Ideas: Intellectual Challenges Facing the American Political Parties*, ed. J.K. White and J.C. Green, pp. 1–10. New York: State University of New York Press.

Gwekoh, S.H. 1949. *Elpidio Quirino: The Barrio School Teacher Who became President*. Manila: Philippine Education Foundation.

———. 1962. *Diosdado Macapagal: Triumph over Poverty: The Common Man from Pampanga Who Became the President of the Philippines*. Manila: G & G Enterprises.

Hansen, A.H. 1953. *A Guide to Keynes*. New York: McGraw Hill.

Hartendorp, A.V.H. 1958. *History of Industry and Trade of the Philippines*. Manila: American Chamber of Commerce of the Philippines.

______. 1961. *History of Industry and Trade of the Philippines: The Magsaysay Administration, a Critical Assessment*. Manila: Philippine Education Company.

Hamilton-Hart, N. 2002. *Asian States, Asian Bankers: Central Banking in Southeast Asia*. Ithaca: Cornell University Press.

______. 2012. *Hard Interests, Soft Illusions: Southeast Asia and American Power*. Ithaca: Cornell University Press.

Hau, C.S. 2000. *Necessary Fictions: Philippine Literature and the Nation, 1946–1980*. Quezon City: Ateneo de Manila University Press.

Hawes, G. 1987. *The Philippine State and the Marcos Regime: The Politics of Export*. Ithaca: Cornell University Press.

Hayden, J.R. 1942. *The Philippines: A Study in National Development*. New York: Macmillan.

Hicken, A. 2009. *Building Party Systems in Developing Democracies*. Cambridge: Cambridge University Press.

Hidalgo, A.A. 2000. *The Life, Times and Thoughts of Don Pio Pedrosa*. Quezon City: Milflores.

Hori, Y. 堀芳江. 1997. "Filipin no eliito kozo henka ni okeru kokka no yakuwari: 1950 nendai no shinko bijinesu eliito wo chushin to shite, フィリピンのエリート構造変化における国家の役割—1950年代の新興ビジネス・エリートを中心として [The Change of Elite Structure and the State in the Philippines: New Business Elite in the 1950s]". *Kokusaigaku Ronshu* 国際学論集 [*The Journal of International Studies*] 38: 29–51.

______. 1997. "1950 nendai Filipin ni okeru tekunokurato shiron 1950, 年代におけるテクノクラート試論 [Some Research Notes on Filipino Technocrats in the 1950s]". *Jyochi Ajia Gaku* 上智アジア学 [*Journal of Sophia Asian Studies*] 15: 259–72.

House of Representatives. 1965. *Constitutional Convention Record*, vol. 11, *Committee Reports*. Manila: Bureau of Printing.

Hutchcroft, P.D. 1998. *Booty Capitalism: The Politics of Banking in the Philippines*. Quezon City: Ateneo de Manila University Press.

______. 2011. "Reflections on a Reverse Image: South Korea under Park Chung Hee and the Philippines under Ferdinand Marcos". In *The Park Chung Hee Era: The Transformation of South Korea*, ed. B.K. Kim and E.F. Vogel, pp. 542–72. Cambridge: Harvard University Press.

Hutchcroft, P.D. and J. Rocamora. 2003. "Strong Demands and Weak Institutions: The Origins and Evolution of the Democratic Deficit in the Philippines". *Journal of East Asian Studies* 3: 259–92.

Ikehata, S. 池端雪浦. 2002. "Filipin kakumei: Visaya no shiten kara, フィリピン革命—ヴィサヤの視点から [The Philippine Revolution: The Visayan Perspective]". In *Tounan Ajia shi 7: Shokuminchi teikou undou to nashonarizumu no tenkai* 東南アジア史7南植民地抵抗運動とナショナリズムの展開 [*Southeast Asian History*, vol. 7: *Anti-Colonial Movements and Emergence of Nationalism*], ed. S. Ikehata, pp. 111–34. Tokyo: Iwanami Shoten.

Ileto, R.C. 1979. *Pasyon and Revolution: Popular Movements in the Philippines, 1840–1910*. Quezon City: Ateneo de Manila University Press.

———. 2001. "Orientalism and the Study of Philippine Politics". *Philippine Political Science Journal* 22 (45): 1–32.

———. 2002. "On Sidel's Response and Bossism in the Philippines". *Philippine Political Science Journal* 23 (46): 151–74.

Jacinto, G.A. et al., eds. 1957. *Tableau: Encyclopedia of Distinguished Personalities in the Philippines*. Manila: National Souvenir Publications.

Jamias, C. 1962. *The University of the Philippines: The First Half Century*. Quezon City: University of the Philippines.

Jimenez, J.D. 1996. "The Pre-war history of the Philippine Bar Association". *Bulletin of the American Historical Collection* 95 (2): 67–70.

Jenkins, S. 1985. *American Economic Policy toward the Philippines*, repr. ed. Mandaluyong: Cacho Hermanos.

Johnson, C.A. 1982. *MITI and the Japanese Miracle: The Growth of Industrial Policy, 1925–1975*. Stanford: Stanford University Press.

JPAFC, Joint Philippine-American Finance Commission. 1947. *Report and Recommendations of the Joint Philippine-American Finance Commission*. Washington: US Government Printing Office.

JPCPA, Joint Preparatory Committee on Philippine Affairs. 1938. *Report of May 20, 1938*, vol. I. Washington: US Government Printing Office.

Jose, R.T. 2003. "Test of Wills: Diplomacy between Japan and the Philippines in the 1930s". In *Philippines-Japan Relations*, ed. S. Ikehata and L.N. Yu-Jose, pp. 185–222. Quezon City: Ateneo de Manila University Press.

Kang, D.C. 2002. *Crony Capitalism: Corruption and Development in South Korea and the Philippines*. Cambridge: Cambridge University Press.

Kasuya, Y. 2008. *Presidential Bandwagon: Parties and Party Systems in the Philippines*. Tokyo: Keio University Press.

Kerkvliet, B.J. 1990. *Everyday Politics in the Philippines: Class and Status Relations in a Central Luzon Village*. Berkeley: University of California Press.

———. 1995. "Toward a More Comprehensive Analysis of Philippine Politics: Beyond the Patron-Client Fractional Framework". *Journal of Southeast Asian Studies* 26: 401–9.

———. 2002. *The Huk Rebellion: A Study of Peasant Revolt in the Philippines*, rep. ed. Lanham: Rowman & Littlefield.

Kitschelt, H. 2000. "Linkage between Citizens and Politicians in Democratic Politics". *Comparative Political Studies* 33: 845–79.

Kuhonta, E.M. 2008. "Studying States in Southeast Asia". In *Southeast Asia in Political Science*, ed. E.M. Kuhonta, D. Slater, and T. Vu, pp. 30–54. Stanford: Stanford University Press.

Kume, I. 久米郁男. 2013. *Gen'in wo suiron suru: Seijigaku bunseki houhouron no susume,* 原因を推論する—政治学的分析のすゝめ [Causal Inference and Political Analysis]. Tokyo: Yuhikaku.

Kusaka, W. 日下渉. 2013. *Han-shimin no seijigaku,* 反市民の政治学 [Anti-civic Politics]. Tokyo: Housei University Press.

Lansdale, E.G. 1972. *In the Midst of Wars: An American's Mission to Southeast Asia*. New York: Harper & Row.

Lande, C. 1965. *Leaders, Factions and Parties: The Structure of Philippine Politics*. Monograph Series No. 6. New Haven: Southeast Asian Studies, Yale University.

Larkin, J.A. 2001. *Sugar and the Origins of Modern Philippine Society*. Quezon City: New Day Publishers.

Legarda, B.J. 1999. *After the Galleons: Foreign Trade, Economic Change and Entrepreneurship in the Nineteenth-Century Philippines*. Quezon City: Ateneo de Manila University Press.

Liang, D. 1971. *Philippine Parties and Politics: A Historical Study of National Experience in Democracy*, new ed. San Francisco: Gladstone Company.

Lichauco, M.P. 1952. *Roxas: The Story of a Great Filipino and of the Political Era in Which He Lived*. Manila: n.p.

Lichauco, A. 1988. *Nationalist Economics: History, Theory, and Practice*. Quezon City: Institute for Rural Industrialization.

Llorente, A. 1935. "Higher Instruction in Economics". *Tribune*, 6 January.

Locsin, J.C. 1960. "The National Economic Council and Economic Planning". In *Planning for Progress: The Administration of Economic Planning in the Philippines*, ed. R.S. Milne, pp. 147–60. Manila: Institute of Public Administration and Institute of Economic Development and Research, University of the Philippines.

Locsin, T.M. 1951. "Cause for Optimism?" *Philippines Free Press*, 17 March.

———. 1956a. "Road to Ruin". *Philippines Free Press*, 7 January.

———. 1956b. "The National Emergency: Slow but Sure?" *Philippines Free Press*, 14 January.

———. 1960. "Nationalism so Far: The Economic, Political, Cultural Fronts". *Philippines Free Press*, 27 February.

Love, J.L. 1980. "Raul Prebisch and the Origins of the Doctrine of Unequal Exchange". *Latin American Research Review* 15 (3): 45–72.

Lowi, T.J. 1964. "Review: American Business, Public Policy, Case-Studies, and Political Theory". *World Politics* 16: 677–715.

Lumba, A.E. 2008. "Materializing the Central Bank of the Philippines: The Uncanny Postwar History of Money and Modernity". Paper presented to the 2008 International Studies Association Annual Convention.

———. 2013. "Monetary Authorities: Market Knowledge and Imperial Government in the Colonial Philippines, 1892–1942". PhD diss., University of Washington.

Macapagal, D. 1968. *A Stone for the Edifice: Memories of a President*. Quezon City: Mac Publishing House.

MacIsaac, S. 1993. "Nationalists, Expansionists and Internationalists: American Interests and the Struggle for National Economic Development in the Philippines, 1937–1950". PhD diss., University of Washington.

Malaya, E. and J. Malaya, eds. 2004. *So Help Us God: The Presidents of the Philippines and Their Inaugural Addresses*. Manila: Anvil Publishing.

Martin, R.P. 1959. "An Ally Angry at U.S.". *U.S. News & World Report*, 27 February 1959, pp. 68–70.

Maxfield, S. and J.H. Nolt. 1990. "Protectionism and the Internationalization of Capital: US Sponsorship of Import Substitution Industrialization in the Philippines, Turkey and Argentina". *International Studies Quarterly* 34: 49–81.

May, G.A. 1980. *Social Engineering in the Philippines: The Aims, Execution, and Impact of American Colonial Policy, 1900–1913*. Quezon City: New Day Publishers.

McCoy, Alfred. 1981. "The Philippines: Independence without Decolonization". In *Asia: The Winning of Independence*, ed. J. Robin, pp. 23–65. London: Macmillan Press.

———. 1982. "A Queen Dies Slowly: The Rise and Decline of Iloilo City". In *Philippine Social History: Global Trend and Local Transformations*, ed. A.W. McCoy and Ed. C. de Jesus, pp. 297–358. Quezon City: Ateneo de Manila University Press.

———. 1988. "Quezon's Commonwealth: The Emergence of Philippine Authoritarianism". In *Philippine Colonial Democracy*, Monograph Series No. 32, ed. R.R. Paredes, pp. 114–60. New Haven: Yale Center for International and Area Studies.

———. 1994a. "'An Anarchy of Families': The Historiography of State and Family in the Philippines". In *An Anarchy of Families: State and Society in the Philippines*, ed. A.W. McCoy, pp. 1–32. Quezon City: Ateneo de Manila University Press.

———. 1994b. "Rent-Seeking Families and the Philippine State: A History of the Lopez Family". In *An Anarchy of Families: State and Family in the Philippines*, ed. A. McCoy, pp. 429–536. Quezon City: Ateneo de Manila University Press.

———, ed. 1994. *An Anarchy of Families: State and Society in the Philippines*. Quezon City: Ateneo de Manila University Press.

Meadows, M. 1962. "Philippine Political Parties and the 1961 Election". *Pacific Affairs* 35: 261–74.

Mendoza, M.P. 2013. "Binding the Islands Air Transport and State Capacity Building in the Philippines, 1946 to 1961". *Philippine Studies: Historical and Ethnographic Viewpoints* 61: 77–104.

Mikamo, S. 2005. "The Politics of Economic Reform in the Philippines: The Case of Banking Sector Reform between 1986 and 1995". PhD diss., University of London.

Mojares, R.B. 1999. *The War against the Americans: Resistance and Collaboration in Cebu: 1899–1906*. Quezon City: Ateneo de Manila University Press.

———. 2006. *Brains of the Nation: Pedro Paterno, T.H. Pardo de Tavera, Isabelo de los Reyes and the Production of Modern Knowledge*. Quezon City: Ateneo de Manila University Press.

Montinola, G.R. 1999. "Parties and Accountability in the Philippines". *Journal of Democracy* 10: 126–40.

MPO, Malacañang Press Office. 1962. *Fair and Equal Opportunity for All, New Hope for the Common Man: Speeches and Statements of President Diosdado Macapagal*. Manila: Bureau of Printing.

Nagano, Y. 永野善子. 1986. *Firipin keizaishi kenkyu: Togyo-shihon to jinushisei,* フィリピン経済史研究—糖業資本と地主制 [A Study of the Philippine Economic History: Capitalism and Haciendas in the Sugar Industry]. Tokyo: Keiso Shobo.

———. 2003. *Firipin ginko shi kenkyu: Shokuminchi taisei to kin'y,* フィリピン銀行史研究—植民地体制と金融 [A Study of Philippine Banking History: Colonial State and Finance]. Tokyo: Ochanomizu Shobo.

———. 2010. "The Philippine Currency System during the American Colonial Period: Transformation from the Gold Exchange Standard to the Dollar Exchange Standard". *International Journal of Asian Studies* 7: 29–50.

———. 2015. *State and Finance in the Philippines, 1898–1941: The Mismanagement of an American Colony*. Quezon City: Ateneo de Manila University Press.

Nakano, S. 中野聡. 1997. *Filipin dokuritsu mondaishi: Dokuritsuhou mondai wo megurru beihi kankeishi no kenky,* フィリピン独立問題史—独立法問題をめぐる米比関係史の研究 (1929 題をめ年) [History of Philippine Independence: A Study on the US Philippine Relations Regarding the Independence Law 1929–1946]. Tokyo: Ryukei Shosha.

———. 2007. *Rekishi keiken to shite no America Teikoku: Beihi Kankeishi no Gunzo,* 歴史経験としてのアメリカ帝国—米比関係史の群像 [American Empire as Historical Experience: History of US-Philippine Relations]. Tokyo: Iwanami Shoten.

NHI, National Historical Institute. 1990. *The Memoirs of Elpidio Quirino*. Manila: National Historical Institute.

National Assembly. 1943. "Act No. 60: An Act Creating the Central Bank of the Philippines". In *National Assembly Year Book*, pp. 132–8. Manila: n.p.

———. 1974. "Filipino First Policy". In *Filipino Nationalism 1872–1970*, ed. T. Agoncillo, pp. 370–2. Quezon City: R.P. Garcia Publishing.

Ocampo, A.R. 2000. "The Malolos Congress". In *Philippine Legislature: 100 Years*, ed. C.P. Pobre, pp. 1–26. Quezon City: Philippine Historical Association.

Ocampo, R.B. 1971. "Technocrats and Planning: Sketch and Exploration". *Philippine Journal of Public Administration* 15: 31–64.

Okada, T. 岡田泰平. 2014. *"Onkei no ronri" to shokuminchi: America shokuminchiki filipin no kyoiku to sono isei* 恩恵の論理」と植民地—アメリカ植民地期フィリピンの教育とその遺制 [Benevolent Assimilation and Colony: Education and its Legacy During the American Colonial Period]. Tokyo: Housei University Press.

Olivera, B.T. 1981. *Jose Yulo: The Selfless Statesman*. Manila: The University Press–Jorge Vargas Filipiniana Research Center.

Orosa, S.L. 1988. *Banking, Anyone?: A Retired Banker Reminisces*. Manila: J.V. Development.

Palma, R. 1985. "The Menace of Economic Efficiency". In *Thinking for Ourselves: A Representative Collection of Filipino Essays*, repr. ed., ed. V. Hilario and E. Quirino, pp. 371–82. Mandaluyong: Cacho Hermanos.

Paredes, R.R., ed. 1988. *Philippine Colonial Democracy*. Monograph Series No. 32. New Haven: Yale University Southeast Asia Studies.

Payer, C.A. 1973. "Exchange Controls and National Capitalism: The Philippines Experience. *Journal of Contemporary Asia* 3: 54–69.

Philippine Assembly. 1908. *Official Directory*. Manila: Bureau of Printing.

Philippine Economic Association. 1933. *The Economics of the Hare-Hawes-Cutting Act: An Analysis*. Manila: Herald.

______. 1934. *Economic Problems of the Philippines*. Manila: Bureau of Publishing.

Pierson, P. 2004. *Politics in Time: History, Institutions, and Social Analysis*. Princeton: Princeton University Press.

______. 2006. "Public Policies as Institutions". In *Rethinking Political Institutions: The Art of the State*, ed. I. Shapiro, S. Skowronek and D. Galvin, pp. 114–31. Cambridge: Cambridge University Press.

Perez-Stable, M. 1993. *The Cuban Revolution: Origins, Course, and Legacy*. Oxford: Oxford University Press.

Polanyi, K. 1957. *The Great Transformation*. Boston: Beacon Press.

Purugganan, T., ed. 1959. *NEPA Silver Anniversary Handbook, 1934–1959*. Manila: National Economic Protectionism Association.

Puyat, G. 1960. "Congress and Economic Planning". In *Planning for Progress: The Administration of Economic Planning in the Philippines*, ed. R.S. Milne, pp. 62–82. Manila: Institute of Public Administration and Institute of Economic Development and Research, University of the Philippines.

Putzel, J. 1992. *A Captive Land: The Politics of Agrarian Reform in the Philippines*. New York: Monthly Review Press.

Quirino, C. 1987. *Apo Lakay: The Bibliography of President Elpidio Quirino of the Philippines*. Manila: Total Book World.

Quirino, E. 1955. *The Quirino Way: Collection of Speeches and Address of Elpidio Quirino*. n.p.

Quimpo, N.G. 2008. *Contested Democracy and the Left in the Philippines after Marcos*. New Haven: Yale University Southeast Asia Studies.

Raquiza, A.R. 2012. *State Structure, Policy Formation, and Economic Development in Southeast Asia*. New York: Routledge.

Reyes-McMurray, M. 1998. "The First Filipino Private Bank". In *Kasaysayan: The Story of the Filipino People*, vol. 6: *Under Stars and Stripes*, ed. M.C. Guerrero, pp. 92–3. Hong Kong: Asian Publishing.

Reynolds, Q. and G. Bocca. 1965. *Macapagal: The Incorruptible*. New York: David McKay.

Risse-Kappen, T. 1994. "Ideas Do Not Float Freely: Transnational Coalitions, Domestic Structures, and the End of the Cold War". *International Organization* 48: 185–214.

Rivera, T. 1994. *Landlords and Capitalists: Class, Family, and State in Philippine Manufacturing*. Quezon City: University of the Philippines Press.

Roces, M.N. 1990. "Kinship Politics in Postwar Philippines: The Lopez Family, 1945–1989". PhD diss., University of Michigan.

Rodriguez, F.C. 1967. *Our Struggle for Power*. Manila: Phoenix Press.

Romero, J.E. 2008. *Not So Long Ago: A Chronicle of Life, Times, and Contemporaries*. Quezon City: Central Books.

Romero, J.V. 2008. *Postwar Political Economy: From Predatory to an Intermediate State towards Take-Off*, vol. 1. Quezon City: Central Book Supply, Inc.

Roxas, M.A. 1936. *Philippine Independence May Succeed without Free Trade*. Manila: n.p.

———. 1947. *The Problems of Philippine Rehabilitation and Trade Relations*. Manila: Bureau of Printing.

———. 1985. "Turning Point". In *Thinking for Ourselves: A Representative Collection of Filipino Essays*, repr. ed., ed. V. Hilario and E. Quirino, pp. 392–402. Mandaluyong: Cacho Hermanos.

———. 2004. "Inaugural Address (28 May 1946)". In *So Help Us God: The Presidents of the Philippines and their Inaugural Addresses*, ed. J.E. Malaya and J.E. Malaya, pp. 128–38. Manila: Anvil Publishing.

Roxas, S.K. 1957. "A Multiple Exchange Rate System for the Philippines". Memorandum submitted to the Senate Committee on Banks, Corporations and Franchises. Mimeograph.

———. 1958a. "The Austerity and Our Foreign Exchange Problems: Introductory Note". In *Christian Democracy for the Philippines: A Re-examination of Attitudes and Views*, ed. S. Araneta, pp. 327–33. Rizal: Araneta University Press.

———. 1958b. "Economic Ideologies and Theories in the Current Philippine Scene". *Comment: A Quarterly Devoted to Philippine Affairs* 5: 3–13.

———. 1962. "Exchange Decontrol in the Philippines". *Philippine Studies* 10: 183–205.

———. 1965. "Lessons from Philippine Experience in Development Planning". *The Philippine Economic Journal* 4: 355–402.

———. 2000. *Jueten Gate: The Parable of a Nation in Crisis*. Manila: Bancom Foundation.

———. 2013. *Bancom Memoirs: With a Compendium of Recollections and Tribute Pieces from Bancom Alumni and Friends*. PLDT Smart Foundation and Bancom Alumni.

Saulo, A.B. 1990. *Communism in the Philippines*. Quezon City: Ateneo de Manila University Press.

Scott, W.H. 1986. *Ilocano Responses to American Aggression, 1900–1901*. Quezon City: New Day.

———. 1982. *Cracks in the Parchment Curtain: And Other Essays in Philippine History*. Quezon City: New Day.

Schumacher, J.N. 1981. *Revolutionary Clergy: The Filipino Clergy and the Nationalist Movement, 1850–1903*. Quezon City: Ateneo de Manila University Press.

———. 1991. *The Making of a Nation: Essays on Nineteenth Century Filipino Nationalism*. Quezon City: Ateneo de Manila University Press.

———. 1997. *The Propaganda Movement, 1880–1895: The Creators of a Filipino Consciousness, the Makers of Revolution*, rev. ed. Quezon City: Ateneo de Manila University Press.

Serrano, C.P. 2005. *Beating the Odds: The Life, the Times, and the Politics of Diosdado P. Macapagal*. Quezon City: New Day.

Schirmer, D.B. and S.R. Shalom. 1987. *The Philippines Readers: A History of Colonialism, Neocolonialism, Dictatorship, and Resistance*. Cambridge: South End Press.

Sicat, G.P. 2002. *Philippine Economic Nationalism*. UPSE Discussion Paper No. 2002-01. Quezon City: School of Economics, University of the Philippines.

Sidel, J.T. 1999. *Capital, Coercion, and Crime: Bossism in the Philippines*. Stanford: Stanford University Press.

———. 2012. "The Fate of Nationalism in the New States: Southeast Asia in Comparative Historical Perspective". *Comparative Studies in Society and History* 54: 114–44.

Skocpol, T. and K. Finegold. 1982. "State Capacity and Economic Intervention in the Early New Deal". *Political Science Quarterly* 97: 255–78.

Skowronek, S. 1982. *Building a New American State: The Expansion of National Administrative Capacities, 1877–1920*. Cambridge: Cambridge University Press.

Smith, J.B. 1976. *Portrait of a Cold Warrior: Second Thought of a Top CIA Agent*. New York: Baltimore Books.

Soberano, J.D. 1963. "The Fiscal Policy Controversy". In *Patterns in Decision-Making: Case Studies in Philippine Public Administration*, ed. R. de Guzman, pp. 321–84. Manila: Graduate School of Public Administration, University of the Philippines.

———. 1961. "Economic Planning in the Philippines: Ecology, Politics and Administration". PhD diss., University of Michigan.

Soliven, M.V. 1962. "The Elections 1961". *Philippine Studies* 10: 3–31.

Stauffer, R.B. 1966. "Philippine Legislators and Their Changing Universe". *The Journal of Politics* 28: 556–97.

Stine, L.C. 1966. "The Economic Policies of the Commonwealth Government of the Philippine Islands". *Journal of East Asiatic Studies* 10 (March): 1–136.

Storer, J.A. and T.L. de Guzman. 1960. "Philippine Economic Planning and Progress 1945–1960". In *Planning for Progress: The Administration of Economic Planning in the Philippines*, ed. R.S. Milne, pp. 5–37. Quezon City: University of the Philippines.

Subramanian, V.D. 1980. "Export Interests in the Philippines: A Study in Political Dynamics". PhD diss., University of the Philippines.

Sudo, I. 須藤功. 2008. *Sengo America tsuuka kinyu seisaku no keisei: Nyu dylu kara acodo he,* 戦後アメリカ通貨金融政策の形成—ニューディールから「アコード」へ [Shaping of the Post-war Federal Reserve Policy: From the New Deal to the Accord]. Nagoya: Nagoya University Press.

Suehiro, A. 2005. "Who Manages and Who Damages the Thai Economy? The Technocracy, the Four Core Agencies System and Dr. Puey's Networks". In *After the Crisis: Hegemony, Technocracy and Governance in Southeast Asia*, ed. T. Shiraishi and P.N. Abinales, pp. 15–68. Kyoto: Kyoto University Press.

Tadokoro, M. 田所昌幸. 2001. *Amerika wo koeta doru: Kin'yu gurohbalizeshion to Tsuuka Gaiko,* 「アメリカ」を超えたドル—金融グローバリゼーションと通貨外交 [The Dollars go Beyond "America": Financial Globalization and Currency Diplomacy]. Tokyo: Chuokoron-Shinsha.

Takagi, Y. 2008. "Politics of the Great Debate in the 1950s: Revisiting Economic Decolonization in the Philippines". *Kasarinlan: Philippine Journal of Third World Studies* 23 (1): 91–114.

———. 高木佑輔. 2009. "Seitou shisutemu to reisen no kokunaika, 1946–1948 nen: Filipin ni okeru nidaiseitou kan no tairitsu to kyochou, 政党システムと冷戦の国内化、1946–1948年—フィリピンにおける二大政党間の対立と協調 [The Emergence of Political Cleavage in the Philippines: The Changing Party System and the Cold War in the Post-independence Era, 1946–1948]". *Aziya Kenkyu* アジア研究 [*Asian Studies*] 55 (3): 18–34.

———. 2014a. "Beyond the Colonial State: Central Bank Making as State Building in the 1930s". *Southeast Asian Studies* 3: 85–117.

———. 2014b "The 'Filipino First' Policy and the Central Bank, 1958–1961: Island of State Strength and Economic Decolonization". *Philippine Studies: Historical and Ethnographic Viewpoints* 62: 233–61.

Ty, L.O. 1948. "'Mike' Cuaderno". *Philippines Free Press*, 5 June.

———. 1955. "The Case of Filemon Rodriguez: Or Should Government Official Engaged [*sic*] in Private Business?" *Philippines Free Press*, 20 April.

———. 1957. "Dangers We Face". *Philippines Free Press*, 25 May.

———. 1960. "Dr. Jose C. Locsin: Father of the Filipino First Policy". *Philippines Free Press*, 6 February.

Uchiyama, F. 内山史子. 1999. "Filipin ni okeru kokumin kokka no keisei: 1934 nen kenpou seitei gikai ni okeru sono houkousei, フィリピンにおける国民国家の形成—1934年憲法制定議会におけるその方向性 [Nation Building in the Philippines: A Study of the Directions and Problems of Nation Building Apparent in Discussions at the Constitutional Convention of 1934]". *Aziya Africa Gengo Bunka Kenkyu* アジアアフリカ言語文化研究 [*Journal of Asian and African Studies*] 57: 195–220.

Valdepeñas, V.B. 1969. "Development Protection in the Growth and Structure of Philippine Manufactures, 1946–1967". PhD diss., Cornell University.

———. 2003. "Central Banking in Historical Perspective". In *Perspectives from Bangko Sentral ng Pilipinas: Money and Banking in the Philippines*, ed. Bangko Sentral ng Pilipinas, pp. 15–91. Manila: BSP.

Wedeman, A. 1997. "Looters, Rent-Scrapers, and Dividend-Collectors: Corruption and Growth in Zaire, South Korea, and the Philippines". *The Journal of Developing Areas* 31: 457–78.

Wickberg, E. 2000. *The Chinese in Philippine Life 1850–1898*, repr. ed. Quezon City: Atene de Manila University Press.

Wong, Kwok-Chu. 1999. *The Chinese in the Philippine Economy, 1898–1941*. Quezon City: Atene de Manila University Press.

Woo, J.E. 1991. *Race to the Swift: State and Finance in Korean Industrialization*. New York: Columbia University Press.

Wurfel, D. 1960. "The Bell Report and After: A Study of the Political Problems of Social Reform Stimulated by Foreign Aid". PhD diss., Cornell University.

———. 1962. "The Philippines Elections: Support for Democracy". *Asian Survey* 2 (3): 25–37.

———. 1963. "A Changing Philippines". *Asian Survey* 4 (2): 702–10.

Yoshikawa, Y. 吉川洋子. 1987. "Filipin no Seijiteki Kuraientelizumu: Daitouryo non Ninmeiken to Ninmei no Seiji Katei, フィリピンの政治的クライエンテリズム—大統領の任命権と任命の政治過程 [Political Clientelism in the Philippines: Presidential Appointment and its Political Process]". *Tounan Aziya: Rekishi to Bunka* 東南アジア—歴史と文化 [*Southeast Asia: History and Culture*] 16: 37–75.

INDEX

KYOTO CSEAS SERIES ON ASIAN STUDIES
Center for Southeast Asian Studies, Kyoto University

The Economic Transition in Myanmar after 1988: Market Economy versus State Control, edited by Koichi Fujita, Fumiharu Mieno, and Ikuko Okamoto, 2009

Populism in Asia, edited by Kosuke Mizuno and Pasuk Phongpaichit, 2009

Traveling Nation-Makers: Transnational Flows and Movements in the Making of Modern Southeast Asia, edited by Caroline S. Hau and Kasian Tejapira, 2011

China and the Shaping of Indonesia, 1949–1965, by Hong Liu, 2011

Questioning Modernity in Indonesia and Malaysia, edited by Wendy Mee and Joel S. Kahn, 2012

Industrialization with a Weak State: Thailand's Development in Historical Perspective, by Somboon Siriprachai, edited by Kaoru Sugihara, Pasuk Phongpaichit, and Chris Baker, 2012

Popular Culture Co-productions and Collaborations in East and Southeast Asia, edited by Nissim Otmazgin and Eyal Ben-Ari, 2012

Strong Soldiers, Failed Revolution: The State and Military in Burma, 1962–88, by Yoshihiro Nakanishi, 2013

Organising Under the Revolution: Unions and the State in Java, 1945–48, by Jafar Suryomenggolo, 2013

Living with Risk: Precarity & Bangkok's Urban Poor, by Tamaki Endo, 2014

Migration Revolution: Philippine Nationhood and Class Relations in a Globalized Age, by Filomeno V. Aguilar Jr., 2014

The Chinese Question: Ethnicity, Nation, and Region in and Beyond the Philippines, by Caroline S. Hau, 2014

Identity and Pleasure: The Politics of Indonesian Screen Culture, by Ariel Heryanto, 2014

Indonesian Women and Local Politics: Islam, Gender and Networks in Post-Suharto Indonesia, by Kurniawati Hastuti Dewi, 2015

Catastrophe and Regeneration in Indonesia's Peatlands: Ecology, Economy and Society, edited by Kosuke Mizuno, Motoko S. Fujita & Shuichi Kawai, 2016

Marriage Migration in Asia: Emerging Minorities at the Frontiers of Nation-States, edited by Sari K. Ishii, 2016